PHYSICAL EDUCATION UNIT PLANS FOR GRADES 3-4

SECOND EDITION

**Bette J. Logsdon, PhD / Luann M. Alleman, MEd
Sue Ann Straits, PhD / David E. Belka, PhD
Dawn Clark, EdD**

Human Kinetics

Library of Congress Cataloging-in-Publication Data

Physical education unit plans for grades 3-4 / Bette J. Logsdon ...
[et al.].
    p.   cm.
    Includes bibliographical references (p.).
    ISBN 0-87322-783-2
    1. Physical education for children--Curricula.   2. Curriculum
planning.   I. Logsdon, Bette J.
    GV443.P477 3 1997
    796' .07--dc20   96-35915
                                    CIP

ISBN: 0-87322-783-2
ISBN: 0-88011-697-8 (set)

Acquisitions Editors: Rick Frey and Scott Wikgren; **Developmental Editors:** Christine Drews and Julia Anderson; **Assistant Editors:** John Wentworth and Alesha G. Thompson; **Editorial Assistant:** Jennifer Hemphill; **Copyeditor:** Bonnie Pettifor; **Proofreader:** Erin Cler; **Graphic Designer:** Judy Henderson; **Graphic Artist:** Julie Overholt; **Cover Designer:** Jack Davis; **Photographers (interior):** Jim Kirby, Matthew Barrick, Terry Fell, Sue Straits, Luann Alleman, Anjum Gillespie; **Cover Photographer:** Wil Zehr; **Illustrators:** Craig Ronto and Paul To; **Printer:** Versa Press

Printed in the United States of America   10   9   8   7   6   5   4   3   2   1

Human Kinetics
Web site: http://www.humankinetics.com/

United States: Human Kinetics, P.O. Box 5076, Champaign, IL 61825-5076
1-800-747-4457
e-mail: humank@hkusa.com

Canada: Human Kinetics, Box 24040, Windsor, ON N8Y 4Y9
1-800-465-7301 (in Canada only)
e-mail: humank@hkcanada.com

Europe: Human Kinetics, P.O. Box IW14, Leeds LS16 6TR, United Kingdom
(44) 1132 781708
e-mail: humank@hkeurope.com

Australia: Human Kinetics, 57A Price Avenue, Lower Mitcham, South Australia 5062
(08) 277 1555
e-mail: humank@hkaustralia.com

New Zealand: Human Kinetics, P.O. Box 105-231, Auckland 1
(09) 523 3462
e-mail: humank@hknewz.com

Contents

Preface

Over the years, we have met a host of caring, capable, and knowledgeable teachers who believed they needed to do more to fully challenge their students' movement potential. Many teachers were quick to point out that they felt their program lacked not only breadth and depth but also progression. Some of them were frustrated by the time required to plan, develop, and evaluate quality programs for children of many different grades and levels of development. Others were overwhelmed by the awesome task of planning for scope and sequence throughout the early childhood and elementary school curriculum.

We have shown many teachers our materials for teaching physical education, and invariably they have expressed appreciation and encouraged us to make the materials widely available. In 1986, we developed a two-book set with lesson plans for grades K through 6. These books have been used by teachers in both public and private schools in urban, suburban, and rural areas in the United States and abroad. Freed from the burden of long-range planning and some of the daily preparation, teachers who use the books have been able to focus more on enhancing their instruction methods to meet their students' individual movement needs. Spending less time on the question, *What am I going to do today, and how will it lead to what I want to do tomorrow?* allows them to spend more time answering the question, *How can I help each of my students benefit most from the time they spend in my class?*

The units in the two-book set served us well for ten years, but it's always the case that the more familiar you become with materials, the more ways you find to improve them. The most obvious changes are that this edition includes units for preschool children and that the set has grown from two books to four, each containing plans for two grade levels: Preschool & Kindergarten, 1 & 2, 3 & 4, and 5 & 6. We have redeveloped, re-edited, and revised the instructional units in three program areas—games, gymnastics, and dance. To help us establish models for quality teaching and program planning, we have developed and tested the units in real-life movement and physical education settings. Each of the four books features an introductory perspective on different aspects of physical education, addressing "Movement as Content" (Preschool & Kindergarten); "Developing the Program Overview" (Grades 1 & 2); "Developing Unit Plans and Lesson Plans" (Grades 3 & 4); and "Accommodating Individual Needs" (Grades 5 & 6).

Our objectives for each unit are consistent with the National Standards for Physical Education (NASPE Standards and Assessment Task Force 1995) and the National Standards for Arts Education (Consortium of National Arts Education Associations 1994). To help you determine whether or not children have met these objectives, we have added assessment tools that correspond to the national standards. These tools will help you collect evidence of student achievement and make judgments about student learning and teaching effectiveness—a process that is essential in order to develop *performance* standards that indicate the level of achievement required to meet *content* standards (NASPE Standards and Assessment Task Force 1995). Assessment can also help you identify content progression, for example, which parts of a unit have been well learned, which skills and concepts require more practice or need revisiting in a different way, or which children show control and variety in their movements and which do not (McGee 1984).

Of course the goal of this edition remains the same as it was for the first edition: To help children fulfill their movement potential in games, gymnastics, and dance and to further their abilities to think and interact effectively with others while promoting an active and healthy lifestyle. To achieve this goal, we have added some physical fitness concepts and assessment tools in many units.

We welcome this opportunity to help you teach. We hope our efforts help you provide your students with the kind of meaningful movement experiences that stimulate development.

ACKNOWLEDGMENTS

We would like to acknowledge the help so willingly given by the following teachers in sensitively critiquing the units in this book and the other three in this series and who also permitted us to interrupt their classes to photograph their students at work: Ann Black, Glendale-Feilbach; Sara Davison, Walbridge; Amy Kajca, Beverly; Karen Keener, McKinley; Jane Lyon, Harvard; Kay Siegel, Franklin; Becky Summersett, Reynolds from the Toledo, Ohio Public Schools and Janet Frederick, Liberty Center, Ohio. We would also like to acknowledge the cooperation of the principals, teachers, parents, and students in the above schools as well as Terry Fell, Director of Media at the University of Toledo for the photographs of children in games and gymnastics.

Our gratitude is extended to Kathleen Landfear, Director of Reston Montessori School, and to teachers and parents affiliated with this private school in Reston, Virginia, for allowing us to photograph the children during dance experiences. Our grateful thanks are given to Brian Ziegler, Theatre and Dance Specialist, Arts Focus Project–Lake Anne Elementary School in Reston, Virginia (and to the administrators, teachers, and parents of this Fairfax County School) for their enthusiasm and support during the dance photo shoots. A special thank you is given to Jim Kirby, photographer, who brought life to our dance units by providing us with a photographic record of learning experiences. Thanks are also due to Ann Erickson, Curriculum Leader, Art Program of Studies–Fairfax County Public Schools, and to Patty Koreski, Visual Arts Teacher, for their assistance in providing children's artwork from Armstrong Elementary School and Lake Anne Elementary School, Reston, Virginia.

We would also like to thank Human Kinetics and their publishing staff, especially Chris Drews, John Wentworth, Julie Overholt, Jennifer Hemphill, and Alesha Thompson, for their infinite patience and professional attitude and expertise during the completion of this instructional series.

Grateful acknowledgment is made to the following authors or publishers for the use of copyright material: Yolanda Danyi Szuch for "The Haunting of Autumn Nights" from *Motion in Poetry*, copyright 1996 by Yolanda Danyi Szuch.

Finally, we are deeply grateful to family and friends for their moral support during the final stages of this project, namely David Vanell, Suzanne Patrick, Carol Ann Riordin, Sharon and Steven Snyder.

> This book is dedicated to
> Emily, Christopher, and Lindsey Alleman
> and to Sara and Alan Vanell

Introduction: Developing Unit Plans and Lesson Plans: Phases 2 and 3 in Planning

MATERIALS NEEDED FOR TEACHING

Creating materials reflecting appropriate progression in physical education is very important and is especially demanding for elementary classroom teachers because they are held accountable for teaching several varied subjects. Once you have designed a program overview as discussed in book two, the next level of curriculum materials needed in preparing to teach is a series of Unit Plans.

This set of four books was developed to reduce the time spent by individual teachers in planning by providing program materials designed to outline an educational approach for the teaching of physical education preschool through grade 6. Each book charts a yearly program through a series of instructional units for the teaching of games, gymnastics and dance for two grade levels. These books collectively were written to:

- outline a scheme of progression for identifying and selecting specific content.
- help teachers develop physical education programs with appropriate scope and sequence by providing a series of unit plans rather evenly divided among three broad program areas: games, gymnastics, and dance.
- define student objectives that challenge motor, cognitive and affective development on a continuing basis.
- illustrate teaching techniques that accommodate individual differences and encourage students to achieve at their highest level of ability.
- enable teachers to concentrate their planning time on the preparation of lesson plans.

In addition, the instructional units in each book have been placed in a logical sequence in games, gymnastics, and dance for each grade level to help teachers with the awesome task of planning for progression. The sequence teachers choose in developing the yearly program may need to vary because of differences in student needs and abilities, school schedules, availability of equipment and facilities, climate, geographic location as well as individual preferences of the teacher, administration, and the community.

A UNIT PLAN—WHAT IS IT?

A unit plan in this series refers to a written outline for teaching a small segment of the physical education program. We include the following discussion to help orient teachers to the format used in this series of books.

The unit format used throughout this series highlights these seven areas of decision making: unit focus, length of unit, theme, content, objectives, suggested equipment and materials, and learning experiences. Besides becoming more aware of the specific movement content to be taught, teachers who have used units with this seven-step planning process report they tend to increase their attention given to planning for progression, improving instruction and their ability to meet the developmental needs of students. Refer to the beginning of a unit in this book as you read the following discussion focused on each of these seven decision-making areas.

1. Unit Focus. A unit focus is written to narrow the content for your plan of study. It identifies the content to be taught. The focus aids in planning for progression and integration by quickly identifying the main content of each segment of your yearly program.

2. Length of Unit. An approximation of the number of lessons is projected for each unit. Estimating the duration of the unit at the outset helps teachers reserve time in their school calendar for each unit when planning a yearly program.

3. Themes. Specific movement themes have been identified for being appropriate for the various grade levels. These are featured on pages ix-xi in the Movement Themes and Basic Content for Third and Fourth Grades. It's important to know when examining this chart that program materials for all grade levels focus on content from Theme 1 and content from the other themes. Theme 1 may be studied alone but all other themes are always studied in conjunction with Theme 1. Selecting the movement theme(s) and the specific content related to the theme(s) to be studied in a unit is made easier by focusing on the answers to these questions:

1. Has your class had previous experiences with content from this theme?
2. If so, what specific content did they experience previously?
3. Was their previous experience with the content in the same program area (games, dance or gymnastics) or in a different program area than the one you are currently planning?

Answers to these three questions are essential to progression and should be determined before proceeding to subsequent steps in unit planning. When writing an isolated unit with little or no knowledge of the program or the children to be taught, your answers to these questions will, out of necessity, be based largely on suppositions. In any situation, remember:

- We do *not* use themes as content.
- We select content representative of specific themes.
- All units focus on content selected from among two or more themes.

An important consideration in theme selection is determining which theme to choose. The theme selected must be appropriate for the students so their developmental needs will be challenged and the progression inherent in the themes will be followed. Movement Themes: A Guide for Planning Teaching Progression (pp. xii) approximates which specific themes in games, gymnastics, and dance are appropriate for each grade level. The content selected from the

Movement Themes and Basic Content
for Third and Fourth Grades

Educational Games

Theme 1   **Introduction to Basic Body and Manipulative Control**

Improving manipulative skills with different body parts or implements while stationary or when performing basic locomotor skills.

Basic Content:

Manipulative activities—triking, throwing, catching, collecting, carrying, dribbling (hand and foot)

Locomotor activities—traveling and stopping, running, jumping, sidestepping

Body parts—hands, feet, shins, knees, hips, shoulders, chest

Theme 2   **Introduction to Space**

Introducing the use of personal and general space-focusing on areas, levels, directions, extensions, and pathways to improve the performance of manipulative skills.

Basic Content:

Areas—general, personal

Levels—high, medium, low

Extensions—near to, far from

Directions—forward, backward, sideward, upward, downward

Pathways—ground, air, curved, straight

Theme 3   **Introduction to Movement Quality (Effort)**

The focus is on the quality of movement-controlling speed, force and the amount of space used to improve efficiency and effectiveness of manipulative and locomotor skills in games.

Basic Content:

Force—strong—light

Speed—fast—slow

Space quality—small-large

Theme 4   **Movement Flow**

This theme focuses on developing flow to improve performance of a skill, combine skills, or increase the ability to keep the movement going. (Taught in conjunction with content from Theme 1.)

Basic Content:

Flow—bound-free

Continuity-(hustle, keeping the ball alive or the game going)

Theme 5   **Introduction to Basic Relationships**

Relationships of the body or body parts to games equipment or between teammates and opponents basic to games play.

Basic Content:

Relationship of individuals—to objects, implements, and equipment arrangements

Relationships of individuals— to individuals and small groups (2 or 3)

Theme 6   **Advanced Body and Manipulative Control**

Combining manipulative skills with locomotion and or non locomotion to enhance effectiveness and efficiency in the performance of the skills.

Basic Content:

Manipulative activities combined with:

locomotion—running, jumping, sidestepping, sliding, rolling,(for recovery of balance) non locomotion—extending, twisting, bending

Theme 7   **Introduction to Complex Relationships**

Passing to spaces (in front of, behind, even with); creating spaces; covering spaces in relation to teammates or opponents.

Basic Content:

Relationships within the environment—passing to spaces, creating spaces, covering spaces.

(continued)

Movement Themes and Basic Content
for Third and Fourth Grades *(continued)*

Educational Gymnastics

Theme 1 **Introduction to the Body**
This theme centers on initiating control of the body through discovering, practicing, and learning locomotor gymnastics activities.
Basic Content:
Locomotor activities— rocking, rolling, sliding, jumping, swinging, flight, step-like actions

Theme 2 **Introduction to Space**
Space content focuses on developing responsibility for the use of space by changing areas, levels, directions, extensions, and pathways all in conjunction with Theme 1.
Basic Content:
Areas—general, personal
Levels—high, medium, low
Directions—forward, backward, sideward, up, down
Pathways—straight, curved, zigzag

Theme 3 **Introduction to Time**
The chief purpose of this theme is to develop the ability to produce and regulate speed in the performance of gymnastic activities.
Basic Content:
Time—fast, slow; accelerating, decelerating; sudden, sustained

Theme 4 **Introduction to Relationships of Body Parts**
This theme places the child's attention on developing relationships with one body part to another, body parts to the floor and to the apparatus. (This theme is always taught in conjunction with content from Theme 1.)
Basic Content:
Relationships of body parts to each other—above, below; along side, apart, together; behind, in front of; near, far; over, under
Relationships of body parts to apparatus—over, under; near, far; above, below, alongside; behind, in front of; arriving on, dismounting from
Roles played by body parts—support body, lead action, apply force, receive force (weight)
Body Shapes—angular, straight; wide, round, twisted; symmetrical, asymmetrical

Theme 5 **Introduction to Weight**
The focus of this theme is to help the child develop the ability to create and control muscle tension in gymnastics and is always taught in conjunction with Theme 1.
Basic Content:
Weight—firm, strong, tension; soft, slight, relaxed

Theme 6 **Flow and Continuity in Movement**
Theme 6 emphasizes the selection and refinement of gymnastic sequences and focuses on improving the totality of the movement response-the movements themselves and the way the are linked. This theme is always used in conjunction with content from Theme 1 and other themes.
Basic Content:
Flow—bound, stoppable; free, ongoing

Theme 7 **Relationships to Others**
Theme 7 gives children the opportunity to relate to partners and small groups in developing gymnastic sequences.
Basic Content:
Relationships of partners and small groups—contrasting, alternating, successive, canon; mirroring-matching, following-copying, above-below, behind-in front of, near-far, over-under-alongside, supporting-being supported lifting-being lifted
Activities of the body—counterbalance-countertension

(continued)

Educational Dance

Theme 1   Introduction to the Body
Improving awareness of the body as an instrument for creating movement by gaining a feeling for producing motion and maintaining stillness.
Basic Content:
Locomotor activities—walking, running, skipping, galloping, leaping, stepping, jumping
Nonlocomotor activities— rising, sinking; opening, closing; turning, spinning
Body parts—leading body actions, supporting weight, receiving weight

Theme 2   Introduction to Weight and Time
Increasing sensitivity for the dynamics of movement by using the motion factors of time and weight for expressive purposes.(This content is always taught along with theme 1 and other themes.)
Basic Content:
Time—sudden, sustained
Weight—firm, fine touch

Theme 3   Introduction to Space
This theme focuses specifically on the environment to encourage the inventive use of space to create a particular mood or feeling.(Space is not taught alone. Like content for each of the remaining themes, space is always taught in conjunction with basic content emphasizing the "Body".)
Basic Content:
Areas—general personal
Directions—forward, backward, sideward, up, down

Theme 4   The Flow of Movement
Creating situations allowing children to experience contrasting sensations involving: bound and free movement; large and small amounts of space; and movement that results from combining various motion factors.
Basic Content:
Flow—bound, free
Space— direct, indirect

Theme 5   Introduction to Relationships
Developing sensitivity by interacting with others to design movement sequences and developing a further awareness of the body by focusing on the relationships of body parts in movement.
Basic Content:
Relationship of body parts to each other
Relationship of individuals and small groups to each other

Theme 6   Instrumental Use of the Body
Expanding and refining body awareness through a more precise look at jumping, the shape of the body in stillness, and movements of the arms and legs in gesturing.
Basic Content:
Jumping—five basic jumps-one foot to the other, one foot to the same foot, two feet to two feet, on foot to two feet, two feet to on foot
Body shape—straight, wide, twisted, round,
Gesture

Theme 7   The Basic Effort Actions
Differentiating and emphasizing the use and nature of the three motion factors: weight, time, and space.
Basic Content:
Thrusting—sudden, firm and direct; Slashing—sudden, firm, indirect;
Floating—sustained, fine, indirect; Gliding—sustained, fine, direct;
Wringing—sustained, firm, indirect; Pressing—sustained, firm, direct;
Flicking—sudden, fine, indirect; Dabbing—sudden, fine, direct

Movement Themes: A Suggested Guide for Content Selection

	PK	K	1	2	3	4	5	6
Theme 1								
Games	Introduced	Emphasized					Continues →	
Gymnastics	Introduced	Emphasized					Continues →	
Dance	Introduced	Emphasized				Continues →		
Theme 2								
Games		Introduced	Emphasized					Continues →
Gymnastics	Introduced	Emphasized						Continues →
Dance	Introduced	Emphasized						Continues →
Theme 3								
Games			Introduced	Emphasized				Continues
Gymnastics			Introduced	Emphasized				Continues →
Dance		Introduced	Emphasized					Continues →
Theme 4								
Games				Introduced	Emphasized			Continues
Gymnastics			Introduced	Emphasized				Continues →
Dance		Introduced	Emphasized					Continues →
Theme 5								
Games				Introduced	Emphasized			Continues →
Gymnastics				Introduced	Emphasized			
Dance				Introduced	Emphasized			
Theme 6								
Games					Introduced	Emphasized		
Gymnastics					Introduced	Emphasized		
Dance					Introduced	Emphasized		
Theme 7								
Games					Introduced	Emphasized		
Gymnastics					Introduced	Emphasized		
Dance					Introduced	Emphasized		
Theme 8								
Gymnastics						Introduced	Emphasized	
Dance						Introduced	Emphasized	
Theme 9								
Dance					Introduced		Emphasized	
Theme 10								
Dance							Introduced	Emphasized

Key for content selection:

· · · · · · · · · · Introduced

▬▬▬▬▬ Emphasized

———→ Continues

theme(s) and the experiences developed to achieve thoughtfully prepared objectives should become more complex for the maturing student.

4. Content. Motor content to be taught in each unit is categorized under the four aspects of movement: Body, Space, Effort, and Relationships. Classifying the unit content in these four categories not only outlines content more specifically but often helps teachers and students recognize concepts or skills previously taught in one program area as they are revisited, expanded, polished, and/or applied in other units even in when the same content is studied in different program areas. Identifying specific content is helpful in narrowing the scope of content to be studied and can aid in planning for progression. Refer to the Movement Framework on pages xiv-xv and try to classify the content of one of the units in this book on the framework before continuing to read. As you classify the unit content on the framework, notice many of the specialized skills of games, gymnastics, and dance are not shown in the framework. Specialized skills have been omitted only because space was limited and the list is too extensive to include all examples relevant to each of the categories. For example, under the heading of "manipulative," to be even partially complete, a list of manipulative skills should include all different kinds and styles of throws—underhand, overhand, sidearm, spiral pass; all the various ways of shooting a basketball—lay up, hook, one-handed jump shot; the toss in the tennis serve . . . and many, many more forms of propelling a ball or other objects with the hands or equipment. You can see how extensive the list of just one entry on the Movement Framework would be when you envision all the manipulative skills that have not been mentioned involving the use of other body parts, such as the feet, as well as the skills required in the use of varying types of sport equipment used in a wide range of sports. It becomes evident that the Movement Framework is a mere outline to trigger the analysis of movement and to organize thinking when planning and while teaching.

5. Objectives. The objectives in this set of books reflect an approach to teaching physical education that recognizes the individuality of the learner, accommodates individual differences and is dedicated to helping each child achieve their full potential. This approach is highlighted in the stating of objectives by the use of the phrase: *In this unit children will (or should be willing to try to) meet these objectives.* As you write your objectives, prepare appropriate objectives that focus on all three learning domains; cognitive, affective, and motor. Make them reflective of the content to be taught as well as the needs and abilities of the class you are teaching. In this book, you will find that most objectives in grade 4 lists a national standard(s) the objective reflects. For detailed information concerning national standards, refer to the appendixes on page 161, as well as to the introduction of book 1 in this series and the references for National Association for Sport and Physical Education (NASPE) Assessment Task Force, 1995 for standards for games and gymnastics; for dance, see National Dance Association (NDA), 1994.

6. Equipment and Materials. The equipment and materials lists suggest what equipment and material should be used for each unit. Use these suggestions to prepare your own list—keeping in mind the type and kind of equipment and materials available in your setting.

7. Learning Experiences. We recommend two levels of learning experiences—major tasks and subtasks—for outlining meaningful teaching progressions. Referring to any one of the units in the book, notice the major tasks when read in order (Examples: 1.0, 2.0, 3.0) are written to sketch an outline of progression for the unit. Subtasks (Examples: 1.1, 1.2, 1.3) are designed to provide the students with additional challenges, information, and practice time needed to

The Movement Framework

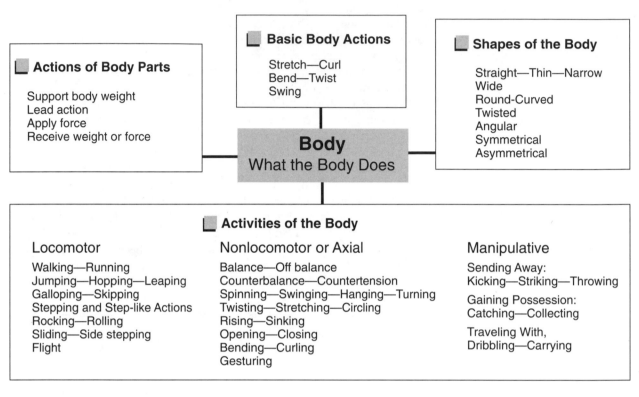

Actions of Body Parts

Support body weight
Lead action
Apply force
Receive weight or force

Basic Body Actions

Stretch—Curl
Bend—Twist
Swing

Shapes of the Body

Straight—Thin—Narrow
Wide
Round-Curved
Twisted
Angular
Symmetrical
Asymmetrical

Body
What the Body Does

Activities of the Body

Locomotor

Walking—Running
Jumping—Hopping—Leaping
Galloping—Skipping
Stepping and Step-like Actions
Rocking—Rolling
Sliding—Side stepping
Flight

Nonlocomotor or Axial

Balance—Off balance
Counterbalance—Countertension
Spinning—Swinging—Hanging—Turning
Twisting—Stretching—Circling
Rising—Sinking
Opening—Closing
Bending—Curling
Gesturing

Manipulative

Sending Away:
Kicking—Striking—Throwing

Gaining Possession:
Catching—Collecting

Traveling With,
Dribbling—Carrying

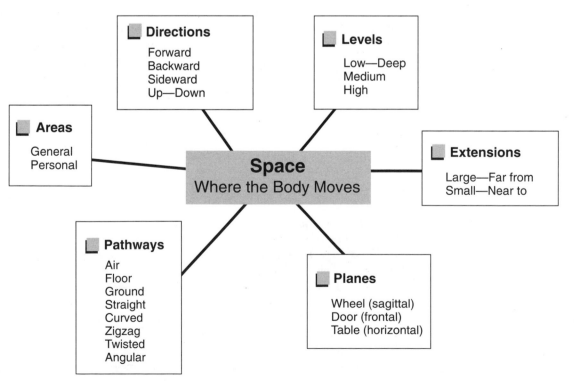

Directions

Forward
Backward
Sideward
Up—Down

Levels

Low—Deep
Medium
High

Areas

General
Personal

Space
Where the Body Moves

Extensions

Large—Far from
Small—Near to

Pathways

Air
Floor
Ground
Straight
Curved
Zigzag
Twisted
Angular

Planes

Wheel (sagittal)
Door (frontal)
Table (horizontal)

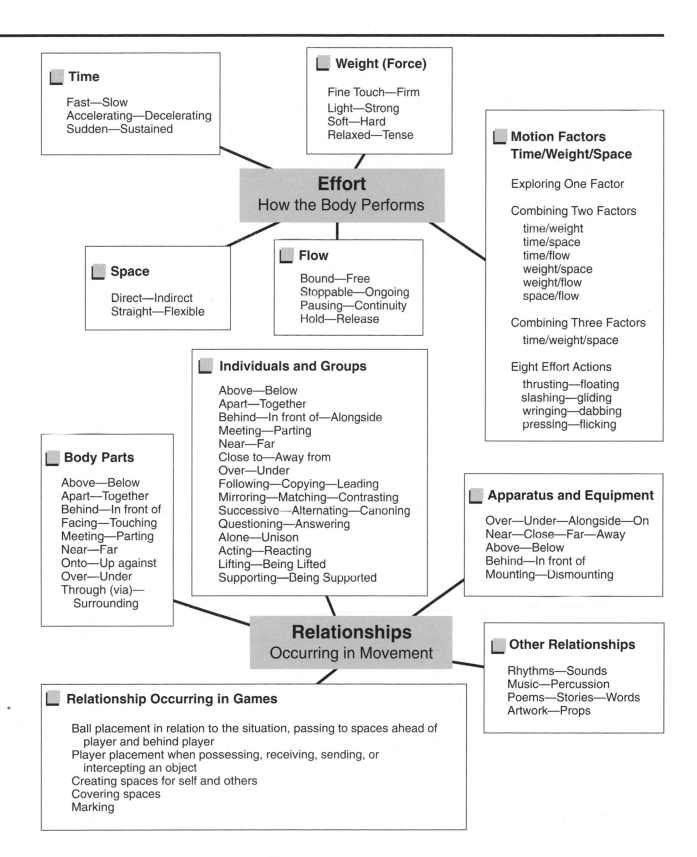

Time

Fast—Slow
Accelerating—Decelerating
Sudden—Sustained

Weight (Force)

Fine Touch—Firm
Light—Strong
Soft—Hard
Relaxed—Tense

**Motion Factors
Time/Weight/Space**

Exploring One Factor

Combining Two Factors
time/weight
time/space
time/flow
weight/space
weight/flow
space/flow

Combining Three Factors
time/weight/space

Eight Effort Actions
thrusting—floating
slashing—gliding
wringing—dabbing
pressing—flicking

Effort
How the Body Performs

Space

Direct—Indirect
Straight—Flexible

Flow

Bound—Free
Stoppable—Ongoing
Pausing—Continuity
Hold—Release

Individuals and Groups

Above—Below
Apart—Together
Behind—In front of—Alongside
Meeting—Parting
Near—Far
Close to—Away from
Over—Under
Following—Copying—Leading
Mirroring—Matching—Contrasting
Successive—Alternating—Canoning
Questioning—Answering
Alone—Unison
Acting—Reacting
Lifting—Being Lifted
Supporting—Being Supported

Body Parts

Above—Below
Apart—Together
Behind—In front of
Facing—Touching
Meeting—Parting
Near—Far
Onto—Up against
Over—Under
Through (via)—
 Surrounding

Apparatus and Equipment

Over—Under—Alongside—On
Near—Close—Far—Away
Above—Below
Behind—In front of
Mounting—Dismounting

Relationships
Occurring in Movement

Other Relationships

Rhythms—Sounds
Music—Percussion
Poems—Stories—Words
Artwork—Props

Relationship Occurring in Games

Ball placement in relation to the situation, passing to spaces ahead of
 player and behind player
Player placement when possessing, receiving, sending, or
 intercepting an object
Creating spaces for self and others
Covering spaces
Marking

improve performance essential for progression. Collectively these tasks are written to outline experiences that can provide students the opportunity for success in achieving the unit objectives.

In using any one of the units in this set of four books, teachers are encouraged to write additional subtasks or major tasks to challenge each group of children they teach. This not only personalizes the unit for teaching specific students it provides teachers with opportunities to adjust the unit to fit their teaching situation and helps to make the unit reflect their personality and style of teaching.

LESSON PLANNING: AN AID TO EFFECTIVE TEACHING

Planning in preparation for teaching is rather universal but the form lesson planning takes can be extremely personal. The format for lesson planning selected by a teacher is subject to change as the teacher acquires deeper understanding of the content being taught and, through experience, develops the ability to anticipate, observe, assess, and respond spontaneously and more effectively to the needs of the students. While the structure of the lesson plan is a decision to be made by individual teachers, we believe, meaningful teaching must always remain focused on the goals of physical education and must be fully committed and attentive to educating the whole child. Too often physical education lessons are designed merely to get the students involved in activities with little or no planning directed toward skill development, cognitive enrichment, or improvement of affective behavior. Planning for physical education as a viable part of educating the whole child requires among other important qualities:

- purposeful planning based on appropriate cognitive, motor, and affective objectives.
- challenging learning experiences designed to help the students achieve their full potential.
- ways to assess progress that helps both the teacher and the students to evaluate achievement and set future goals.

Planning Day-to-Day Progression

The first suggestion we recommend for teachers using these units is to refer to and read about the content of the unit. Depth of knowledge for the content to be taught helps in preparing meaningful learning experiences and builds confidence in providing appropriate feedback when teaching the unit.

We prepared the sample lesson plan format shown on page xvii to guide teachers through the planning process. It outlines an approach to lesson planning developed to encourage teachers to prepare each plan based on knowledge of the developmental level of the students and the content to be included in the lesson.

Simplifying the Initial Stage in Lesson Planning

Teachers who have developed an awareness of the developmental needs of students and an understanding of the content and unit objectives often simplify this initial stage in planning by jotting down only a brief synopsis of the tasks they plan to teach in each lesson. For example, instead of listing learning expe-

LESSON PLAN FORMAT	
Unit Focus:	**Lesson Content:**
Lesson Number (Within Unit):	**Body:**
Observations Influencing Planning:	**Space:**
Main Purpose of the Lesson:	**Effort:**
	Relationships:

Objectives:

•Learning Experiences	•Accommodating Individual Differences (ways to simplify or extend a task)	•Improving Cognitive and Affective Behavior	•Improving Motor Responses

rience 1.8 verbatim for refining the forearm pass in volleyball, you might recall this task by jotting down these few words: *Sit in make-believe chair. Stand as ball contacts forearms. Say, 'sit . . . stand'.* (Grade 3, Games Unit 4)

When your initial stage in lesson planning includes greatly abbreviated tasks taken from the unit and other tasks you design, you reduce the work involved in preparing the initial stage in lesson planning giving you more time to devote to personalizing the teaching of the unit.

Many varied reasons can cause teachers to alter even the best prepared plans. Example of some possible reasons include:

- Unplanned changes in the daily schedule
- Large number of absentees
- Progressing more or less rapidly in a lesson than planned
- Differences in abilities among classes using the same unit
- Variation of teaching styles among teachers

The abbreviated format with fewer words written by the teacher teaching the unit can provide the total recall for the longer, original task. Including the task number as it appears in the book helps in the event the teacher may need to check where the task fits into the progression of the unit or wants to review the exact phrasing of the task.

SUMMARY

In preparing plans at all levels, Program Overview, Unit Plan, or Lesson Plan, it is essential to read, study, and learn as much as possible about the content and the children you are planning to teach. Obviously, practice and experience in teaching help to develop confidence but, for the beginning teacher, in addition to monitoring and analyzing your behavior as you teach, nothing can substitute for an in-depth, sensitive approach to planning.

Third Grade Games

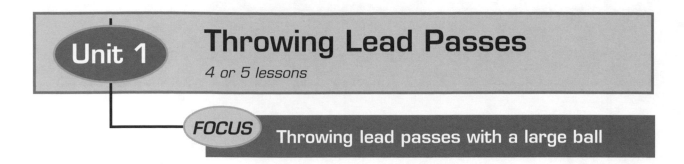

Unit 1 — Throwing Lead Passes
4 or 5 lessons

FOCUS Throwing lead passes with a large ball

MOTOR CONTENT

Selected from Theme 3—Introduction to Movement Quality (Effort) and Theme 5—Introduction to Basic Relationships

Effort

Speed—getting rid of the ball quickly; changing directions quickly

Relationships

Ball placement—throwing passes ahead of a running receiver; receiver repositioning to show front of body to ball

OBJECTIVES

In this unit, children will (or should be willing to try to) meet these objectives:

- Elude a guard by repositioning to make a clear path between the guard and the ball by altering their speed and by making sudden changes in direction and size of step.
- Complete lead passes by watching for the breaking team member and a clear path, passing the ball only as hard and as far away from the receiver as the receiver can catch.
- Explain and show that a lead pass is executed by throwing the ball into the space ahead of the receiver so the ball and the receiver reach the same point at the same time.
- Work to improve their lead passes by timing the pass so the receiver catches the ball without having to break stride or alter direction.
- Make their best effort to catch *every* ball thrown to them to help create the best learning situation for themselves and others.

EQUIPMENT AND MATERIALS

8- to 10-inch ball (foam, plastic or rubber) one for each one or two children.

LEARNING EXPERIENCES

1.0 Completing passes in game situations takes two cooperative people. The person with the ball has to throw the ball carefully so it can be caught, and the receiver has to work hard to catch the ball. Show each other you care by trying hard to complete every pass. Join with someone, get one ball for the two of you, and begin.

1.1 Tossers, remember you have to take responsibility for making the throw catchable. Watch the speed of your throw. If the catcher misses the ball, the incomplete pass may be due to your mistake in judging the speed of your throw. [Monitor the distance between partners and alter if necessary.]

1.2 Catchers, think of your partner as a learner, too. The pass might not come right to you, even though your passer is trying very hard to make the pass catchable. Help make your passer look like the best passer in the class by adjusting your position when necessary to catch the ball.

1.3 Passers, send the ball directly to the catcher's chest. Throwing the ball chest or shoulder high makes the ball easier to catch because the catcher doesn't have to bend to catch.

1.4 Work seriously. Make an extra effort as a thrower or a catcher to complete each pass. Be proud of your work!

1.5 Let's see how many completed passes you can make in 15 seconds. You and your partner count, and I will time you. Stand about ten big steps away from each other. Ready? Begin! [Repeat, having them try to beat their record.]

1.6 Discuss what caused any throw to be missed. Was the throw too hard, did the catcher fail to reposition to catch the ball when it didn't come right to them, or was the throw too low—not up about chest high? Discuss the reasons the ball was missed, and let's see if you can correct them and break your record. Ready? Begin!

Cooperate with your partner and try hard to catch every pass.

2.0 [Have each pair find a working space about 15 to 20 feet square so both can run to catch a pass without interfering with others.] Those of you who made several completed passes may want to try something a little harder. Receivers can start to jog and have the passers see if they can pass the ball in the space ahead of the receiver so the receiver can catch the pass on the run.

2.1 Does anyone know what name we give to passes that are thrown ahead of a running receiver? Right! They are called *lead passes*, and they are harder to complete than the passes you have been practicing. When throwing to a running receiver, aim your pass about chest height and time your pass so the ball and your receiver reach the same place at the same time.

2.2 As soon as you throw the ball, dart toward a new spot so you are already running to receive the next pass. Only pass when the catcher is on the move.

2.3 Passers, watch your catcher. If your catcher is having to stop or slow down to catch the ball, you need to pass the ball a bit farther out in front of the receiver.

2.4 Catchers, try desperately to catch every ball. If you feel you and the ball are not going to meet at the same spot, help complete the pass by slowing down, speeding up, or maybe even changing your direction when necessary to come back to the ball to catch it.

2.5 If you are completing your passes, dart to a different place away from your partner each time you complete a pass. Passers, watch the receivers. Remember to pass the ball ahead of the receiver.

3.0 [Observe for children who are successful in throwing and catching lead passes and combine them into groups of three (or four). Don't rush and expect all children to go to this task at the same time.] This time, after you pass the ball, see if you can travel to a new place by cutting across the center of your working space. Because you are now working in small groups, you will not know when you are going to be the receiver so everyone has to keep their eyes focused on the passer, ready to receive the ball.

3.1 As you cut across your working space, keep looking at the ball. You never know when the pass will be coming to you.

3.2 Quickly dash to an open spot by crossing the center of your group space after you pass the ball to a running teammate.

3.3 Receivers, try to pass the ball as quickly as you receive it. Throw the ball immediately. Do not run with the ball.

Passes thrown ahead of a running receiver are called *lead passes*.

3.4 Receivers, be ready to catch the pass by changing your speed or direction.

3.5 Make your working space a little bigger so you have to run faster and a bit farther when receiving a pass. If you begin to miss because your space is too big, move a little closer. Keep in mind that completing each pass is the most important thing. A missed pass now causes your work to stop; later it can cause your team to lose the ball to your opponents.

4.0 [Organize individuals to play two versus one keep-away when you feel they are ready. Later, you might use one of these groups to demonstrate the following task to help move the class into game play faster.] Now you are going to have to be even more committed to completing passes because now there will be one person trying to intercept your pass. Two of you will try to keep the ball away from the one in the middle by completing lead passes. When the pass is intercepted, the person who threw the pass changes places with the one in the middle.

4.1 Receivers, try to reposition away from the person in the middle so there is a clear path between you and the ball.

4.2 Receivers, show the entire front of your body to the ball. Don't let the player in the middle get between you and the ball.

4.3 Pass the ball as soon as you see an opening between you and your receiver. Hesitating to throw the ball gives the middle player time to move in front of your receiver to intercept the pass.

4.4 [Demonstrate as you question.] Receivers, think. Is it easier for the person who is guarding you to stay with you as you run if you make sharp corners in your pathways or curved, rounded pathways? OK, let's make quick, sharp changes in pathways, not rounded ones that opponents can easily guard.

4.5 [Go to two versus two or three versus three for children who are ready. Don't be too hasty and reorganize the whole class. Practicing cutting, showing the front of the body to the ball, and using lead passes are the most important skills. The children can practice all of these effectively in two versus one situations.]

4.6 Guards in the center, some of you are standing in the middle of the space. The passes are being completed easily by sending the ball high over your head. Stay closer to the receiver to catch the ball when the ball drops lower.

4.7 Count and see how many completed passes your team can make before the ball is intercepted. When the ball is intercepted, the other team tries to beat your record.

4.8 Watch your passes. Throwers don't permit your throws to get too low. Make your throws about chest high. Catchers, make sharp corners as you change directions and keep your whole body front open to receive the ball.

4.9 Each time you intercept the ball, see if your team can increase the number of completed passes.

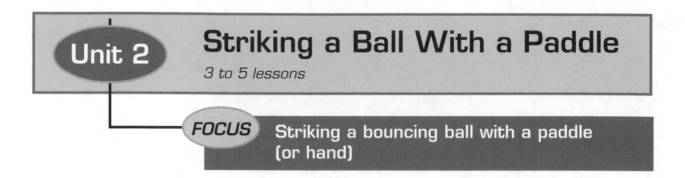

Unit 2 — **Striking a Ball With a Paddle**

3 to 5 lessons

FOCUS — Striking a bouncing ball with a paddle (or hand)

MOTOR CONTENT

Selected from Theme 1—Introduction to Basic Body and Manipulative Control; Theme 2—Introduction to Space; and Theme 3—Introduction to Movement Quality (Effort)

Body

Manipulative activities—stroking a bouncing ball with a short-handled paddle, racquet, or hand

Effort

Force—varying the force of the stroke

Space

Levels—sending the ball to different levels, especially medium

OBJECTIVES

In this unit, children will (or should be willing to try to) meet these objectives:

- Control their strokes by willfully altering the level and speed of a ball as they serve or return a bouncing ball.
- Adjust their feet to position the body sideways.
- Increase the number of times they can repeatedly return a bouncing ball when working alone or with others.
- Apply knowledge by showing that the angle of the racquet and the force of the swing has a direct relationship to the height (level) of the path of the ball and the distance and speed the ball travels.
- Create a safe working environment for everyone by controlling the racquet, being watchful when retrieving or striking a ball, and not entering the space of others.
- Accept responsibility for modifying the force and level of the stroke to accommodate the skill of the receiver.

EQUIPMENT AND MATERIALS

Each child needs one paddle or short-handled racquet and one ball. (While you can use various kinds of racquets and balls, you must take care to ensure the weight and size of the ball are consistent with the durability of the racquet and needs of the children. For example, 8- to 10-inch vinyl or plastic balls and strong wooden paddles are exceptionally useful in introducing this unit to third grade children. The unit has also been meaningful for children who strike the ball with the hand or work with improvised racquets made with a nylon hose stretched over coat hangers, bent into the shape of a paddle, hitting plastic golf balls.) *Optional:* Nets and standards; ropes, or benches to hit over; floor tape to mark wall targets.

LEARNING EXPERIENCES

1.0 Today you are going to see how successful you can be in trying to return a ball that has been tossed and comes to you on a bounce. You will stroke it with a racquet [or hand], trying very hard to make the ball bounce right in front of your tosser. Each of us is responsible for not hitting someone or getting hit. Never swing your racquet wildly and remember to always look before you swing when someone has gone out of their own space to retrieve a ball. Get a partner. One of you get a racquet for the two of you, one of you get one ball for the two of you, and begin. [For safety, arrange the children in two facing rows, partners across from each other. Have children change roles several times. More experienced children often change roles on their own.]

1.1 Tossers, toss the ball so it lands in front of your partner and bounces up to about the waist of your partner. Those with racquets, make sure you have free space about you before you swing.

1.2 As you strike the ball, make it land in front of your partner by directing the racquet face toward your partner.

1.3 Tappers, take pride in seeing if you can stroke just hard enough to make it land in front of your partner. If it is bouncing past your partner, you are swinging your racquet too fast.

1.4 Watch the ball and see where it lands. If you are really controlling your racquet and trying to place the ball, your partner will not have to move their feet to strike or catch the ball.

1.5 Put your hand on the flat part of your racquet. This is called the face of the racquet. Keep the face of your racquet reaching out toward the spot in front of your partner where you want the ball to bounce.

1.6 See how many times out of five tosses you can make the ball bounce in front of your tosser so they can catch it without having to take any steps.

2.0 If both of you have been successful in making the ball land right in front of your partner, let's see if the two of you can hit the ball back and forth to each other. Still remember to be caring partners and make the ball bounce in front of your partner. Get a racquet if you do not have one and begin.

2.1 When you stroke the ball, work to keep the face of the racquet reaching out toward a spot in front of the receiver so the receiver has an easy chance to send it back. If you make your partner chase the ball, you are giving them practice in running and not hitting a ball. It is your responsibility to give each other good practice in hitting the ball so you both improve your stroking skills. [Observe: Is the racquet swung in a horizontal plane?]

2.2 See your racquet contact the ball, then follow the ball with your eyes and see it bounce. Talk to yourself and say, 'I can control this racquet and make that ball go anywhere I want it to go if I keep looking at the ball and care where it goes.'

2.3 Receivers, focus your eyes on the ball and be ready to reposition your feet to move your body so your nonstriking side is pointed toward your receiver as you return the ball. If your body isn't in the right position to control your return, just catch the ball and drop it carefully so you can stroke the ball so it bounces where your partner can hit it.

2.4 Count to see how many times you and your partner can hit the ball back and forth, remembering to reposition your feet so the ball bounces in front of you each time before you return it.

3.0 [Place a horizontal line of tape about four feet above the floor on the wall.] Notice the tape line on the wall. This time, each person will practice controlling the height of the ball by striking the ball so it hits close to the line of tape. Remember to move to let the ball bounce in front of you each time before you hit it.

3.1 Watch how the tilt of your racquet helps determine how high your ball goes. If the face of your racquet is tilted up too high toward the ceiling, your ball will go way above the line. [Path of racquet should be parallel.]

3.2 Try to make your arm and racquet swing out away from the side of your body horizontal [explain or demonstrate] with the floor. Don't let the tip of the racquet drop down toward the floor.

3.3 Some of you are ready to see if you can intentionally make your ball go to a medium level, right near the masking tape, and then, on your next hit, tilt your racquet face up a bit and stroke up, making the ball go only a little higher.

3.4 I hope you have noticed it is what you do with the racquet that changes the level of your hits. Try harder to control your ball by tilting the racquet face a little to hit the ball just above the tape. Say, 'Drop ball and stroke.'

4.0 Let's see how well you can control the ball and keep it in your own area as you send it back and forth to a partner. [Children may like to send the ball over a rope, net, bench, or the like.]

4.1 Receivers, be ready to make your feet take you toward the ball. You may have to run fast forward, backward or to the side.

4.2 See how many times you and your partner can hit the ball, keeping the ball going in your own space.

Strike the ball so it hits close to the horizontal line of tape.

4.3 When hitting the ball, act like you will lose a point if you send it too hard. Try to control the power and the tilt of your racquet so your partner never has to travel backward to receive a ball.

4.4 Find another set of partners near you and challenge them to see which set of partners can keep the ball going the longest. Don't be discouraged if your first try is unsuccessful. Team play takes a lot of practice! [Some children may need to spend more time on refining tasks 3.4 and 4.3 before joining in team play. Offer a choice of tasks to accommodate a wide range of developmental levels.]

ASSESSING STRIKING A BALL TO A PARTNER WITH PADDLE RACQUET

Class list	Adjusts feet to turn sideways to the target.	Controls hit to land in front of partner.	Adjusts angle of racquet face so ball hits near intended target.	Is considerate of others, watching out for their safety.	Adjusts speed and force of hit so partner can return the ball.
Craig Rice	3	3	4	3	3
Julie Lynn	5	5	5	4	5

Scale: 5 = Almost always 4 = Consistent 2/3 or more of tries 3 = Erratic consistency but improving 2 = Successful 1/3 or less of tries 1 = No success; needs task and equipment changes

[Revisit this unit and challenge students to gradually increase the force or power of their stroke. Assess the developmental level of sidearm striking (racquet action), see Hayward, 1993, p. 69.]

MOTOR CONTENT

Selected from Theme 3—Introduction to Movement Quality (Effort) and Theme 5—Introduction to Basic Relationships

Effort

Speed—passing the ball quickly

Relationships

Ball placement—passing ahead of a receiver; receiver repositioning to show the front of the body to the ball

OBJECTIVES

In this unit, children will (or should be willing to try to) meet these objectives:

- Pass the ball ahead of a running receiver, repositioning quickly to an open space to receive a pass.
- Improve their skills in passing, dribbling, collecting, and trapping a ball with their feet.
- Know that a lead pass is executed by kicking the ball into a space ahead of the receiver so the ball and the receiver meet at the same time; a well-timed pass allows the receiver to begin dribbling without having to break stride or alter direction.
- Accommodate the skill of others by passing the ball only as far as the receiver can travel and reach comfortably.
- Accept anyone in the class as a teammate.

EQUIPMENT AND MATERIALS

For every three or four children: one soccer or playground ball; two cones.

LEARNING EXPERIENCES

1.0 Let's see you make nice quick passes while you are on the move, trying hard to keep the passes soft and in your own working space. Get one ball, a partner, a space to work, and begin.

1.1 When receiving, collect the ball with one foot and pass it with the other. You will need to shift your weight onto the foot that received the ball, then pass the ball with the inside of the other foot.

1.2 Practice passing with all parts of your foot. Pass the ball with the outside of your foot, the inside—even the heel—occasionally.

1.3 Let's see how many completed passes the two of you can make in 30 seconds without letting the ball get out of your working space. Ready? Count your passes. [Repeat the task often throughout the unit, having the children try to break their records.]

1.4 What is going wrong when there are passes being lofted in the air? Right! Passers are kicking under the ball with their toes. Let's use only the inside or outside of our feet to pass the ball.

1.5 Passers, the receiver is on your team! Watch the speed of your pass. You want each pass easily collected. Some teammates may need soft passes and others, harder passes because they are farther away.

1.6 Everyone, try to remember we are all learners and we will make mistakes. If the pass does not come right to you, try desperately to hustle to collect the ball to make the passer and you look good.

2.0 Receivers, start to run. Passers, see if you can pass the ball into the space ahead of your receiver so the ball can be collected without stopping.

2.1 The minute you pass the ball, cut across your space to receive a pass. Passers, watch the direction of your runner and send the ball ahead of them.

2.2 Does anyone remember from our basketball unit what passing ahead of the receiver is called? Good for you! *Lead pass* is right. The ball is thrown ahead of the receiver and the receiver and the ball must meet at the spot at the same time. It is also important to make the ball roll on the ground so the receiver can collect the ball easily on the run.

2.3 Try to control the ball with different parts of your feet when you collect it. Sometimes use the inside of your foot, the outside, and even try using the top of your foot by pointing your toes down and back as the ball approaches your foot.

2.4 Passers, after you pass the ball, run across your working space to a new place. Don't pass the ball to a receiver who is standing still.

2.5 Watch the speed of your pass and how far ahead of the receiver you are aiming. Try not to make your receiver slow down or stop to get your pass.

2.6 Receivers, practice collecting the ball with one foot and passing it with the other.

2.7 Receivers, when you see that you and the ball are not going to meet at the same spot, help to complete the pass by slowing down or speeding up to meet the ball.

2.8 Receivers, as you receive the ball, keep it close in front of you.

3.0 [Observe for children who are ready and place them in groups of three or four.] Your group is on the same team sharing the space and one ball. After you pass the ball, reposition away from both teammates, but keep your eyes on the ball, ready to receive the pass.

3.1 Passers, try to send the ball to a teammate who didn't pass to you. All receivers, be alert to receive the pass.

3.2 Passers, remember to pass the ball in front of a running receiver. Then run to a new space to receive a pass. Hustle!

3.3 Collect and pass the ball quickly. Make no more than one or two touches before passing.

3.4 Keep settling that ball. Control it before you pass.

3.5 Make the ball roll. Pass it with the side of your foot—not your toes—because a rolling ball is easier for your teammate to collect.

3.6 Receivers, be ready to make the passer look good by speeding up to get to the ball when you see you and the ball aren't going to meet.

3.7 Make your working space a bit bigger so you have to run faster to still complete those passes. If you begin to miss, move in a little closer.

4.0 Let's play three versus one Soccer Keep-Away in our own working space and practice our best lead passes. Get into groups of four with one ball. The tallest person will start as the defender trying to intercept the pass. Defenders, don't try too hard at first to take the ball away. (See figure below.)

4.1 Receivers, be alert. Always try to show the front of your body to the person with the ball. Run out to the side, away from the defender, so the passer can see your whole body. Don't get behind the defender.

4.2 Collect the ball and glance about. Watch each team member moving and pass the ball quickly to an open space in front of a receiver.

4.3 See how many times you and your partners can pass the ball back and forth without the defender intercepting the ball. Defender and passer change places when the defender intercepts the ball or when you complete four passes.

4.4 After you pass the ball, reposition quickly to an open space away from the person with the ball because sometimes the ball may be passed back to you.

4.5 [Go to a three versus one or two versus two game with any group of children who are ready. All students will not be ready for this at the same time. Don't rush them.]

4.6 [When the children are ready, set up goal lines with cones at least 12 feet apart at both ends of the playing area for every six or eight children.] See how your team can take the ball down your playing area, practicing lead passes and kicking for a goal when you are near the cones.

5.0 [Organize the class to work four versus two in different playing areas. Arrange each area with a goal by placing two cones about four to five feet apart and one ball. A defensive player starts the game with a kickoff to the offensive

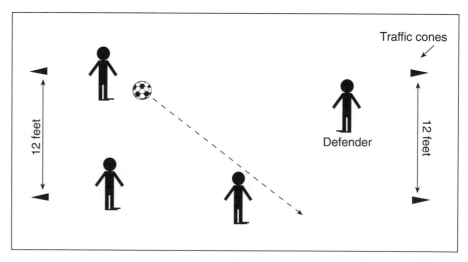

Practice lead passes with your team and kick for a goal when you are near the cones.

ASSESSING KNOWLEDGE AND AFFECTIVE BEHAVIORS

Class list	Knows that lead passes are used in many games.	Knows how to reposition for strategy advantages.	Contributes willingly to others' chances for success.	Is aware of and respects others' working spaces.	Shares equipment with partners and adjusts to their skill levels.
Shane Dye	5	5	4	4	5
Jeff Lewis	4	3	3	2	3

This assessment guide applies to many units in third grade as well as to previous units in first and second grades.
Scale: 5 = *Almost always* 4 = *Most of the time* 3 = *Improving* 2 = *Needs to improve* 1 = *Never*

team. The offense tries to pass the ball toward the goal, using lead passes as the defense tries to intercept. Score one point when the offense sends the ball over the end line between the cones. Change the two defensive players after each goal.] Let's see how your team can work the ball toward the goal line using lead passes. The defense tries to intercept the ball as it is passed from one player to the next. Defense, start your game with a kickoff to the offensive team. Get in groups of six with four offensive and two defensive players. Go to a playing area and begin.

5.1 Defenders, try to keep the person closest to the goal line from receiving the ball by constantly repositioning between the passer and the receiver to block the path of the ball.

5.2 Receivers, develop a passing lane for the ball by traveling toward your goal, away from your teammates and the defensive players and then break toward the goal to receive the pass.

5.3 Try to keep big spaces between you and your teammates so everyone can see your passing lanes. [You may go to three versus three or four versus four for those who are ready.]

ASSESSING LEAD PASS KNOWLEDGE

Children draw or find pictures in newspapers and magazines that illustrate any or all of the following: (1) timing lead passes to a running receiver; (2) adjusting lead distance and force of pass in relation to speed of receiver, and (3) sending lead passes so that the receiver can collect the ball successfully at nearly full speed. Post these pictures in the gymnasium with descriptive captions.

Unit 4 — Forearm Pass

4 or 5 lessons

FOCUS Introducing the forearm pass

MOTOR CONTENT

Body

Manipulative activities—bumping and passing a ball with the forearm

Relationships

Player and ball placement—traveling to align the body directly in front of the oncoming ball and tossing or passing the ball to the side of the receivers to make them travel to return the ball

OBJECTIVES

In this unit, children will (or should be willing to try to) meet these objectives:

- Execute a forearm pass by placing the back of one hand inside the palm of the other, bending the wrists down to keep the forearms flat and close together while maintaining a bent-knee forward stride position.
- Send the ball to a partner or an open space by allowing the ball to rebound off the flat surface of their arms as they go from a bent-knee sitting position to a straight-leg standing position, raising the arms to meet the ball.
- Consciously try to help others improve their skills by (1) sending the ball high enough so the ball bounces, enabling the receivers to position their arms under the ball, (2) sending the ball to both sides of the receivers so they can practice aligning themselves with the ball, and (3) accepting the responsibility for equalizing the amount of practice for everyone in their group.

EQUIPMENT AND MATERIALS

One vinyl or foam ball for every two children; nets and standards for each group of four children (you may substitute benches or ropes and cones for nets).

LEARNING EXPERIENCES

1.0 [Demonstrate as you talk.] Today, one person will toss the ball up about 10 feet and make it land in front of the receiver. The receiver lets the ball bounce and then tries to send the ball back to the tosser by letting the ball rebound off both forearms held close together and very flat. Partners will change roles every 10 tosses. Choose a partner, one ball, a space to work in, and begin. [Use an organizational plan suited to your situation.]

14

1.1 Tossers, try very hard to make the ball land about one step in front of your receiver and bounce about waist high.

1.2 Receivers, try to make the ball bounce right in front of your tosser by contacting the ball with flat arms held close together and shrugging your shoulders on contact with the ball.

1.3 Direct the ball to your partner by keeping your flat forearms facing toward your partner as you send the ball back. Pointing your fingers and thumbs down toward the floor will help you keep your forearms flat.

1.4 Do you know what this skill is called? Right, it's called the 'forearm pass' or 'bump,' and it is used in the game of volleyball. Passers, watch the ball and see if you made the ball land in front of your receiver. You can tell if you controlled your pass if your receiver's feet do not move when catching the ball.

1.5 Your legs will do almost all the work if you remember to bend your knees, then straighten them as you contact the ball. Act like you are sitting in a straightback chair and say to yourself, 'sit—stand' as you contact the ball. Keep your back straight against the back of the imaginary chair as you bend your knees to sit.

1.6 See how many times out of 10 tosses you can make the ball bounce in front of your receiver without having the receiver take any steps to return the ball. [Change roles.]

1.7 Receivers, if you were successful in sending [bumping] the ball back in front of your tosser, you may want the tosser to intentionally toss the ball one or two feet to one side of you so you have to reposition your feet to return [bump] the ball.

1.8 Return to your ready position with your weight on the balls of your feet and your knees bent so you can move quickly to either side to align yourself with the ball.

2.0 When the sender makes the ball bounce softly up to the middle of your waist, try to bump it back. Remember to be caring partners, returning the ball in a nice arc so it always bounces to your partner's waist.

2.1 Remember, it is up to each of you to make your partner look like a pro. When you make the ball land right in front of your receiver, it is easier to send the ball back. Let's give our partners practice in bumping the ball—not in chasing or catching the ball.

2.2 Be sure you remember to keep your fingers and thumbs pointed down to make your arms flat to help you send the ball straight to the magic spot in front of your partner.

2.3 Begin to notice you are getting good enough to send the ball almost any place you want. To help you aim your pass, try pointing your forward foot toward the spot where you want the ball to land.

2.4 Receivers, watch the ball coming and adjust your feet quickly so the ball bounces in front of you to help your sender look like a pro, too. Just catch the ball and start again when the ball is too far off target.

2.5 Remember to sit in that straightback chair and stand to lift your arms by straightening your knees. Say 'Sit—stand.' Count how many times you and your partner can bump the ball back and forth.

3.0 [Set up nets about three to four feet high. You can tie ropes to chairs or benches as a substitute for nets.] This time, as you work on your forearm pass, try to make the ball land on an exact spot as you pass it over a low net. Practice trying to make the ball land on the floor so it bounces to the middle of your receiver's body.

3.1 Think of your arms as a rebound surface, not as a batting surface. Hold your arms straight out in front of you with the back of one hand held in the palm of the other and fingers pointed down. Concentrate on bending your knees as you wait for the ball and straightening your knees as the ball contacts your arms.

3.2 Some of you may be ready to make your partner travel by sending the ball over the net so it bounces to the side of your partner. Receivers, move your feet quickly to get to the ball by staying on the balls of your feet.

3.3 If you and your partner are passing the ball back and forth several times without missing, challenge each other by intentionally directing the pass to land to the side or farther in front of the receiver to make each other move your feet to line up the middle of your body to the ball.

3.4 Be sure you move quickly to get in front of the ball, letting it bounce to give you time to get in your sitting position, prepared to return the pass.

3.5 Some of you may want to begin to share the space on your side of the net with a partner. When working with others on the same side of the net, return the ball when it comes into your space, allowing your partner to return the ball when the pass lands in their space. Be sure you give everyone equal practice. [Increase the difficulty of this task by having them send the ball higher to make the receiver move backward to line up with the ball.]

3.6 [Those working in fours may be able to alternate hits. This will make them have to hustle to adjust their positions to get to the ball.] Some of you are ready to accept a greater challenge. Take turns returning the ball each time it comes over the net. When it isn't your turn, move away from the ball quickly to make room for the receiver to get in line with the ball.

3.7 You really have to hustle when alternating turns by running quickly to get the middle of your body in line with the ball. Always try to contact the ball with your arms positioned in the center of your body.

3.8 When it is your turn to receive the pass, quickly take the center position of your area so you can move quickly in any direction to play the ball.

4.0 [Observe for groups of four to six who are able to keep the ball going over the net several times.] Your group might like to begin to play a cooperative game of One-Bounce Volleyball. Count to see how many passes your two teams can make, always letting the ball bounce before it is returned.

4.1 Everyone, be on the balls of your feet and watch the ball. When the ball isn't coming to your space, move quickly out of the way of the receiver. Good team players give their partners space to play the ball.

4.2 This is a cooperative game. Pass the ball carefully so it can be returned easily. Each time you miss, start over and see if your two teams can complete more passes.

4.3 You may challenge another group to see which group can keep their ball going back and forth over their net the most times. [Continue to reinforce passing the ball from the midline of the body and moving to give the receiver space to return the ball.]

4.4 [Observe children carefully and select those who may produce greater effort when challenged by competition against an opposing team on the opposite side of the net.] Your group might like to see which group can make the most points in a competitive game. Your team makes a point when the opponents fail to return the ball. Decide whether you want your game to end when one team reaches 7, 11, or 15 points and begin.

4.5 Whether you are playing a cooperative or competitive game, commit yourself to lining up the middle of your body to the ball, bending your knees and contacting the ball with two flat arms.

4.6 Let's share our three different kinds of games. As we watch, look for quick feet aligning the center of the body with the ball and the knees, bending and straightening to help the arms return the ball over the net. [Have each of the groups participating in the three different types of games share their games with the class (cooperative with two teams, competitive with two teams, or cooperative-competitive with four teams).]

4.7 Now, some of you may want to change the kind of game you are playing or make up a new one. [Continue to revisit tasks 1.3, 1.5, 1.8, 3.1, and 4.1. These tasks reinforce aligning the middle of the body with the ball, arms together, and the sitting and lifting with the knee action.]

ASSESSING FOREARM PASSING				
Class list	Uses arms as a rebound, surface (not for striking).	Keeps fore-arms flat to complete pass.	Uses legs to lift through the ball.	Aligns to meet balls when stationary or when moving 1 to 2 steps.
Tamara Lloyd	3	4	4	3
Kyle Gaskin	4	5	5	4

Scale: 5 = Almost always; 4 = Very frequently; 3 = Sometimes; 2 = Rarely; 1 = Never

Unit 5 — Unilateral Throw and One-Handed Catch

3 to 5 lessons

FOCUS — Introducing the unilateral throw and one-handed catch with a deck tennis ring

MOTOR CONTENT

Selected from Theme 1—Introduction to Basic Body and Manipulative Control and Theme 5—Introduction to Basic Relationships

Body

Manipulative activities—flat, unilateral throw; one-handed catch
Nonlocomotor and Locomotor activities—extending or traveling to catch

Relationships

Deck tennis ring placement—throwing into empty spaces about and away from the receivers (in front of, behind, along side of)

OBJECTIVES

In this unit, children will (or should be willing to try to) meet these objectives:

- Throw a deck tennis ring with either hand.
- Catch the ring with either hand.
- Be alert with weight on the balls of their feet, ready to travel in any direction to catch the ring.
- Understand that sending the ring in a high arc gives the receiver more time to travel to catch the ring than a ring thrown parallel to the floor.
- Know that the preparation for the unilateral throw starts with the throwing arm crossing over in front of the body, taking the hand and ring down near the opposite knee, and, *unlike* any throw they have learned previously, they will be stepping on the same foot as the throwing hand.
- Work with as many different classmates as they can to help them become better throwers and catchers.

EQUIPMENT AND MATERIALS

One deck tennis ring for every two people in the class; standards and nets or ropes to throw over. (You can easily make a deck tennis ring by tightly rolling up a page or two of newspaper and forming it into a circle. Wrap the circle many times with masking tape to make it firm. Have the nets or ropes set up on the side so they can be set up easily by the children.)

LEARNING EXPERIENCES

1.0 Today, many of you will be throwing a deck tennis ring for the first time. This throw will be different mainly because of four things. [You or a child demonstrate while you talk.] First, you hold the ring with your thumb on top and your fingers on the bottom. Second, you turn and point your whole throwing side toward your target. Third, your throwing arm crosses your body so the ring starts way down near your opposite knee. Fourth, as you throw, you step forward on the foot on the same side as your throwing hand while reaching your throwing hand toward your target. Get a partner, one ring, and stand opposite each other, ready to begin, as I talk you through the throw a couple of times.

1.1 As you throw the ring to your partner, make your throwing side and shoulder point toward your partner. Try to make the ring spin flat with the floor. It shouldn't wobble or spin like a tire.

1.2 See if you can make the ring travel horizontally to [flat as] the floor and go right to your partner by holding it flat with your thumb on top of the ring with the hole in the ring facing the floor when you start your toss.

1.3 This time make your ring travel in a high arc by taking your ring down near your opposite knee to start and releasing the ring above your shoulder as you toss it to your partner. This throw always starts low and finishes high.

1.4 Can anyone tell me what is different about this throw than most throws? You are really smart! Right, you step on the foot on the same side as your throwing hand, rather than on the opposite foot. Let's all step toward our receiver with the foot on the same side as our throwing hand when we throw the ring to our partners.

1.5 Watch the distance between the two of you. Don't get too far apart. Both of you take great pride in seeing the ring travel in an arc to give your catcher time to catch the ring. Remember—your throwing hand starts low and finishes high. [Monitor the space. Some may need to move farther away or closer together.]

1.6 Some of you are having trouble getting the ring to go to your partner. Make your hand release the ring and stop when your hand is pointing right to your partner. Check your throwing hand. Did you stop it when you released the ring? Are your fingers pointing to your partner.

1.7 Take a step toward your partner on your throwing-side foot as you throw the ring.

1.8 How many times can you and your partner toss the ring back and forth in high arcs without missing, making the ring spin horizontally to the floor?

2.0 Catchers, more of you are ready to try to make a one-handed catch. Open your fingers and thumb so the ring will slide right into your hand.

2.1 Keep your fingers up when the ring is caught above your waist and point your fingers down when you catch the ring below your waist.

2.2 Always have your hand ready to catch the ring by having it look like it's ready to gobble up the ring.

2.3 Be sure to watch your partner's hand holding the ring from the minute they catch the ring until they throw the ring back to you. This may help you judge where the ring will go in case you have to travel to catch it.

2.4 The minute you throw the ring back to your partner, get in a ready position with knees bent and your weight on the balls of your feet so you are ready to travel in any direction to catch the next throw.

2.5 If your partner has been successful in catching the ring one-handed, try to toss the ring to either side so your partner will have to travel to catch it.

2.6 Are you still remembering to make your hand like an open mouth, ready to gobble up the ring wherever it goes?

2.7 Give each other really high and really low tosses so you can practice changing the position of your fingers in relation to the height of the ring. Remember, fingers point up to catch when the ring is above your waist and fingers point down to catch when the ring is below your waist.

2.8 The two of you may like to set up a net and practice your throwing and catching over a net. [Have the nets or ropes set up on the side so they can be set up easily by the children.]

Remember to start the ring low.

3.0 Let's concentrate on our throwing so we can be the very best throwers possible. A good thrower makes the ring travel flat and sends it right where they want it to go by pointing their throwing hand to their target as the ring is released.

3.1 Toss the ring a bit higher and softer so it floats in the air to give the receiver more time to run to catch it.

3.2 Focus your eyes on a spot where you wish to send the ring. Try very hard to reach out toward that spot as you release the ring.

3.3 Pick out several different spots about and away from your partner and see if you can toss your ring exactly to each of these spots.

3.4 Try to step toward the spot where you want your ring to go. Are you still remembering to step forward on the foot that is on the same side as your throwing hand?

3.5 Mix up your target spots so your partner must travel and reach into many different empty spaces to catch the ring.

3.6 Keep track of your completed catches for 30 seconds. I'll time you. Stand about 12 steps away from each other and try to make the ring travel flat like a Frisbee, not spin in the air like a tire. Ready? Begin.

4.0 [Set up ropes or nets about five feet high. Create enough room for groups of two or four to work together.] This time we all have nets or ropes to toss the deck tennis ring over. See if you can continue to make each other travel to catch the ring. Get a partner, a ring, and begin.

4.1 Keep in mind that a high, horizontal [flat] toss starts from your hip and is released when the ring is high above your shoulder. Toss the ring from the very place where you caught it. Feel your whole arm and body extend—throw!

4.2 Intentionally try to make the ring spin flat close to the net, then the next time, in back of your receiver. Make your receiver travel forward and backward to catch the ring.

4.3 [Observe for children being successful in traveling to catch and group four or six together.] Now see if the four [six] of you can keep the ring going. Watch and share the space to be sure everyone is getting a chance to throw and catch the ring.

4.4 Carefully think before you throw the ring and see if you can make the receiver travel to an open spot to catch.

4.5 Let's all play a cooperative game of deck tennis and see how many successful catches we can make before someone misses. If the ring is dropped or thrown out of bounds, start your count over from one. I'll stop you in one minute to see how many good throws you have made.

4.6 This time, some of you may want to play a competitive game to see how many points you can score against your opponents. [Make sure that everyone in the group agrees to playing competitively before they begin. You may have to do some rearranging of partners.] The team that drops the ring or sends the ring out of bounds gives the other team one point. Decide whether you want to end the game when one team reaches 6, 10, or 12 points.

4.7 Trade partners with the two people across from you and play another game. Do you need to change any rules to make your next game work even better?

4.8 If you are playing a competitive game of deck tennis, try to throw the ring away from the receivers so they must travel to catch the ring. In a cooperative game, try your very best to place the ring high and in front of the receiver so they can make an easy catch.

ASSESSING THROWING DECK TENNIS RING					
Points throwing shoulder toward receiver.	Starts ring below knee opposite the throwing hand.	Shifts weight from the back to the front foot.	Steps forward with throwing-side foot.	Sends ring in a high arc, making ring spin parallel to the floor.	Throwing hard follows through toward intended target.

Scale: List the names of children who do *not* perform the criteria more than half the time.

ASSESSING CATCHING DECK TENNIS RING

Shows "ready" position before all catches.	Grips with open hand. Reaches to catch with open hand.	Positions fingers on top for high catches; thumb on top to catch low.	Absorbs force during the catch by bringing ring back on line of flight.	Uses either hand to catch and throw.	Travels to align body with ring to catch.

Scale: List the names of children who do *not* perform the criteria more than half the time.

Unit 6

Throwing and Fielding

4 or 5 lessons

FOCUS   Throwing and fielding a ball

MOTOR CONTENT

Selected from Theme 3—Introduction to Movement Quality (Effort) and Theme 5—Introduction to Basic Relationships

Effort

Time—getting rid of the ball quickly
Flow—blending the catch and the throw into a continuous movement

Relationships

Player placement—running toward the ball (sometimes at an angle) to meet the ball quickly

OBJECTIVES

In this unit, children will (or should be willing to try to) meet these objectives:

- Blend the catch and throw into one continuous movement by joining the give in the catch with the preparation of the throw.
- Take less time to retrieve a ball by running at an angle to meet the ball.
- Demonstrate an awareness for the skill level of others by trying to throw hard enough to challenge without intimidating the receiver.

EQUIPMENT AND MATERIALS

One softball-size ball for every child; batting tees; plastic bats; and bases.

LEARNING EXPERIENCES

1.0 Let's all try to throw a ball overhand and hit the wall low to make the ball roll back so you can field it quickly and throw it again. Get a ball, find a working space about 15 steps from the wall, and begin.

1.1 Wait until the person has thrown the ball if you must go into someone else's space to retrieve your ball. Then, the next time you throw, be careful when releasing your ball. Point your throwing hand down low toward the bottom of the wall, right out in front of you, so the ball stays in your space and rolls back to you.

1.2 Quickly move to get directly in front of the ball to see how soon you can catch the ball.

1.3 Hustle and run up to meet the ball. Don't wait for it.

1.4 Does anyone remember the *ready* position? Show it to us, [Leonardo]. Notice his weight is forward on the balls of both feet, his knees and hips are bent, his arms hang down in front of him, his palms face forward, and his fingertips almost touch the ground. Does anyone notice something else important in his ready position? Right! Look at his eyes. He is looking forward. You can tell he is alert and ready to run to meet the ball. Let's all practice that ready position every time we wait to retrieve the ball.

1.5 After you throw, don't take your eyes off the ball. Still be looking at that ball when it rolls into your hands.

1.6 Remember what we did to retrieve the ball quickly? We worked on charging up to the ball, instead of standing, waiting for the ball to come to us. See how fast you can throw, catch, and throw again. Hustle!

2.0 You are getting good at fielding balls you have thrown. Now let's see if your catching skills are as sharp when you practice fielding a ball thrown by someone else. Join with someone near you, put one ball away, and take turns throwing the ball to each other and fielding the ball.

2.1 When you throw, point your hand down to the floor as you release the ball to make the ball roll or bounce along to your catcher. This will give your partner lots of practice fielding grounders.

2.2 Remember to charge the ball. Don't wait for the ball to come to you.

2.3 Throwers, aim your throw a step or two to the side of your retrievers, and let's see what they do to get to the ball more quickly.

2.4 Great! You are all hustling. Let's watch [Meredith and Lucinda] hustle and notice how they are aligning themselves to the ball. Everyone try to figure out what we all need to do to get to the ball sooner. I am going to come around and ask you to show me your solution.

2.5 Have a seat. See if you can tell what [Brandy and Meesha] do to get to the ball more quickly. Right, they charge the ball at an angle. They are aligning their bodies to the ball as they run up rather than moving to the side and waiting for the ball to come to them. Everyone, see if you can go at an angle to meet the ball.

2.6 Some of you are forgetting that wonderful, ready position you had when you were practicing alone. Everyone keep your eyes on the ball and try to take your ready position in the middle of your space immediately after every throw so you can move quickly to get to the ball.

3.0 When you are playing a ball game, you need to learn to throw the ball immediately after you catch it. Holding the ball after you catch it gives the base runner more time to run. Let's practice throwing the ball quickly back to your partner as soon as you catch it.

3.1 Prepare your feet as you catch the ball by turning your side to your partner. Step out on the foot opposite your throwing hand and throw quickly.

3.2 See how quickly you can field the ball and return it to each other.

3.3 As you hustle to return the ball to each other, try to give your partner good practice in charging the ball at an angle. Make every throw fun for your partner to catch. It isn't any fun if the throws are too far to your side and you have to chase it after it passes you.

3.4 Let's see how many throws you and your partner can make while I time you for 30 seconds. Ready? . . . Begin!

3.5 When I time you again, see if you can charge those balls at an angle more quickly to help you and your partner get even more throws this time.

4.0 You have been working on fielding the ball by charging it at an angle and returning it quickly to your partner. Begin to think about smoothing out your throw. Blending your catching action into your throwing action makes catching and throwing one single motion with no stops. [Demonstrate.]

4.1 As you give with the ball when you catch, go right into your preparation to throw by not letting your throwing hand stop until after you release the ball.

4.2 When you catch the ball, let the speed of your hands giving with the catch take your throwing hand and arm right into the preparation of your throw.

4.3 Think about what your feet are doing just as your hands make contact with the ball. Step back with the foot on your throwing side as you give with the catch so your weight is shifted backward, then step forward on your opposite foot as you throw.

4.4 Don't hesitate between your catch and your throw. Continue practicing fielding the ball and throwing it back to your partner in one big, smooth, flowing motion.

4.5 This half of the class sit and watch and see if you can find someone who has learned to make the catch and throw one big, continuous motion. [Ask someone to name a student who caught and threw in one nonstop motion and have that child demonstrate.]

4.6 Let's go back and see if everyone can take out all stops between the catch and throw. Try to feel one big, smooth motion.

4.7 Now, let's observe the other half of the class and count how many are making one, big, smooth, no-stop action when they catch and throw.

5.0 [We suggest batting tees to maximize practice in fielding the ball.] There will be three in a group: one catcher, one batter, and one fielder. Sit in groups of three and watch closely. This group stand up. One of you get a ball and go over and place it on top of one of the tees. This person is the catcher and always takes three big steps back behind the tee. Listen carefully to what the rest of you will be doing. The second player is the fielder who will practice fielding the ball and throwing it back to the catcher when the batter hits the ball. The third player is the batter and gets a bat and takes a batting position facing the tee with their nonthrowing arm and side pointed toward the fielder. Each batter gets to hit the ball five times. After five hits, the batter goes out to be the fielder, the fielder becomes the catcher, and the catcher is the next batter. Carefully, the rest of you may take your positions, and everyone may begin.

5.1 [Make sure all catchers are standing three long steps in back of the tee.] Batters, face the tee with your nonthrowing arm and side pointed toward the fielder. Step sideways with the foot nearest the fielder as you swing flat with the ground to hit the ball. Try to hit the ball so it doesn't bother another group.

5.2 Fielders, remember you'll need your best overhand throw to get the ball back to the catcher. Get into the ready position with your weight forward, hips and knees bent, hands and arms low, ready to charge that ball. Don't wait for the ball—run to get it.

5.3 Hustle to the ball and try to make your catch blend right into your throw. Remember, don't stop your catching-throwing action until after you see the ball flying back to the catcher.

5.4 Catchers, be ready to run out to meet the throw from the fielder. You always have a chance to practice fielding each time the fielder throws it to home base so stay alert.

6.0 [Provide opportunities for children to be engaged in this game several times throughout this unit. Point to children and have them count off by seven (boys and girls combined). Have them sit down in groups of seven.] Two people in each group will start as fielders. Three will play the bases and one will be the catcher. One will be the starting batter. Each batter gets five hits so we call this game Five-Hit Softball. After hitting the ball, the batter places the bat down and runs to touch each of the bases before the ball reaches home or before a player with the ball steps on the base before the runner reaches the base. Score one point for each base reached. [In their individual games, children may choose to count caught fly balls as automatic outs with no points earned by the batter.] The score for the batter is the sum [total] of the bases reached in the five tries. Rotate from batter to right field, to left field, to third base, to second base, to first base, to catcher, to batter. [After everyone is in place on their diamonds, walk them through the rotation once or twice to teach this.]

6.1 Watch where the runner is and try to throw the ball so the ball reaches a baseman ahead of the runner.

6.2 First and third basemen, while waiting for the batter to hit, stand three or four steps to the side of your base. This spacing will help you field more balls and get the runner out sooner.

6.3 Runners, run as fast as you can and see how many bases you can reach.

[*Note*: Many tasks listed earlier in the unit need to be revisited when the children are involved in Five-Hit Softball to keep the students focused on improving blending the catch into the throw.]

Third Grade Gymnastics

Rolling, Stepping, and Moments of Flight

Unit 1

4 or 5 lessons

FOCUS Combining rolling, stepping, and moments of flight with changes in speed and levels

MOTOR CONTENT

Selected from Theme 1—Introduction to the Body; Theme 2—Introduction to Space; and Theme 3—Introduction to Time

Body

Locomotor activities—flight, rolling, and stepping with different body parts

Effort

Time—changing and contrasting (speed; slow, fast, and accelerating)

Space

Levels—changing and contrasting; (high, medium, and low)

OBJECTIVES

In this unit, children will (or should be willing to try to) meet these objectives:

- Increase their versatility in gymnastics by developing a series of short gymnastic sequences, which include different combinations of rolling, flight, and stepping actions with different body parts; achieving variety in each sequence by altering speed and level.
- Improve their abilities to perform self-selected or self-created stunts by purposefully practicing the same gymnastic movement at contrasting speeds.
- Know that they can increase their gymnastic skills when they are able to change the level and speed of a single skill and perform skills in ever-changing combinations.
- Be conscious of their responsibility for maintaining a safe working environment by sticking to the task, challenging themselves to do their best work, and allowing others freedom to have the space they need.

EQUIPMENT AND MATERIALS

Tumbling mats; a selection of gymnastic apparatus (if you believe the addition of apparatus could motivate children to sustain their efforts toward increasing skill and versatility). (If you include apparatus, be sure to use landing mats.)

LEARNING EXPERIENCES

1.0 Over the past few years you all have shown improvement in your gymnastic skills. During these gymnastic lessons, we want to continue to improve on staying away from the mat until it is your turn so the gymnast in front of you can begin to feel the mat and the space behind it really belongs only to them. Each of you will select one gymnastic way of traveling down the mat and perform it two times. Think and select wisely so you can start with your very best work. [Plan the organization of the students and the mats to fit your teaching situation. The diagram below illustrates one way you might organize a class to start this unit.]

1.1 Choose a different gymnastic movement on your next turn if the way you have been traveling hasn't been challenging you to do your best gymnastic work. Always challenge yourself to do your best. [You may need to name skills for the students to perform; however, many students will challenge themselves.]

1.2 Now you are beginning to look like gymnasts. To help you develop more control of your body, see how slowly you can do your movement the first time and then, the second time, increase your speed but keep control of your movement. Maintain muscle tension and your best performing attitude all of the time.

1.3 Begin to watch the other people in your group. Notice how their changes in speed almost make them look like they are doing two different things! Changing your speed helps you add beautiful variety to your gymnastic work.

1.4 Can anyone think of why we should work to add variety to our gymnastics moves? Right, there are several reasons. One, it makes it more fun for you when you perform because you get to keep changing things. Two, it makes it more exciting for the observers because they never know just how you are

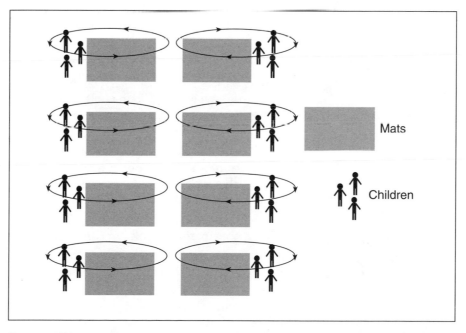

One possible arrangement for a group of 24 students. This organization plan has all children traveling toward the center of the teaching station. This creates an active environment that makes it easier for the teacher to focus on the responses of all children.

going to perform your movement. Three, changing and controlling your speed to make variety can be more challenging because it makes you work harder and it helps you become more skillful.

1.5 Select a different way to travel down the mat and see if you can feel yourself traveling both slowly and quickly. Demonstrate your best work for your group every time you take a turn.

1.6 This has gotten too easy for you. Now every time you take your turn, see if you can perform a different gymnastic movement. And don't forget: Do it two times on the mat. See how slowly you can do it and how quickly you can do it, always looking like a gymnast under control. [Some children may need more direct teaching, benefiting from you making the decision as to how they should travel. You can name ways to travel, such as on hands and feet, rolling, forward roll, cartwheel, depending on the capability of the individual, group, or class.]

2.0 Show a big contrast in the level of your body this time as you travel down the mat. See if you can perform one movement that takes you low, then make your next movement take you high. Think before you start your turn.

2.1 Try to figure out ways you can exaggerate your high level to make it even higher so it makes your low level look even lower. Those of you who are waiting, take care not to inch closer to the mat. Let the performers feel that the space behind the mat is all theirs. Some gymnasts may even get more height if you stay back and give them room to make a running approach to the mat.

2.2 Some of you who are traveling onto your hands to take you into a high level can give more height to your body by really stretching the tip of your toes toward the ceiling. [Observe the children, noticing what body parts the children have the highest, encouraging them to reach even higher with those body parts.]

2.3 See if you can add a high pop-up in between your two moves. Extend your arms, ankles, and legs by reaching up with your hands, pushing off the floor with your feet, and pointing those toes toward the floor.

2.4 [Have half of the class demonstrate some of their responses developed in 2.0-2.3. This can be done several times as warranted.]

2.5 Let's see how many of you can do 'a backward roll, pop up high, and go right into a cartwheel' or 'a forward roll, high balance and headstand.'

2.6 [Novices tend to 'open up' by straightening the back, taking the abdomen away from the knees.] When you are finishing your backward roll, stay tucked and land on your feet, not on your shins, so you can make your pop-up come right after your roll.

2.7 See how many of you can start with a pop-up, sending your fingertips high into the air, land on your feet, go into a backward [or forward] roll, and finish with a trick of your own, which you can definitely feel takes some part of your body very high.

2.8 Try combining a high pop-up, rolling, and something on your own that takes a body part to a high level. [Handstand, high lifted balances, etc.]

2.9 Really make your work exciting for you by combining different movements each time. Don't permit yourself to make one trip down the mat look like one you have already performed.

3.0 Remember, all of you stay back to give each performer the pleasure of freedom of space to approach the mat. In your group, quietly and showing your best work, begin to play 'Can You Top This?' The first person will do their best change in levels, then the second one will do one, and so on, until it is the first person's turn again. Everyone in each group tries to outdo themselves by creating different combinations that show definite changes in levels.

STRENGTH AND ENDURANCE

To increase abdominal (stomach) strength needed to stay tucked while rolling, try 10 sit-ups each day at home. Lie on your back with your hands folded across your chest and your chin tucked just like in the roll. Bend your knees, resting your feet on the floor. Curl up part way, hold two to three seconds, and then slowly return to lying on your back. If you complete 10 sit-ups successfully, you can add one or two more.

3.1 Check your muscle tension, making each trip a true performance by feeling firm and lifted throughout your demonstration. Begin to add a good, lifted pause to start, then stop completely and freeze, slowly counting to five before you walk away at the end.

3.2 People at these four mats, have a seat and observe closely. See which classmates at the other four mats are taking their demonstration really seriously and are true performers all the way. [Have observers comment. Then reverse roles.]

3.3 Since you have done such a fine job on the levels, let's add more excitement and more skill to your show by bringing in those changes of speed you perfected, too!

3.4 Keep all your body parts firm throughout your performance. No limp dish towels allowed in your gymnastic performance!

3.5 Exaggerate the changes in levels and the changes in speed. Make your high movements really high, and the slow movement very *slow*.

3.6 Let's take a moment to enjoy the skill you developed in contrasting levels and speeds. As we watch, see if you can tell me which group has truly conquered their desire to inch up to the mat by standing way back, giving the performers the pleasure of having the mat all to themselves.

ASSESSMENT OF SPEED AND LEVELS IN GYMNASTICS

Class list	Combines rolls, flight, and stepping actions into sequences.		Alters speed and levels to produce variety.		Repeats a sequence at contrasting speeds.		Changes a sequence while emphasizing level and speed changes.		Changes levels and speed while repeating the same sequence of skills.	
B. Cole	3	11/9	5	11/9	5	11/9	4	11/15	4	11/15
C. Dill	3	11/9	4	11/9	5	11/9	3	11/15	4	11/15
H. Johns	3	11/9	4	11/9	5	11/9	4	11/15	4	11/15

Scale: 5 = Always 4 = 2/3 or more of the time 3 = Half the time 2 = 1/3 or less of the time 1 = Rarely or never

Relationships of the Feet With Weight on Hands

4 to 6 lessons

FOCUS Changing relationships of the feet while taking weight on hands, rolling, and traveling on, off, and over apparatus

MOTOR CONTENT

Selected from Theme 1—Introduction to the Body and Theme 4—Introduction to Relationships of Body Parts

Body

Locomotor activities—rolling; traveling on the floor, over, on, and off apparatus
Nonlocomotor activities—taking weight on the hands

Relationships

Body parts to each other and to apparatus—changing relationships of feet and legs to the floor, apparatus, and one to the other

OBJECTIVES

In this unit, children will (or should be willing to try to) meet these objectives:

- Create and maintain sufficient arm and shoulder strength to support themselves while mounting and dismounting the apparatus and change relationships of feet and legs in the air when dismounting and when rolling to improve greater gymnastic ability and versatility.
- Name the relationships created by feet and legs occurring in the performances of themselves and others.
- Understand that changing relationships of legs and feet while executing rolls, vaults, and step-like actions is essential to performing known gymnastic skills and to creating variations.
- Increase their versatility and skills by concentrating on controlling the relationships of their legs and feet.

EQUIPMENT AND MATERIALS

A selection of vaulting boxes; benches; blocks or traffic cones; newspaper rolls (wands); at least one tumbling mat for every four to six children plus landing mats by boxes.

LEARNING EXPERIENCES

1.0 Place your palms flat on the floor. Take your feet into the air and notice where your feet land. [Close to one hand? Both? Behind? To the side?]

1.1 Know where your feet land and how they land. Make them land one at a time or two at a time. Make them land apart, sometimes together.

1.2 Place your feet softly back on the floor by tightening your tummy and upper leg muscles to help slow down your feet. Don't let gravity bang them on the floor.

1.3 See if you can keep your feet close together as you place them down in different places near your hands.

1.4 Place both feet near the heel or back of one of your hands. Then, next time, place them very close to the side of one of your hands.

1.5 Listen to the sound your feet make as they land. Remember this sensation of your feet touching the floor. Get rid of any sound. Be gentle when you place your feet on the floor. You can eliminate the sound made by your feet and the floppy feeling of your body if you tuck your knees to your chest while in the air. Stay tucked until your feet touch the floor. [Observe children's legs. Uncontrolled descending legs usually have straight knees. The children let their feet fall, rather than placing them, almost a body length away from hands. It takes concerted effort on the part of the learner and close, sensitive instruction to reduce this problem. Make this task a part of almost every lesson.]

1.6 [When children become skilled in placing their feet on the floor while tucked, encourage them to work on the pike position by bending only at the hips and keeping their knees straight.] Keep your knees straight throughout the movement. Bend sharply at your hips so you can softly place both feet close to your hands.

2.0 Practice perfecting your backward and forward rolls by keeping your body tucked and coming to your feet quickly. Get in groups, choosing people who help you be serious as you work, carefully pick up the mat, and carry it to a working space away from other mats. [The size of the group will depend on the number of mats available. If the quantity of mats is insufficient to have six or fewer at a mat, we advise you to divide the class and have half of the class work on weight on hands on the floor while the other half works on their rolls on the mats, then rotate groups. Note placement of mats on page 35.]

2.1 Watch the placement of your hands when rolling forward or backward. Always place the palms of your hands flat on the floor, fingers spread, with your thumbs pointed toward each other. Push firmly with your hands on the mat, trying to keep your arms strong.

2.2 [If children have not voluntarily practiced the backward roll, encourage them to work on the hand placement and tucking of the body while executing the backward roll.]

2.3 As you roll, begin to notice and to feel where your feet are in relation to each other when you start your roll, during your roll, and when they touch the mat again. Be able to know if they are both close together, far apart, one out in front of the other, crossed and close together, or whatever relationship you see and feel your feet have.

2.4 As you work on thinking about the relationship of your feet, don't forget to make your whole body look alert like you are giving a special performance. Tighten your muscles to sharpen each line of your body. Get rid of any feeling of droopiness or weakness in your muscles.

2.5 Now, try to change the relationship of your feet as you start your roll. Sometimes start your roll with your feet close together, sometimes with them far apart. Exaggerate the relationship you select so observers can accurately name each relationship.

2.6 This time, change the relationship of your feet as you roll by starting with your feet in one relationship, then ending up with them in another relationship.

2.7 Listen carefully. I am going to tell you which relationships you should have at the beginning and at the end. Then I am going to see if you can make your feet do them. [Name various relationships for the children to practice, such as "start with your feet close together and end with your feet far apart; start with your feet far apart and end with your feet close together; start with your feet close together and end with them one in front of the other." Give this task while the children are focusing on their forward and backward rolls.]

2.8 Take turns telling each other whether the roll should be a backward or forward roll and the relationship the feet should have to start and to finish the roll.

2.9 You all have gotten to be quite masterful at controlling the relationships of your feet at the beginning and at the end of your forward and backward rolls. See if you can intentionally change the relationship of your feet in the middle of your roll. [For example, they could start with their feet close together, then take them far apart, and end with them back close together.]

3.0 As you roll, concentrate on the relationship of one foot to the other so you know where they are when you start, during the roll, and when you end.

3.1 Do a backward straddle roll and, pushing hard with your hands, see how far apart your feet can be throughout your entire roll. [Teach for straight knees throughout.]

3.2 Tell the person in back of you exactly what relationship you plan to have for your feet when you start, during the roll, and when you finish. Observer, listen and then notice carefully to tell the performer exactly what relationships they actually created in the beginning, middle, and end of their sequence.

3.3 One person at each mat be the leader and change the relationships of your legs as you roll. Everyone else watch your leader's legs very carefully as they change relationships. See if each of you can copy the roll and the relationships of the leader's legs exactly. [Rotate leaders.]

3.4 As you continue practicing, everyone take pride in doing your best work. Set a standard of performance for your group that will make your group champions for today.

3.5 Each of you see if you can combine at least two rolls, varying the relationship of your feet.

3.6 Try to perfect what your body looks like as you perform your series of rolls. Exaggerate the relationships you are creating with your feet and pop up when you finish your last roll. End holding your tall, stretched, standing position very still.

4.0 [Add at least one piece of apparatus per group close to the mat so the mat can cushion the children's landings. Add more incentives for children to make shapes in the air by spacing blocks (traffic cones) with newspaper rolls on top of them to go over before they reach the mat and after they leave the mat. See p. 35.] As you travel on, off, or over the apparatus and the newspaper rolls, see what relationships you can create with your feet while they are in the air.

4.1 Work hard to show nice strong muscles in the air to help you make your body shape very clear. Then land softly by giving in your knees and ankles.

4.2 When you go over the apparatus, place only your hands on the apparatus and land on your feet on the other side of the apparatus. Before you start to practice again, ask yourself if you are really being serious about giving your best

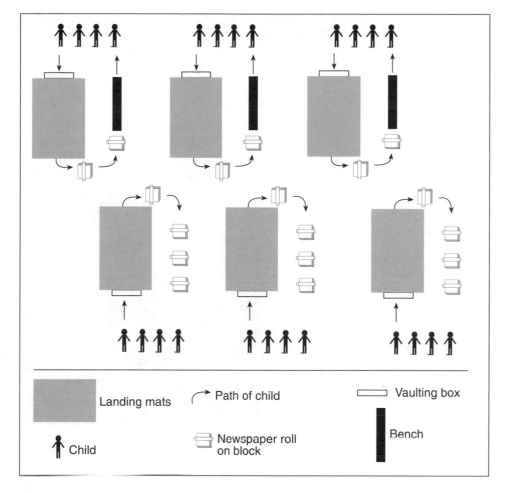

One possible arrangement of apparatus, mats, and children.

effort. If you are not, think about if there is someone in the group you find yourself tending to laugh at or trying to make laugh instead of being serious. If so, one of you may want to move to a new group so you can really give yourself and your friend the best chance of doing serious work.

4.3 As you go over the apparatus touching it only with your hands, begin to pay very close attention to where each foot is in relation to the other foot.

4.4 See if you can go over the apparatus while keeping your feet and ankles very close together.

4.5 Each time you land on the mat, practice a roll where you intentionally change the relationship of your feet as you roll, then spring up very high to finish your roll.

4.6 Let's share some of the relationships you have been making with your feet to each other, to the apparatus, and to the newspaper rolls. Focus your attention on the relationship of the feet of each performer and maybe the ideas of others will give you something new to try. [Recall some of the relationships the children have made and call upon children to show variety in the relationships created by the feet and the relationships the feet have to the apparatus.]

4.7 All of you select a new relationship you haven't tried with your feet and see if you can control your feet to make that relationship. Follow the landing on the mat immediately with a roll, changing the relationships of your feet as you roll, and create different relationships with your feet each time you go over a newspaper roll.

4.8 After finishing your roll, go right into taking your weight on your hands, intentionally planning and controlling the relationships of your legs while they are in the air and the placement of your feet back onto the floor. Plan to control the relationship of your legs when going over the newspaper rolls, too.

See if you can control the relationship of your feet when they are in the air.

5.0 Each of you, begin to make up and remember a planned sequence that involves changing the relationships of your feet while you roll, take weight on hands, and travel off or over the apparatus and newspaper rolls.

5.1 Take care and make every moment a planned part of your sequence. Get rid of the little unplanned, nongymnastic movements that take away from your lovely performance. [Should you notice someone not working to potential, move them to another group or you might make this suggestion: If any of you find yourself not taking your practice serious, perhaps you need to move away from the group you are in and work at another apparatus arrangement.]

5.2 Let's look at some of the routines for things we all need to do in our sequences to help them look more polished and skillful. [To avoid discouraging anyone, keep the suggestions directed to the entire class. Include in the remarks ideas such as, "We need to make our starting posture nice and tall by lifting our bodies up from our waist to our shoulders; we could really soften our landings by giving more in our ankles, knees, and hips; we could try to make our routines more challenging for ourselves by trying to include our most difficult gymnastic movements, especially if we think our sequence is too easy for us."]

5.3 Show variety in your sequence by including different relationships of your feet as you travel off or over the apparatus, when you take weight on your hands, and as you travel forward and backward.

5.4 Keep the order of your sequence the same. Work on perfecting your sequence by exaggerating the relationship of your feet to make the relationships clearer to an observer.

5.5 Take care and control your feet after you take weight on your hands. Don't let your feet crash to the floor. Work hard to feel those stomach muscles tightening up to control your legs.

5.6 [Let some or all of the children demonstrate. To save time, have two groups, performing at different arrangements of apparatus, demonstrate at the same time.] Sit up tall on the floor, away from the apparatus, and appreciate the relationships of the feet that all of you have created in your sequence.

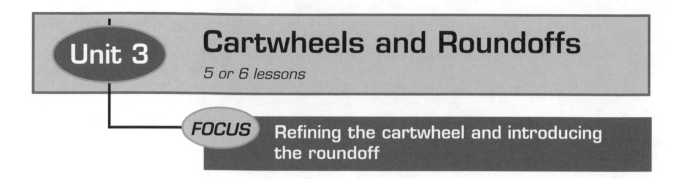

Cartwheels and Roundoffs

Unit 3

5 or 6 lessons

FOCUS Refining the cartwheel and introducing the roundoff

MOTOR CONTENT

Selected from Theme 1—Introduction to the Body; Theme 2—Introduction to Space; and Theme 3—Introduction to Time

Body

Locomotor activities—step-like actions (cartwheel, roundoff, hurdle step)
Nonlocomotor activities—twisting

Space

Direction—changes of direction

OBJECTIVES

In this unit, children will (or should be willing to try to) meet these objectives:

- Travel sideways in a straight line to perform a cartwheel by transferring weight from one hand to the other, then to one or both feet, pushing hard off the floor with the feet and legs in order to bring their hips, their center of weight, vertically over their hands.
- Attempt a roundoff by pushing off forcefully from the floor with their hands, twisting the hips one quarter turn while their legs are in the air, and bringing their legs together simultaneously to land on two feet.
- Incorporate a hurdle step in the approach to produce a more powerful takeoff when performing a cartwheel or a roundoff.
- As they gain confidence, accelerate the approach and elevate the height of the hurdle to increase momentum for the takeoff.
- Understand that each phase of the movement—the approach, the action, and the recovery—are necessary and important in a skilled performance.
- Feel the stretch in the body from the hands to the tips of the toes to help create and maintain a vertical line with the entire body. [Expect a wide range of ability. Children come with varying backgrounds. Be prepared to note individual progress and development occurring during this unit.]

EQUIPMENT AND MATERIALS

A selection of equipment for children to travel over or along: hoops, newspaper roll (wands), or short ropes. Tumbling mats are recommended.

LEARNING EXPERIENCES

1.0 Place your hands on the floor, try to take your hips up over your hands, then carefully bring your feet down quietly in a new place on the floor. Try not to let your feet fall. Keep your arm and leg muscles strong.

1.1 Remember to spread your fingers as you place your hands flat on the floor. Bring both feet down near the side of one hand.

1.2 Tighten your leg and hip muscles to bring your feet down slowly close to your hands. Bend at your hips to keep your seat high over your hands until your feet are near the floor.

1.3 Place your first hand down very near your takeoff foot. You won't have to work so hard to push those hips up over your hand if you place your first hand close to where your takeoff foot is.

1.4 Traveling sideways in a straight line, see if you can make your hips go straight over your hands and place your feet one at a time on the other side of your hands. [Watch closely, they need to be traveling sideways, not forward as in a walkover. Repeat cue often: 'Point the side of your body in the direction you wish to travel.'] Feel the entire weight of your body over each hand and foot as you place them on the floor.

1.5 Land one foot after the other and you have done a cartwheel. If both feet land together, you are beginning to do a roundoff. [The following figure shows the floor pattern of the cartwheel, hands and feet landing one at a time, and the roundoff, both feet landing at the same time.]

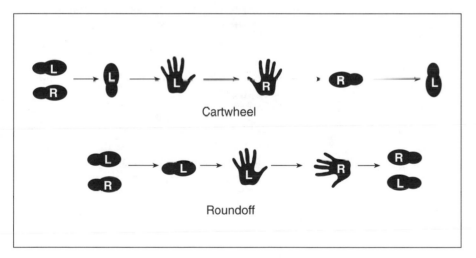

Hand and foot placement in the cartwheel and roundoff.

2.0 Get a hoop and place it on the floor [mat]. Stand on one side of the hoop and travel over it to the other side, making your hands touch inside the hoop and your feet finish on the other side.

2.1 Think of a clock and stand where the '6' is on the clock. See how you can place your hands inside the hoop, take your feet up high in a straight line over the hoop, and land near the '12' on the clock.

2.2 Place one hand, then the other, in the hoop as you take your hips and feet high over your hands to travel across your hoop.

2.3 If you are having trouble supporting your weight on your hands while your feet are in the air, work on keeping your arms straight by not bending your

Place one hand, then the other, in the center of the hoop as you take your hips high over your hands.

elbows, making your arms strong, and by keeping your knees tucked. Don't straighten your legs until you can hold your weight up on your hands without falling.

2.4 Stretch and reach with your legs, pointing your toes to the ceiling as you travel in a straight line across the hoop. When you bring your first foot down, see if you can make the toes on that foot point to the center of the hoop [to do a cartwheel], or make the toes on both feet point to the center of the hoop when they land at the same time [to do a roundoff].

2.5 To help you get momentum to lift your hips up over your hands, walk or run three or four steps, then transfer your weight to your hands one at a time inside the hoop. If you think your running or walking approach has helped to give you extra momentum, try doing two cartwheels before you stop.

2.6 Work on pushing off forcefully with your hands and standing up quickly. This forceful pushoff helps you take your feet higher.

3.0 Let's work in twos with one of you marking 'Xs' with chalk on the floor [mat] where the other is to place each hand and foot as weight is transferred from feet to hands to feet when attempting a cartwheel. [Change roles often in 3.0 to 3.2.]

3.1 See if you can draw one straight line connecting the four marks your partner put on the mat [floor]. [Having them pick an existing line to travel along, such as the line made by a board or a line marking a court, aids in developing straight pathways. Some teachers have had success in copying the hand and footprints as shown in the illustration on page 39 on a long sheet of shelf paper and taping it to the floor.]

3.2 Performers, get your hips over your hands and stretch and reach with every body part. Some of you are still placing your first hand down too far from your foot. Putting it closer makes it easier to send your hips over that hand onto the next hand.

4.0 Find an open space in the room and practice your hurdle step to help make your cartwheel or roundoff easier to do. Take no more than three running steps and then hop straight up, seeing how high you can raise your lifted knee before the foot on the other leg.

4.1 Really thrust that free knee way up as high as you can. Feel it lifting you off the floor as you swing both arms way up to get greater height.

4.2 [Encourage children to practice on both sides, not only on the dominant or easier side.] Many of you have found doing a cartwheel in one direction is easier for you than the other. Practice your hurdle, lifting your left knee high, followed by taking a step on the left foot. Then practice your hurdle by lifting your right knee high and stepping on your right foot. Practice until the hurdle feels comfortable when you lift either knee.

4.3 Continue practicing your cartwheel on the floor or the mat. Start far enough away from your mat so you finish your running steps and hurdle before reaching the mat, saving the mat for your cartwheel.

4.4 Prepare your hands and arms to support you by stretching them upward and outward as you lift your knee in the hurdle step. If your left knee comes up, your left hand will be the first to take weight.

4.5 Spread your fingers and make your palms flat so that, when you push off into your hurdle, your hands are ready to receive your weight. Remember to place your hands close to your feet to help get your hips into the air.

4.6 When the foot that went high with the knee lands, flex [bend] that knee and ankle and push hard against the floor with that foot to create power to lift your legs and hips high up, straight over your hands.

4.7 The rhythm of the hurdle step is difficult to capture, and you will have to practice it many times. [Many children will not become proficient at performing a cartwheel during this unit. Praise each child for progress made.]

5.0 Take weight on the hands and make your feet meet at some point in the air. Carefully place them down on the floor. [Childen struggling with the cartwheel *may choose* to remain focused on it instead of moving on to the roundoff.]

5.1 Notice the wall you are facing. As you bring your feet together, twist your hips so that you end up facing the opposite wall.

5.2 Turn to face the opposite wall as you place your second hand down.

5.3 Push off fast with your hands and bend in the hips to snap both feet down together quickly, close to the spot where your hands were.

5.4 After you bring both feet down, see if you can quickly take your hands high into the air above your head. Taking your hands high quickly will help you land standing facing the opposite wall.

5.5 Start your run with small, quick steps, leading to that big, high hurdle.

5.6 Some of you are ready to run faster in your approach so you get a faster swing of the legs up and then can snap them down as you prepare to land.

5.7 You are remembering to run fast. Now give a lot on the landing by bending your ankles, knees, and hips to land more softly. Bounce up as soon as those feet touch the floor and reach high with your arms. Land, springing right back up, making one straight line in the air with your arms and body. Act like you just won a gold medal in the Olympics.

6.0 Begin to develop a short gymnastic phrase where you start with your cartwheel or roundoff and go directly into a roll. Some of you may like to roll, spring up, and go right into a cartwheel or roundoff.

6.1 As you are working, make the cartwheel or roundoff the 'spark' of your sequence. Stretch long and make it a very clear shape.

6.2 Eliminate any extra movements in between your weight transfer from your feet to your hands to your feet and your roll.

6.3 Make a clear beginning and a solidly held ending. You all have worked hard. Make a big show of your accomplishments.

6.4 Exaggerate the extension throughout your body, arms, and legs while taking your weight on hands and feet, then see how tightly tucked you can roll.

6.5 Some of you may enjoy increasing the length of your gymnastic phrase by repeating what you have done or by adding something new. Be sure to show your best stretches and nicely tucked roll.

ASSESSING THE CARTWHEEL					
Class list	Takes hips and legs over hands in a wheeling action.	Attempts a roundoff with 1/4 turn in air after beginning cartwheel.	Uses a hurdle step to take off into a cartwheel or roundoff.	Accelerates hurdle step to increase momentum as confidence increases.	Shows full stretch to create and maintain a vertical line with entire body.
Kriss Ding	3	3	4	4	3
Kent Reel	2	2	3	2	2

Scale: 5 = *Almost always* 4 = *Consistently evident 2/3 or more of the time* 3 = *Evident about half the time; needs instruction and additional practice* 2 = *Sometimes to seldom evident; may need special instruction* 1 = *Never; major modification needed for success*

Traveling on Hands and Feet, Mounting and Dismounting

4 to 6 lessons

FOCUS Traveling on hands and feet; mounting and dismounting apparatus, emphasizing contrasting speeds

MOTOR CONTENT

Selected from Theme 1—Introduction to the Body and Theme 3—Introduction to Time

Body

Actions of body parts—applying and receiving force (transferring weight from hands to feet in the air and upon landing)
Locomotor activities—step-like actions; jumping (mounting and dismounting)

Effort

Time—contrasting speeds (fast, slow; accelerate, decelerate)
Weight—firm, strong, tension; soft, light, relaxed

OBJECTIVES

In this unit, children will (or should be willing to try to) meet these objectives:

- Change speed by following coaching cues and practicing.
- Try to do their best work so they remain challenged and can see personal progress.
- Observe the performance of others, identifying when a change in speed occurs; identify in advance when a change of speed will occur in own performance.
- Know that (a) they must create muscle tension to increase or decrease speed; (b) when in an inverted position, they must exert muscle tension, especially in the hip and abdominal areas, to slow down or speed up the descent of their feet; (c) some gymnastic movements are easier when performed slowly, while others are easier performed more rapidly and, for the most part, their movements to date have tended to be neither fast nor slow; and (d) it takes hard work to develop the skill to intentionally control the speed of their movements.
- Recognize that the same movement takes on a very different look when it is performed at a variety of speeds, adding variety to a performance.

EQUIPMENT AND MATERIALS

For each four to six children: one tumbling mat; one bench. For each child: one rope or newspaper roll (wand); paper and pencil; a selection of other available apparatus (landing mats required if apparatus is higher than 16-18 inches).

LEARNING EXPERIENCES

1.0 Let's see how you can transfer your weight from your feet to your hands to your feet. Find a space on the floor big enough so you won't kick others and begin. If you want a rope [newspaper roll] to travel back and forth over, you may get one.

1.1 Repeat your movement several times. Pay attention to that moment when your legs and feet are in the air. See if you can control exactly what your legs are doing with them while they are in the air and when they land. [Select one child who is making the feet travel very fast through the air and still not collapsing or banging the feet to the floor, one whose feet are taken up very slowly and brought down very slowly. Pick a third whose speed is in between the fast and slow pace of the other two. Tell these children you want them to demonstrate later and to continue practicing their fast, slow, or medium movement. In selecting the children, choose children with similar skill abilities to make the speed of the movement stand out.]

1.2 Sit down for a moment and watch the speed of [Marcy, Samuel, and Hosea] and see whose legs travel very fast while in the air, who makes their legs go the slowest, and whose movement is sort of medium speed. [All three perform at one time.] Watch again, and let's ask the fast mover and the slow mover to exaggerate their speed but not change their kind of movement. [All three perform again at the same time.] Can you see when we exaggerate and make the speed very fast as [Marcy] did and really slow the movement down like [Hosea], it makes the movement done at medium speed like [Samuel's] stand out? Exaggerate your speed to make your choice very clear.

1.3 You may change your movement but perform the movement you select three times at three different speeds. You can decide the order but, once you decide, keep repeating the speed of the movement in the same order.

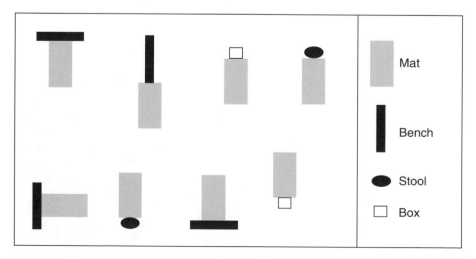

Sample arrangement of mats and apparatus.

1.4 Be in command of your body when you are changing speeds. You have to tighten up those muscles to be prepared to produce and cope with that extra speed or to slow your movement down.

1.5 Scoot next to someone. One of you will be the observer. Look for the muscle tension that helps to slow down or speed up the movement of the legs. The other partner will be the performer and will demonstrate the muscle tension present in three speeds. Observers, be honest and see if your performer is speeding up [accelerating] or slowing down [decelerating] their fast or slow movement. Tell them which speed they need to exaggerate. [Change roles.]

2.0 [Group four to six children at each arrangement of apparatus. Because various pieces of apparatus will provide different learning opportunities, you may need to rotate groups within a lesson or assign different groups daily if apparatus arrangements vary.] Let's safely show a clear contrast in speed as you travel over the apparatus and on the mats.

2.1 Think before you start. Know where your movement will be fast and where it will be slow. Make sure you show both fast and slow movements each time you take your turn.

2.2 Tell the person behind you exactly what gymnastic movement you will be doing as you travel very slowly and where in your sequence your slow movement is going to come. Observers, look to see if the performers do as they say they will.

2.3 Work on slowing down your slow movement. Exaggerating your slow speed will make your fast movement look even faster.

2.4 Now, as you arrive onto your apparatus on your feet, don't stop—but really slow down your mount—then dismount fast, and safely go into a fast roll. Remember, always land feet first when dismounting.

2.5 Take care as you work on showing the contrast in your speed. You should have enough tension in your muscles to support your weight so you don't collapse.

2.6 Think about what body part is going to be your next base of support as you mount the apparatus and prepare your base to take your weight.

2.7 Let's reverse the order of your speed. Safely mount the apparatus fast and then slowly transfer your weight onto the mat. You could change your base of support while on the apparatus before dismounting.

2.8 Some of you may like to add a fast movement to your short sequence while going from your feet to your hands to your feet.

2.9 Think about what your whole body feels like during your sequence, trying to feel lifted and tight, making sharp, clear lines with your body.

3.0 Begin to work on a gymnastic sequence, trying hard to show different ways of traveling, such as different forms of rolling, step-like actions, or flight, arriving onto or off of the apparatus. You may like to include a balance as well.

3.1 Decide what to include in your sequence and the order of those movements. Then repeat the exact same things in the same order each time you perform.

3.2 [To avoid embarrassing students, speak to the whole class without singling anyone out.] Some of you have unplanned movements that are distracting. Try hard to get rid of all unplanned movements.

3.3 Some of you have moments in your sequence where you are forgetting that you are preparing a gymnastic performance. Maybe you are collapsing your knees or your ankles aren't straight, or you have sagging shoulders. See if you can feel and look great throughout your whole sequence.

COOLDOWN AND FLEXIBILITY

Sitting or standing when waiting a turn in class, do your favorite leg stretch, silently counting to fifteen. Repeat one for the upper body. Do one more. When muscles are warm, it's good to stretch them. Muscles can stretch more when they are warm. It's good to stretch after vigorous activity, too.

3.4 When waiting for your turn, come get a pencil and paper. On the paper, number from one to five from top to bottom. Across from the numbers, list in order each of the ways you travel or balance in your sequence. You may need several turns on the apparatus before your checklist is complete. Keep checking your performance against your list until you have each part of your sequence listed in the exact order they appear in your performance.

3.5 When waiting your turn, put an 'F' after each fast part of your sequence. Put an 'S' after parts you do slowly. When you finish labeling everything you do fast or slow, go back to work and exaggerate the fast and slow parts of your sequence by really working on your muscle tension and thinking about your speed.

3.6 Who would like to read their sequence to their group and then perform it for your group. Observers, watch and see if you can tell which of the movements are very fast and which are very slow. Check the performer's list. Do you think they went fast and slow when their list said they would? [Change performers several times until everyone has had a chance to be observed.]

3.7 Look at your own list. Does it include any weight transfer from your feet to your hands, back to your feet? If it doesn't, see if you can add it before you mount the apparatus or at the very end—or at both places.

3.8 Pause and take a big breath to lift your chest to stand nice and tall. Look straight ahead and don't be distracted [don't pay attention to anything else]. When you are in total control, do your new sequence.

3.9 [Call on individuals from various groups or let whole groups demonstrate, one at a time.] Before you demonstrate, tell which movements are very fast and which are very slow. Observers, watch and see if you agree with the speed of the movements.

ASSESSING KNOWLEDGE OF SPEED

Write a note to someone at home, explaining how you have learned to control speed to help you move better. Include at least three suggestions you have learned in class to improve the quality of your performance.

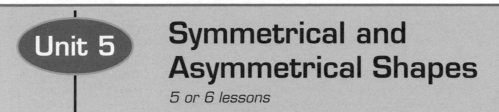

Symmetrical and Asymmetrical Shapes

Unit 5

5 or 6 lessons

FOCUS Creating and maintaining symmetrical and asymmetrical shapes

MOTOR CONTENT

Selected from Theme 1—Introduction to the Body and Theme 4—Introduction to Relationships of Body Parts

Body

Nonlocomotor activities—balancing
Locomotor activities—student selected forms of locomotion
Body shapes—symmetrical and asymmetrical

Relationships

Body parts—relationship of body parts on one side of the body to corresponding body parts on the other side of the body

OBJECTIVES

In this unit, children will (or should be willing to try to) meet these objectives:

- Create and refine a gymnastic sequence containing symmetrical and asymmetrical body shapes while traveling and when performing a variety of balances on different bases of support on the floor, mats, and apparatus.
- Understand that they can create symmetrical shapes when identical body parts on both sides of the body perform the same movement and take the same position at the same time, and they can create asymmetrical shapes when the identical body parts on both sides of the body perform different movements or the same movement at different times.
- Create and maintain (a) symmetrical body shapes while traveling forward, backward, up, and down, (b) asymmetrical body shapes while traveling in any direction as well as when moving sideways.
- Accept the differences in others' abilities, working hard to achieve their own potentials by listening and developing personally challenging solutions to the tasks and by staying on task, thereby making the class an effective learning experience for themselves and others.

EQUIPMENT AND MATERIALS

For every four to six students: one tumbling mat; at least one other piece of apparatus; a selection of objects that clearly illustrate symmetry and asymmetry, such as most new pencils, a pair of glasses, or a picture of someone doing a jumping jack, a round cookie, a seashell, and a pitcher with a handle. (If the children have had any work in art with symmetry and asymmetry, include their artwork when selecting objects to illustrate the concept. Perhaps enlist the cooperation of the art or classroom teacher in conveying these concepts. In addition, if more equipment is available, give the children increased practice time by giving them their own equipment or by reducing the size of the group working at each piece of apparatus.)

LEARNING EXPERIENCES

1.0 [Have a group of objects on the floor such as those mentioned in this unit's equipment list.] Come in and have a seat over here so you can see these small objects I have here. Today we are going to try to work in gymnastics on body shapes, trying to make both sides of our body look and perform alike. Can you see an object that, if you lined up a string with the center of the object, the string would cut the object in half from top to bottom with both sides of the object looking exactly alike? [Hold up a string with a small weight attached to it to demonstrate. A pencil is a good object to start with. Continue this discussion, introducing both symmetry and asymmetry. Point out to the children that sometimes an asymmetrical object has symmetry when you look at it from a specific direction, such as a water pitcher if the handle is turned so it is directly in front of you. If the children have studied symmetry and asymmetry in art before the introduction of this unit, have them name the objects representing each category and only review the concept with them.] Think a moment what your body shape should look like when you are in a symmetrical balance. When you think you have an idea for a symmetrical balance, go to a mat and see if you can make that balance on the mat [or floor]. Do not have more than [one to six] to a mat so each of you can have more opportunities to practice and improve your gymnastic skill.

1.1 Come out of your balances by bringing new body parts down to take your weight. Do not hold the balance so long that you collapse.

1.2 Keep trying new bases of support. As you select your base, to be symmetrical remember the same body parts from both sides of your body must serve as your base.

1.3 Keep thinking about that string we held up in front of the pencil [or other object]. If I come around with a string and hold it up, will both sides of your body look just the same?

1.4 As you go into your balance, think about symmetry, trying to make both sides of your body look alike as you form your balance. For example, you can't kick up into a headstand with one foot. You will have to take both feet off the floor exactly at the same time to keep your symmetrical shape.

1.5 If you can go into the balance performing a symmetrical movement, hold your balance just for a moment and then see if you can come out of the balance while still making both sides of your body look exactly alike.

1.6 Check each other's balances. See if the one performing partner is indeed going into the balance, balancing, and coming out of the balance with the same body parts on both sides of the body doing the same thing exactly at the same time.

1.7 [Repeat experiences 1.0 to 1.6, having the children work on asymmetry, pointing out that the two sides of the body must be different.]

Think about symmetry; make both sides of your
body look exactly alike.

2.0 Now that you really have the idea of symmetry and asymmetry, see if
you can travel, keeping your body shape symmetrical all of the time. This will be
fun because it makes you think about every body part on both sides of your
body all of the time.

2.1 Some of you are trying to roll and keep that fine symmetrical shape. That
is a great idea. Let's all try to roll symmetrically. Watch your hands, your feet,
your knees—everything.

2.2 As you start to roll symmetrically, make sure your body shape is symmetrical from the very beginning.

2.3 Can you make a symmetrical ending when you finish your roll?

2.4 Try different kinds of rolls—forward, backward, straddle—and keep your
body in a symmetrical shape as you do all of them.

2.5 Ask someone close to you to watch and see if the shape of your body is
symmetrical throughout your entire roll. Sometimes, you feel that the same

Now make your body shape asymmetrical.

body parts on each side of your body are directly opposite each other, doing the same things, when maybe they aren't. By watching carefully, the observer can help you improve the relationship of like [similar] body parts.

2.6 See if you can roll symmetrically and then go immediately into a symmetrical balance. Try very hard to keep your body shape symmetrical throughout your entire performance.

2.7 Watch your posture as you perform. Really try your best to pull in your tummy and feel your body curl and stretch tightly.

2.8 [Repeat all or any of the tasks 2.0 to 2.7, having the children concentrate on asymmetry.]

2.9 Now see if you can travel with your body maintaining only symmetrical shapes, go into an asymmetrical balance, and come out of the balance symmetrically. [Keep designing different combinations, giving the choices to the student performing the work or to children working in partners, designing combinations for each other. Children also enjoy copying the combinations others design and perform.]

3.0 [Arrange the apparatus before the instruction begins or bring it out and add to the mats when needed. In either case, closely supervise the children, instructing them as to how to carry the apparatus safely. Have enough children work together to lift the apparatus so the weight does not put excess strain on any one child. Plan this part of the lesson just as carefully as any gymnastic task given to the children. Children can work on one type of apparatus for the entire unit, or you may decide to change apparatus periodically or rotate groups.] We have added some pieces of apparatus near the mats. Think carefully about symmetry and asymmetry as you arrive on the apparatus, as you work on it, and as you dismount from it. I am going to be watching, and I will come around and ask you which kind of body shape you were making at different times in your performance. Those of you waiting a turn on the apparatus, in your own space, see if you can work on making your body shape symmetrical or asymmetrical while transferring your weight from your feet to your hands, back to your feet. [Make it obvious you are observing those waiting a turn also by asking different children whether they remember what shape their bodies were in during specific parts of their sequences. This is a good technique to use to see if the children are cognizant of what you are teaching. When children are able to describe what they are learning and differentiate within a concept, they probably understand the concept you are teaching.]

3.1 Sit down a moment and number off in your groups. You are going to play the role of an observer like I just did. Be prepared to name a part of the performer's work and see if he can remember whether his body was in a symmetrical or asymmetrical shape. Remember the sides are alike in a symmetrical shape and different in asymmetrical shapes. Number twos begin your sequence.

3.2 Take a balance on the apparatus and hold your body shape long enough for you to determine whether it is symmetrical or asymmetrical.

3.3 Some of you need to challenge yourself by including more difficult balances, rolls, and ways of traveling on your hands and feet. You must learn to try things that are a bit hard for you to become more skillful.

3.4 Think about how you mount and dismount the apparatus and see if you can make your body shape in both your mount and dismount symmetrical. [Repeat, having them do both with asymmetrical shapes. You could also allow children to choose to do one shape for the mount and one shape for the dismount.] Remember to always land feet first on the mat.

3.5 Did you know you cannot keep a true symmetrical shape and travel sideways? Every time you travel sideways, one set of muscles works on one side of the body that doesn't work exactly the same way on the other side, and your shape becomes asymmetrical. While you are waiting your turn on the apparatus, work on doing true symmetrical movements on your hands and feet, remembering that you can travel up, down, backward or forward—but not sideways—to make true symmetrical shapes.

4.0 Develop a short gymnastic sequence, trying to create symmetrical and asymmetrical shapes with your body. You may start your sequence on the apparatus or on the floor, but let's all end the sequence on the floor with a lifted, symmetrical, stretched balance.

4.1 Include both symmetry and asymmetry in your sequence while you're traveling and when you're balancing. [Use your judgment as to how much the children can handle to determine the number of requirements you give to the children each time they do this task. As it is written, it may be asking too much of some children.]

4.2 Don't make your sequence too long because you need to be able to repeat it in exactly the same order each time you take your turn.

4.3 Think about how you travel into and out of your balances. These moments going into and out of the balances are great opportunities to show you have mastered the idea of symmetry and asymmetry. Make the shape you have chosen very clear. If it is supposed to be asymmetrical, make both sides very different. If it is to be symmetrical, don't let one little finger on one hand do some things different than the other hand.

4.4 Now begin to take out some of the unplanned little nonperforming movements you do, like taking two or three unplanned walking steps to get to the apparatus, or crawling up on the apparatus on your knees when you haven't planned it, or brushing the hair out of your eyes. These little unplanned movements take away from the wonderful gymnastic ideas that you've been working so hard on.

4.5 Check your sequence. Do you have traveling? Have you included both symmetrical and asymmetrical shapes while you travel? Maybe the sequence is too long if you can't remember exactly what you are doing. If it is, leave some parts out. [Ask questions often to encourage self-assessment.]

4.6 You have thought really hard and can make both symmetrical and asymmetrical body shapes while traveling and while balancing. Take a moment to think about how sharp you look from the beginning to the end of your performance. Remember to hold that stretched, symmetrical balance at the end to show you have finished.

4.7 [Use this task several times in the unit. Don't wait until the last lesson to use this task.] Number off in your groups at your apparatus. Number threes, please take a nice, standing position near the spot where you start your sequence. Observers, let's watch for the clear symmetrical and asymmetrical shapes while traveling and while balancing. When I say, 'begin' all of the threes will do their sequence. When each has finished, see if you can hold that nice, stretched, symmetrical balance until I say 'thank you.' Ready threes? Begin. Remember to hold the nice, stretched, symmetrical shape at the end. Thank you. [Call each number, until every child in the class has had a turn to share.]

Third Grade Dance

Symmetry and Asymmetry

3 or 4 lessons

FOCUS Exploring symmetry and asymmetry while creating body shapes and while traveling

MOTOR CONTENT

Selected from Theme 3—Introduction to Space and Theme 6—Instrumental Use of the Body

Body

Body shapes—symmetrical and asymmetrical
Locomotor activities—traveling using a variety of locomotor movements; stepping; and step-like actions

Space

Pathways—air, floor

OBJECTIVES

In this unit, children will (or should be willing to try to) meet these objectives:

- Demonstrate symmetry and asymmetry while creating body shapes (still positions) and while designing pathways in space as they travel.
- Demonstrate kinesthetic awareness and focus by concentrating on the stillness of body shapes and spatial relationships of body parts (reflects National Standard in Dance 1g).
- Design simple movement sequences, contrasting symmetry and asymmetry while traveling and while staying in place; identify the beginning, middle, and ending of sequences (reflects National Standard in Dance 2a).
- Improvise, create, and perform dances based on their own ideas and on concepts from other sources (reflects National Standards in Dance 2b and 7a).
- Understand that symmetry occurs in movement when both sides of the body perform exactly the same way at the same time; asymmetry occurs when both sides move differently.
- Work effectively alone and with a partner or small group by demonstrating an awareness of others' positioning (reflects National Standard in Dance 2e).

EQUIPMENT AND MATERIALS

Drum. Optional: musical Selection A: slow and quiet as in "The Swan" from *Carnival of the Animals* by Saint-Saens; Selection B—lively march by Sousa;

Selection C—classical selection such as "Menuet in G" by Handel; Selection D—energetic, explosive score such as *The Rite of Spring* by Stravinsky.

LEARNING EXPERIENCES

[Briefly explain the meaning of symmetry and asymmetry and provide visual aids to enhance understanding of the concepts of line and shape (form). Consult the art teacher in your school for possible examples of student's work on symmetrical and asymmetrical design.]

1.0 In your own space, let's explore a variety of symmetrical body shapes on many different bases of support and at many different levels. With each tap of the drum, change your symmetrical shape. Here we go: '[Tap:] Change, [tap] a new shape, [tap] both sides the same.'

1.1 As you design your symmetrical body shapes, imagine that the right half is exactly the same as the left half. Try to match up every body part on both sides of your body in each new shape.

1.2 Change your base of support each time you make a new symmetrical shape. Change *slowly*—now hold! Concentrate on how the shape feels in your muscles.

1.3 [The appearance of the shape will be different, depending on the relationship of the performer to the audience.] Let's look at [Marty's] shape. As she faces us or has her back to us, her shape appears symmetrical. What would her shape look like if the side of her body was facing us, the audience? [Turns to hold shape.] Notice how the design looks completely different. Everybody face me, and I will be your audience. Continue, making only symmetrical body shapes for the audience to see.

1.4 [Accompany by tapping a drum.] Let's see if we can maintain our symmetrical shapes as we rise and sink through space. Begin in a low-level symmetrical shape. As I tap the drum slowly, gradually rise and sink on the spot, keeping your symmetrical body shape. '[Tap:] Rise, [tap] higher, [tap] higher stretching, [tap] to your highest shape; [tap] now sink, [tap] lower, [tap] lower down, [tap] to your lowest shape.'

1.5 When you rise, slowly uncurl all your body parts, stretching away from your body's center [middle]. Feel your energy radiate [spread] outward—feel the extension! When you sink, tighten your stomach muscles and feel your ribs and hips pulling inward toward your body's center. This is called a *contraction*.

1.6 We can also design symmetrical pathways. Travel to your right, doing a movement idea. Then travel to the left side, doing exactly the same movement. [For example, slide to the right and jump into the air; repeat to the left.] When you repeat the same movement, traveling first to one side, then to the other, you are making a symmetrical pathway in space [on the floor and in the air].

1.7 Select four symmetrical shapes that you can perform one after the other to show the class. As you practice these shapes, think about how you can move between the shapes to make transitions [changes] smooth from one shape to the next. [Play quiet, slow music (such as Selection A or C in equipment list) to accompany children's movement as you critique their symmetry and smooth transitions. Use this feedback to design and introduce a scoring rubric for task 1.9 (see NASPE 1995, p. 107).]

1.8 Some of you are hooking shapes together by rocking onto new body parts [for example, from knees to hip to seat] or by rolling smoothly to transfer weight onto new bases of support. Others are traveling by stepping, jumping, or running. Try different ways.

1.9 [Divide the class in half. Have half perform and half observe.] As we look at your symmetry dances, the audience will be continually impressed by how smoothly you move from one symmetrical shape to the next with amazing concentration. I will accompany the performing group with quiet music, and when all dancers are finished, the audience will become the performers.

2.0 to 2.6 [Repeat tasks 1.0 to 1.6, substituting asymmetry for symmetry, pointing out dissimilarities between right and left sides of the body created by asymmetry.]

2.7 Select four asymmetrical shapes and practice your shapes at different levels. Try to move quickly from one shape into the next in light, controlled ways. [For example, a fast roll or rocking action or sudden leap, skip, or jump. Play music D.]

2.8 Move in different directions to hook or link your shapes together—forward, backward, sideways, up, down. Do this quite unexpectedly. [Divide class in half to demonstrate and observe.] Audience, look for concentration and stillness when creating shapes and sudden, but controlled, transitions between shapes. [Reverse roles.]

Move in different directions to connect shapes.

2.9 [Read a story or poem of enchantment or mystery, see pg 57.] Travel with slow stepping actions and an awareness of all that is about you. Follow, lead, pass by others. Sometimes when you meet someone, suddenly make a shape—symmetrical or asymmetrical! Your movement and shapes should be mysterious, unexpected. Surprise us with your actions and reactions!

The Haunting of Autumn Nights

In fall, the moon shines through the window screen.
Strange shadows come inside and disappear.
Irregular and dancing shapes perform
across the walls, no image in my mirror.

   Come, come. Come this night. Unexpected things to see.
   Come, come. By moonlight. Solve the night's sweet mystery.

The breeze picks up and curtains swing and flap.
Sounds beckon me to rise and lend an ear.
The hooting owls and hunting bats fly by.
I brush a spider from my face in fear.

   Come, come. Come this night. Unexpected things to see.
   Come, come. By moonlight. Solve the night's sweet mystery.

Imagination's playing tricks on me.
I scare myself this haunting time of year.
I feel a chill and jump back into bed.
I cover up and hope that nothing's near.

   Come, come. Come this night. Unexpected things to see.
   Come, come. By moonlight. Solve the night's sweet mystery.

—*Yolanda Danyi Szuch*

In the artroom, children use cut paper to create landscapes that show imagined sounds, sight, and motion. Artwork by Alex, age 8.

3.0 Now that we have worked with symmetrical and asymmetrical designs, let's combine the two. With each tap of my drum, alternate symmetrical and asymmetrical shapes. See how many different body parts you can use to support your weight in your shapes. [Play slow, steady taps on drum.] '[Tap:] Symmetrical shape, [tap] asymmetrical shape, [tap] symmetrical shape.' [Repeat many times. To simplify, alternate two asymmetrical shapes with one symmetrical shape. Pause, then repeat.]

3.1 Move from symmetrical to asymmetrical shapes by rising or sinking. Begin in a low symmetrical shape and, as you rise, gradually change into an asymmetrical shape, then gradually sink into a different symmetrical shape.

3.2 Let's move from an asymmetrical shape to a different asymmetrical shape with symmetrical traveling to link the shapes. For example, take an asymmetrical shape. Now travel to the right and travel to the left the same way, then pause in a different asymmetrical shape. Show the audience how your asymmetrical shapes on the spot look completely different from symmetrical travel.

3.3 Tighten your muscles to hold each shape firm and still. Notice differences in the lines of your asymmetrical shape. How does the right side look different from the left?

3.4 Remember the meaning of asymmetrical and symmetrical body shapes or traveling pathways? If there is any difference between your movement [and shape] on the right side *and* your movement [and shape] on the left side, then we have asymmetry.

3.5 This time, let's link symmetrical shapes with asymmetrical travel. Begin in a symmetrical shape and travel in some direction—either forward, backward, sideways. Now, travel in a different way altogether and end in another symmetrical shape.

3.6 As you travel, prepare for your next position. Rather than travel and stop and make a shape, plan in advance what the shape will be and on what body part[s] so there will be smooth transitions. Your shapes should be a smooth outcome of your traveling, not just something tacked on.

4.0 Let's design a dance that is longer and more complicated. Part 1 will be a symmetrical shape with symmetrical travel. Part 2 will be an asymmetrical shape with asymmetrical travel. We'll practice each part separately, then combine parts 1 and 2. Let's begin by designing part 1—our symmetry section. Right where you are [in your own space], perform a symmetrical shape. Now, travel some way to the right and the same way to the left. [For example, do a series of small, quick jumps to the right and to the left.] You've just designed part 1.

4.1 Some of you have such fabulous symmetrical shapes in your body you could probably hold that position frozen and still travel symmetrically. [Practice part 1.]

4.2 Now for part 2. Perform your favorite asymmetrical shape. Hold it strong! Clearly show us the details in your shape. 'Travel to the right . . . now do a different movement to the left.' You've just designed part 2.

4.3 [Have everyone scatter throughout the empty space.] Let's practice both parts so our movement becomes automatic. This half of the class perform part 1. After part 1 is finished, the other half will perform part 2. Part 1 dancers stay motionless [still] until everyone in part 2 is finished. [Reverse roles after several tries.]

4.4 We're ready to put parts 1 and 2 together and conclude our dance. Everyone will perform both parts at the same time. Remember to end with asymmetrical traveling, then hold very still. Here we go: 'Symmetrical shape . . . and symmetrical traveling . . . asymmetrical shape . . . and asymmetrical traveling . . . now hold your still shape.' Try to feel the exact moment when all traveling or motion in the room has stopped. [Pause.]

5.0 We're going to call this dance 'Odds and Evens.' Whenever you make a symmetrical shape or travel with symmetry, move for an *even* number of counts [for example, four, six, eight]. Move for an *odd* number of counts [for example, three, five, seven] whenever you make an asymmetrical shape or travel with asymmetry. I will tap the drum [or play a march tempo; see music Selection B]. You will need to count your sections by yourself.

5.1 Everyone who is now an *even* age [eight years old] will make a symmetrical shape or travel symmetrically. All of you who right now have an *odd* number of years [seven or nine years old] make an asymmetrical shape or travel asymmetrically. After some tries, we will change our roles.

5.2 Join with a classmate. One of you perform the symmetrical phrase, then watch your partner perform the asymmetrical phrase. After four practices, exchange parts.

5.3 Let's perform our 'Odds and Evens' duets for the class in groups of four or five pairs at a time. Audience, we are looking for clear symmetry or asymmetry in body shapes and traveling.

5.4 Rather than one person moving at a time, let's see if you and your partner can move at the same time and end by linking or joining your symmetrical and asymmetrical shapes. Take a bit more time to allow for traveling to your partner if you need to.

5.5 Some of you may want to dance both parts. Begin by learning one person's phrase and rehearse it until you know it well. Then learn the other person's. Decide which person's phrase should start the dance.

5.6 As you work with a partner, focus all your attention on what they are doing. Dancers, clearly show what each body part is doing while you teach your phrase to your partner.

5.7 Let's watch our duets. Audience, we are looking for clear differences between symmetry and asymmetry while traveling and staying on the spot. We are also looking to see how well our partners can work together being respectful of each other's ideas.

RELATING DANCE CONCEPTS TO ART

[During art class.] Draw or design one or more pictures or a mural to show how symmetry and asymmetry are used in art and in everyday life. Write words to describe what you are showing in the drawing(s). Create a dance that demonstrates the concept of symmetry and asymmetry. Choose music, design a costume, or arrange the environment to further reflect your idea.

Moving Alone and With a Partner

2 to 4 lessons

FOCUS Traveling and moving in place, alone, and with a partner, emphasizing lively, bouncy movement

MOTOR CONTENT

Selected from Theme 4—The Flow of Movement and Theme 5—Introduction to Relationships

Effort

Time and flow motion factors—sudden, free

Relationships

Interpersonal—meeting, parting, passing by and circling in relation to music and hand-body sounds

OBJECTIVES

In this unit, children will (or should be willing to try to) meet these objectives:

- Demonstrate a variety of step, hop, and jump combinations while traveling or while staying in place.
- Demonstrate accuracy in moving to a musical beat by repeating locomotor combinations in four- or eight-count phrases (reflects National Standards in Dance 1b and 1f).
- Feel the staccato quality of selected music and translate this into lively, bouncy movement to create and vary a repeatable movement sequence with a beginning, middle, and end (reflects National Standards in Dance 2a and 2d).
- Demonstrate an ability to work alone by exploring movement in their own space and to work cooperatively with a partner on matching rhythmic movement phrases (reflects National Standards in Dance 1d, 2e, and 2f).

EQUIPMENT AND MATERIALS

Tambourine (or handle castanets, bells, or the like); drum (or wood or tone block); music (select one): Selection A—"Chitty Chitty Bang Bang" by Myron Floran; Selection B—"Patty Cake Polka" and "Heel and Toe Polka"; Selection C—"Polka" from the *Age of Gold Ballet* by Shostakovich; Selection D—"Polka" by Kabalevsky (piano arrangement) or any light, quick dance music, such as Cajun or fiddle tunes (see *Cajun Spice* or *Riverdance*).

LEARNING EXPERIENCES

WARM-UP AND FLEXIBILITY

Sitting in your own space with legs stretched long, slowly draw 20 small, imaginary circles with both feet, making each circle a little bigger. Repeat in the other direction. Now bend your ankles, bringing your toes toward your knees until you feel a stretch and hold for 10 seconds. Do the complete opposite so your toes stretch away from your knees and quietly count to 10.

1.0 Let's all bounce in place, sometimes on both feet, sometimes on one, then the other. Feel just your heels lifting off the floor. [Practice.] Now bounce a little higher—take small jumps on the spot.

1.1 Let your whole body bounce like a ball or spring. Keep your bounces light and your body very tall. Begin to push off with the balls of your feet, jumping higher, and higher, and higher! Feel the rebound! And extension!

1.2 Try hopping on one foot. See if you can take your other foot to spaces around you . . . in front of you, behind, to each side. Change feet often.

1.3 Swing the free leg up and stretch or shoot it out. Dab the air with your toes. Keep the foot action light and crisp. It's a bright, cheerful, hopping movement! [Beat a quick, even, staccato rhythm on tambourine.]

1.4 [Accompany with soft percussion.] Let your free heel or toe point to spots on the floor in front of you . . . behind you . . . to the right . . . left. Do this as you hop or step in place. It's a small, quiet, tapping or patting movement of the feet.

1.5 Be very careful to stay in your own space for this next part. Suddenly, swing your legs up high and cut the air like scissors all about you! Make those legs look long and strong! [Louder drumbeats.]

1.6 Again, bounce lightly in place. Let your shoulders, elbows, and hands poke, dab, shoot out, or jab the space all around you. Keep each gesture small, like quick jolts or flashes of energy.

1.7 [Accompany with lively percussion.] Choose different body parts to explore the space around you. Remember to keep your jumps and hops light and bouncy and to change feet often.

2.0 Keep your whole body dancing and begin to travel. Step and hop and bounce and poke and hop and step—keep the rhythm going. Enjoy using all the

Swing your legs up, cutting the air like scissors.

space! [Play music Selection A, B, C, or D. Encourage spontaneous traveling—galloping, hopping, skipping, jumping.]

2.1 Let's try just bouncing and hopping along. Keep your whole body dancing—don't forget your head, hands, arms, and knees. [Play music for three to four minutes. Divide class in half and have each group demonstrate their own ways of traveling. Challenge children to try more difficult combinations, such as "a-skip-run-run" or "a-slide-and-skip," repeating each phrase several times. Or, have them try galloping with a right foot lead, then change to a left foot lead: "A-gallop right (two gallops and change), a-gallop left (two gallops and change)." Repeat many times, alternating lead foot. Soon children will be doing the polka.]

2.2 Fill the room with movement as you travel. Feel and enjoy every open, available space! [Music.] Explore different ways to hop, step, skip, slide, and gallop along. Keep your traveling light and lively.

2.3 Your movement reminds me of a bright-colored ball, bouncing about the room. Really work on making those actions even livelier. Think of the lightest ball imaginable—bouncing, bouncing, bouncing.

2.4 Feel your whole body dance, darting from here to there, shooting up high, stirring up the air, bouncing down low, rolling and stopping. [Continue music, then fade out.] Give yourself a rest.

2.5 Let's put our bouncy actions into a short movement phrase. Begin on the spot: 'A-bounce and bounce, a-bounce and bounce; a-travel and travel, a-travel and travel.' [Repeat several times, tapping a short-long, short-long rhythm, then add music. Encourage children to keep their bouncy movement going and to change directions often.]

2.6 Join with a partner and make up your own bouncy dance. Surprise us. As you bounce, sometimes stay in one spot and sometimes travel. Remember, feet can meet and part, then meet again in so many different ways. Heels and toes can tap the floor while bouncing. Fingers or toes can dab the air. Off you go! [Play your choice of music.]

2.7 [Ask children to share their favorite ways of moving with a partner. Help them select and combine ideas into one or two repeatable phrases with or without music.] Decide how you will begin and end your movement phrase. Run through [practice] the sequence two or three times. Keep your movements lively and upbeat. Who would like to perform their sequence? [Share with other partners or entire class.]

3.0 [Choose music with clear, repeatable four- or eight-count rhythmic phrasing. In dance, the standard tempo is counted in eight beats. Do not expect children to move "up to tempo" or at full speed in the beginning. Practice phrases without the music to teach responding to cues, then gradually move up to tempo with the music.] Today, I will call cues and tap a [short-long, short-long] rhythm to tell you when to dance on the spot and when to travel. *Ready*? On the spot,

'A-bounce [1], and bounce [2], a-bounce [3], and bounce [4], a-bounce [5], and bounce [6], a-bounce [7], and bounce [8]; a-travel [1], and travel [2], a-travel [3], and travel [4], a-travel [5], and travel [6], pause on [7], a new spot [8].' [You can change the words to acknowledge a variety of children's responses. Practice several times, then reduce cues to "a-bounce and bounce" or "a-travel and travel" on counts one and two only.]

3.1 [Play music Selection A, B, C, or D to 3.0, at first saying words rhythmically along with the lively, buoyant music. As soon as possible, reduce or omit these words to encourage children to feel the rhythmic phrase changes for themselves.]

3.2 See if you can make the changes without my help by listening carefully to the music when you move. Ready? Eight counts on the spot and eight counts to travel! Feel each phrase change coming.

3.3 Keep your movements light and quick. Remember to let your shoulders, elbows, and hands dance along with your feet.

3.4 Let's start again. This time remember your starting place. We are going to dance on that spot for eight counts; travel eight counts; dance on a new spot for eight; and return to our starting place in eight counts. Ready? 'Dance in place, 2, 3, 4, 5, 6, 7, 8; travel to a new spot, 2, 3, 4, 5, 6, 7, 8; dance on your new spot, 2, 3, 4, 5, 6, 7, 8; travel back to your starting place, 2, 3, 4, 5, 6, 7, 8.' [Repeat many times with music.]

3.5 With a partner or group of three, see if you can dance on the spot close to each other for eight counts; travel away from each other for eight counts; dance by yourself on the spot for eight; and travel back to meet your partner[s] in eight. [Play music of your choice. Call out cue words just before each action.] 'Dance together; travel away; dance alone; back together.' [Part A, see below.]

3.6 Watch your partner[s] and help each other. With a hand gesture or glance of the eyes, you can signal your partner[s] to meet and dance close together or to separate and dance far apart. [Many square dances and mixers use simple dance patterns of meeting and parting, passing by, or dancing around a partner. Create new tasks by exploring adaptations of your favorite dances with the children.]

4.0 Find ways of counting eight beats by making sounds with your hands. [Snapping or clicking fingers, clapping hands, slapping body parts.] Has anyone clapped or slapped a hand to their leg, chest, arm, or feet to make a rhythm? Slapped the floor? Find many different ways to make your hand-body sounds match the music. [Play music softly.]

4.1 Choose one way to keep the rhythm [eight-count phrase] going with hand-body sounds and actions.

4.2 Try to repeat your sounds and actions in the same order several times. Make your hand-body sounds as light and quick as your feet can dance.

4.3 Let's all start our eight-count phrase at exactly the same time and end it together. Repeat your sound pattern twice. Ready? On the spot, 'Clap [or snap or slap], 2, 3, 4, 5, 6, 7, 8; clap [or snap or slap], 2, 3, 4, 5, 6, 7, 8. Hold!'

4.4 With the same partner[s] we had before, let's repeat part A of our dance, then add our sound pattern, calling it part B. [Count and talk children through the dance several times with music.]

Part A	8 counts dancing on the spot
	8 counts traveling away
	8 counts dancing on new spot
	8 counts traveling to meet partners
Part B	8 counts for sound pattern
	8 counts repeating sound pattern

4.5 We'll add one final part C, *circling,* to our dance. Then you and your partner(s) can practice putting the polish on your steps. You can circle by yourself, with a partner, or in a small group. Quickly decide how you want to circle. The circling will last for 16 counts.

4.6 [Invite some children to demonstrate.] You can hook right elbows with your partner and skip in a circle [for eight counts]; hook left elbows and skip the other way around [for eight counts]; or join hands, facing each other, circling around [for eight counts]. [If eight counts are easy for the children, challenge them to change the way they circle every four counts. Children need to experience the joy of working with a partner(s) and creating dance variations together. Ask them how they could make their formations or patterns even more exciting.]

4.7 You have all worked so hard matching your actions with your partner's and with the music. [Divide class into groups of six to eight children and have each group share their dances while others enjoy watching the many variations performed. Remind partners to spread out and use the dance space wisely so the audience can see everyone.] Ready? With the music.

Children enjoy dance patterns of meeting, parting, passing, and circling.

ASSESSMENT: PEER OBSERVATION

Evaluate progress toward unit goals by having children observe and informally rate peer performances: [Have each set of partners in the audience watch one set of partners perform in a group setting. Focus on one criterion for each group to give children practice in observing, responding to, and discussing movement.]

Performance criteria include

- a variety of step, hop, and jump combinations demonstrated while traveling and staying in place;

- movements that match the music, showing a lively, bouncy, "staccato" feeling and movements that match a partner's movements;

- hand-body sounds repeated in the same order, keeping the rhythm going.

Meeting and Separating

3 or 4 lessons

FOCUS Changing directions while traveling to meet with and separate from a partner or small group

MOTOR CONTENT

Selected from Theme 1—Introduction to the Body; Theme 3—Introduction to Space; and Theme 5—Introduction to Relationships

Body

Locomotor activities—stepping, walking (marching)

Space

Directions—forward, backward
Pathways—floor

Relationships

Interpersonal—meeting and parting; circling (accompanied by folk song)

OBJECTIVES

In this unit, children will (or should be willing to try to) meet these objectives:

- Combine precise marching steps with directional changes while meeting and parting from a partner or small group (reflects National Standard in Dance 1b).
- Demonstrate accuracy in moving to a musical beat at a fast tempo (reflects National Standard in Dance 1f).
- Listen while moving, responding quickly and appropriately to calls or instructions.
- Work cooperatively with a variety of classmates in pairs and small groups while copying, leading, and following movement (reflects National Standards in Dance 2e and 2f).
- Describe the time period and setting of a Civil War folk song and perform variations of marches originating in the United States (reflects National Standard in Dance 5c).

EQUIPMENT AND MATERIALS

Drum; instrumental recording of the Civil War song "Marching Through Georgia." *Optional:* Revisit this unit in fourth, fifth, or sixth grade by introducing dances of the period with more complicated march or step patterns, for example, "When Johnny Comes Marching Home Again," "Lancaster Barn Dance" (barn dance step), "Hull's Victory," "Jennie Lind Polka" (Schottische step).

MARCHING THROUGH GEORGIA

"Marching Through Georgia," by New England composer Henry Clay Work, is a famous song recalling General William Tecumseh Sherman's notorious march from Atlanta to Savannah in 1864.

LEARNING EXPERIENCES

1.0 [Tap a steady 4/4 or 2/4 meter.] As I tap the drum, travel with marching steps through open spaces and stop right where you are when I say, 'And stop.' Ready? *And*, 'Travel, two, three, four, move through empty spaces . . . . And stop.' [Repeat many times, having children walk to the beat, staying far apart.]

1.1 Make your feet important by carefully and quietly placing each foot on the floor as you go. [Tap drum softly.] Can you lift each knee high and still step quietly? Show proud marching steps. [Briefly introduce historical facts from above caption.]

AEROBIC ACTIVITY

The activity in this unit raises your heart rate but still allows you to pace your work so that you can take in all the oxygen you need while you are moving. That is called *aerobic activity.*

1.2 When I say, 'Go back the other way,' or, 'You are going the wrong way,' take an about-face [turn halfway around] and march forward the other way! If you hear me say, 'You are going the right way,' keep traveling forward the same way. Listen carefully to my calls [instructions] as you march to open spaces. [Repeat many times, varying calls to surprise.]

1.3 Each time you pass a classmate, give a big, cheery salute [say "hello" or give a "high five"] and continue on your way! Ready? Begin, 'March . . . march . . . hello [salute] . . . . You're going the right way. March . . . walk . . . walk . . . . You're going the wrong way—about-face [turn sharply and continue marching]!' [Repeat.]

1.4 Let's all travel for eight counts [taps] to meet a classmate across the room [area]. Circle this partner round, passing back to back [demonstrate], for another eight counts and, without stopping, travel again to meet a different person. Listen as you go. 'March, 2, 3, 4, walk to meet someone, 7, 8; circle round your partner, 2, 3, 4, 5, 6, 7, 8; and march on to the next.' [Repeat.]

1.5 This time, when you meet a partner, join hands or link right elbows and circle round by swinging your partner for eight counts, then march on to find someone else. Off you go, meeting and circling round with many different partners! [Repeat several times.]

1.6 Let's combine all the parts we've learned: marching through empty spaces, making quick changes in facing, meeting and parting, and circling. Listen carefully to my calls and follow each action. [Call instructions in a clear, strong voice while tapping a drum. Then, add music selection A (instrumental side).]

VERSE *(Eight measures of 4/4 played 8 times.)*

"Everybody march around, march around and sing;"

(march through empty spaces [4 counts], walk toward partners, saluting [4 counts])

"Step up to a partner and give them a great big swing."

(step and swing partners round, 8 counts)

"Everybody march around, march around and sing."

(leave partner and continue marching, 8 counts)

"While we go marching through Georgia."

(continue marching, 8 counts)

CHORUS *(Eight measures of 4/4 played 8 times.)*

"HIP-HIP! Hooray! Go back the other way"*

(turn halfway and march forward another way, 8 counts)

"HIP-HIP! Hooray! Go back the other way"*

(turn halfway and march forward another way, 8 counts)

"Travel through our dance space now, everybody sing,"

(march through open spaces, saluting, 8 counts)

"While we go marching through Georgia!"

(continue marching, 8 counts)

(*Substitute "You're going the right way" or "You're going the wrong way.")

1.7 As you march, try hard to take one step per beat. March lightly in time with the drumbeat. [Clap or play the underlying beat as music plays. Allow extra time to practice marching. See assessment on page 70].

1.8 Continue traveling as I call out the instructions—don't stop to hear them. Listen *while* moving and keep stepping to the beat. [Verse and chorus.]

1.9 Move near different classmates as you hear me call, 'Step up to your partners,' so you can immediately swing your new partner round! [Practice the whole dance to the music. The verse and the chorus will repeat seven times.]

2.0 Let's vary [change] our dance by moving in a different way on the final verse. [See verse below.] Quickly find a partner, face each other, and separate a little [two body lengths]. Be ready to march toward each other. This time, as you march forward [to meet] *stamp* your feet four counts, then back up [or part] with four quiet steps [counts], ready to start again. 'Forward all and *stamp* your feet [four counts], back up a little as I repeat [four counts]; now forward all.' [Repeat meeting and parting several times. Tap loud drumbeats on the forward cues and soft beats on the backup cues.]

2.1 Let's add circling around our partner after we meet and part. Step up to your partner and circle round. Go all the way around! See if you can make a complete circle safely in eight beats. Ready? [Check to see if partners are near each other.] *And*, 'Circle, two, three, four, five, six, seven, eight.'

2.2 Let's try a more difficult circling pattern called *do-si-do*. Step up to your partner, walk around each other, passing right and then left, shoulders back-to-back, and return to your own space. [Have two children demonstrate, then everyone practice the do-si-do with partner.] Watch your partner as you circle. First, look over your right shoulder, then your left. You need to be aware of each other's position at all times. Be close, but not touching.

2.3 Let's try our new movements with a small group. Make a circle with another couple. Be next to your partner, but give yourself plenty of space to move. [Check for four children in each circle and good spacing.] Listen to my calls and be ready to march into the center of your circle.

LAST VERSE

"Forward all and stomp your feet"
(march forward into the center to meet for four stamping counts and quietly walk back out for four soft counts),

"Forward again and everybody shout!"
(repeat forward and back, except shout "Hurrah" in center circle.)

"Do-si-do your partner"
(face partner and do-si-do for a full eight counts),

"Do-si-do again"
(face person on your other side and do-si-do).

3.0 Let's try meeting and parting and the do-si-do with two more couples [eight in a group]. Stand beside your partner with each couple forming one side of a square. We are working on listening while moving, on meeting and parting, and on changing our pathway or direction. [Initially, talk children through the calls in 2.3 and accompany on the drum at a pace slightly slower than the music. Repeat at same tempo as music, then add music.]

3.1 Remember, when you hear the call, 'Do-si-do your partner,' face your own partner and circle round. When you hear, 'Do-si-do again,' turn away from your partner to face your corner; that's the person nearest you on your other side [walk them through]. 'Do-si-do your corner, taking a full eight counts.'

3.2 Now for the final chorus and the most difficult part—'A grand right and left.' Turn away from your corner, back toward your partner. Reach out, extending your right hand to your partner [as if shaking hands]. Keep walking forward and pass by your partner to meet the next person with your left hand. Pass by and go on to the next with a right hand. On to the next with the left hand all the way around the circle until you meet your partner back home. Swing your partner round and round!

3.3 Let's try the entire dance from the very beginning. Remember how we marched all about the room when we said, 'Everybody march around, march around, and sing?' When you are in a square formation, you need to stay near the other three couples so we can walk and circle to the left [clockwise], following each other around the clock. See if you can walk all the way around your circle and back home in eight counts. [Tap drum and sing or call out words of the verse (line 1) of learning experience 1.6.]

3.4 Pause to swing your partner [line 2], then continue marching clockwise [lines 3 and 4]. And be alert for changes of direction on the chorus, 'Hip, hip, hooray! Go back the other way.' Quickly reverse. Make a half-turn and walk counterclockwise [to the right] around the circle. Be prepared for these surprises and several changes of direction! [Repeat the first verse and chorus seven times, then finish with the last verse (see page 69) and final chorus—a grand right and left!]

ASSESSING DANCE KNOWLEDGE

Explain or show how you would help someone listen and move to the underlying beat (steady, continuous pulse) of the music. Work with a partner. Try to explain as clearly as possible. (Clap the underlying beat as march music is played; walk out the beat; say the words 'walk, walk . . .'; move different body parts to the underlying beat.)

Unit 4 — Creating Group Shapes at Different Levels

4 lessons

FOCUS Traveling with simple steps, turns, and pauses to create group shapes at different levels

MOTOR CONTENT

Selected from Theme 3—Introduction to Space and Theme 5—Introduction to Relationships

Space

Directions—forward, backward, sideways
Levels—high, medium, low (deep)
Extensions—small, large

Relationships

Interpersonal—leading and following (canon)
Spatial positioning—above, below; near to, far from; in front of, behind

OBJECTIVES

In this unit, children will (or should be willing to try to) meet these objectives:

- Explore and discover many different ways to travel and pause to a 2/4 or 4/4 rhythmical pattern.
- Demonstrate clear body shapes by extending body parts far away from the body's center (large extensions), pulling body parts in close to center (small extensions), and holding these contrasting shapes firm and still.
- Show and describe that body shapes at high levels lift up through the whole body; at low levels, occupy space on or near the floor; at medium levels, take up space in the middle (reflects National Standards in Dance 1c and 1h).
- Discuss how dances are similar and different in regard to pathways traveled, body shapes created, and levels used (reflects National Standards in Dance 3b and 4b).
- Lead a small group safely to open spaces with steps and turns and follow partners closely to create group shapes with contrasts in levels (reflects National Standard in Dance 2f).

EQUIPMENT AND MATERIALS

Drum or tambourine (or a rap stick, guiro, maracas, hand castanets, or shaker characteristic of African and Latin music and dance). *Optional:* Musical selections with a moderate tempo in 2/4 or 4/4 time, such as "Polly Put the Kettle On" (piano arrangement compiled by Appleby and Pickow, 1993) or play African-American, Caribbean, or Latin percussion music with a strong beat.

LEARNING EXPERIENCES

1.0 There are so many different ways to travel and pause. Show some ways. Ready? *And*, 'Travel, travel, travel, and stop!' [Repeat phrase many times, playing an even rhythm on the drum or tambourine.]

1.1 Change how you travel by taking larger steps, jumps, and turns. [Practice.] Now, take smaller steps—toes out, toes in, knees straight, knees bent, tiptoe. Find many ways. [Repeat phrase in 1.0, playing slow, strong beats for big movements and quick, light beats for small movements.]

1.2 Let your arms stretch or extend far away from the body as you travel with large steps—cover a lot of space! [Slow, strong drumbeats.] Now, pull arms in tightly, close to your sides, as you travel with small steps. [Quick, light drumbeats. Repeat slow and quick sequences several times.]

1.3 Let's take our traveling to different levels. Travel low, close to the ground. Your movement says, 'Watch me travel, travel, near the ground, and stop.' [Play moderate tempo on drum. Repeat at medium and high levels.]

1.4 Let your arms follow your movement naturally. When you travel low, swing your arms low and reach downward. Travel high and swing your arms upward, pulling you off the ground!

1.5 What can your arms do at a medium level? Yes, reach out away from the body in all different directions. [Practice on the spot, then while traveling.]

What can you do with your arms at high levels? Medium? Low?

1.6 Keep changing your level each time you travel. High. Medium. Low.

1.7 Can you turn as you travel and arrive at a new level?

2.0 Repeat after me [rhythmically], 'Turn, and turn, and turn, and stop.' Say this phrase three times as we move together, then hold your last still shape for four more counts. [Accompany with a moderately slow tempo on drum, repeating phrase throughout.]

2.1 Explore different ways to travel and turn around as you go. Do you see open spaces where you can travel farther with bigger turns? Find spaces that are close to you. Turn around on a spot nearby. [Warn children about turning too long or fast and getting dizzy. Encourage children to repeat words slowly as they move, using their voices as accompaniment.]

2.2 Go to a new spot each time you repeat the phrase.

2.3 As you travel and turn to distant spaces, extend your arms outward to help you balance. Bring your arms in closer when you travel and turn nearby.

2.4 Think about your pauses. Let your arms, eyes, chest—your whole body—tell us where you are. Look there and go! [Repeat.]

2.5 Are you traveling to different levels? High. Medium. Low. [Have a child demonstrate.] Ready? *And*, 'Low-level turn, and turn, and stop; high-level turn, and turn, and stop; medium-level turn, and turn, and stop; now hold a strong firm shape!' [Repeat sequence several times with whole class, encouraging children to explore different levels.]

2.6 Let's try our turning dance to the rhyme [song] 'Polly Put the Kettle On.' We will repeat the movement phrase, 'Turn, and turn, and turn, and stop,' three times, arriving at a new spot and at a different level each time. Hold your last shape very still for four counts. This gives you time to get ready to repeat the whole sequence again. [Talk children through the sequence by saying the following verses (or movement phrases) without, then with, music. Music is not necessary to make this an enjoyable dance experience.]

'Polly put the kettle on,'	[Turn, and turn, and turn, and stop],
'Polly put the kettle on,'	[turn, and turn, and turn, and stop],
'Polly put the kettle on,'	[turn, and turn, and turn, and stop],
'We'll all have tea.'	[now all hold still].
	[Repeat entire sequence again.]
'Sukey, take it off again,'	[Turn, and turn, and turn, and stop],
'Sukey, take it off again,'	[turn, and turn, and turn, and stop],
'Sukey, take it off again,'	[turn, and turn, and turn, and stop],
'They've all gone away,'	[now all hold still].

[See Appleby and Pickow, 1993, for music]

ASSESSMENT: DIALOGUE AND DEMONSTRATION

Do you remember what spot and level you stopped at first? Second? Third? Did you hold your last shape firm and still? Try repeating the whole sequence again exactly the same way. Choose a partner and watch each other to see if you repeat movements and levels accurately.

3.0 Now that you know the sequence of the dance, let's try something more difficult. I will start by traveling and turning on the first phrase or line of the song [voice number one]; [Cameron] will travel on the second phrase [voice number two]; then all of you will travel together on the third phrase of the song [voice number three]. Everyone will hold a still shape for the final four counts. [Repeat several times with verbal cues.] I go, 'Turn, and turn, and turn, and stop.' [Cameron] 'Turn, and turn, and turn, and stop.' [Whole group.] 'Turn, and turn, and turn, and stop. Now we all hold still.'

3.1 Let's all stop at different levels so our dance will be more interesting. [Demonstrate.] If I stop low [voice number one], [Cameron] needs to stop at either a high or medium level [voice number two]. If he chooses high, what level will all of you [voice number three] stop at? Right, medium. We will end the sequence holding shapes at three different levels. [Repeat with cues.]

3.2 We need to take turns leading and following. Let's say that whoever arrives at the high level to hold a still shape will be the leader next. This person has two important jobs: to lead others safely to open spaces [far away or nearby] and to remember to arrive at a medium or low level the next time so someone else can be the next leader. [Assign different children the voice number one and voice number two roles.]

3.3 Remember that sometimes the whole group [voice number three] will be the leader. You need to watch each other, move together, and arrive at a medium or low level at the same time. [Repeat several times to link phrases together, developing smooth transitions.]

3.4 [Vary 3.2 and 3.3 by playing three distinct sounds on percussion, for example, tap drumhead or tambourine skin (voice number one); tap rim of drum or tambourine (voice number two); rub drumhead or shake tambourine (voice number three).] Move when you hear your sound.

3.5 [Optional: Repeat 3.0 to 3.4, substituting different traveling activities, for example, hopping, jumping, or skipping. Sing verses and/or play music while moving.]

4.0 We're ready to try the dance; everyone will have a chance to lead. Quickly decide what level you want to start at and show me on the count of one. Ready? *And,* 'One!' Look around the room. Do we have too many highs? Lows? You may want to change your level so we have different levels scattered about the room. Make your level clear and beginning shape strong. People who are holding shapes at a high level, be ready to move first! Medium level moves next. Low level, last. [Play percussion or music, if you wish.] *Ready and,* 'High-level turn, and turn, and stop. Medium-level turn, and turn, and stop. Low-level turn, and turn, and stop. Now all hold still!' [Repeat sequence several times to give all children a chance to arrive at different levels as leader and follower.]

4.1 *Trio* means three. Quickly find two other people you work well with and sit down together, listening. [Encourage mixed groups.] Each of you select a number—one, two, or three. Number one, stand up and demonstrate a shape that we can clearly identify as high, medium, or low. Number two, make a shape above or below number one. Number three, can you fill in at the level where you are needed? Now, hold your group shape very firm and still. Be close, but don't touch. This will be your starting position.

4.2 Dancers at the high level will move first. What levels could they travel to next? Right, a medium or low level. Be sure that your group plans ahead so everyone has a chance to lead and to follow. [Play percussion or music with rhyme; cue as needed.]

4.3 Let's take it with the music [or percussion]. Use strong muscles to hold your starting position for four counts. *Ready and,* 'High-level turn, and turn, and stop; medium-level turn, and turn, and stop; low-level turn, and turn, and stop. Hold your group shape very still!' New leader. [Repeat sequence several times.]

4.4 Leaders, discover new, open spaces. Sometimes cover a lot of space while turning! Other times step and turn in a little space, stopping nearby. Try not to go back and forth between the same two places. Find new open spaces! [Music.]

4.5 Think ahead. Know what shape you will make next. Leaders, will you extend arms and legs out from the body or bring them in close? Will you make a long, narrow shape or a wide, spread-out shape? A round, curved shape or pointy shape with angles? [Music.]

4.6 Followers, how will you relate to your leader's still shape? Look for large spaces to fill or reach around. Small, tiny places to squeeze into. Spaces in front, behind, right-left, above or below your partner[s]. [Play music to end. Share dances, discussing similarities and differences in pathways traveled and body shapes or levels used.] What makes a group shape interesting and why?

4.7 [Vary this dance experience in many ways to help children learn to dance responsively with others, both in duets and trios. Children can make up everyday rhymes and chants, or substitute names for "Polly" and "Sukey" or "kettle" and "tea" (or other familiar rhymes and songs) to create movement studies of their own. Post (on chalkboard, poster, or computer printout) the following possibilities for dancing together in a duo or trio: leading or following, meeting or parting, passing by, going around each other, joining together; linking and splitting apart, going between or passing through others, and circling around. Have children accompany each other by singing rhymes or playing percussion instruments.]

ASSESSMENT: GROUP PROJECT (COORDINATE WITH A FIRST GRADE TEACHER)

Working in partners or trios, tape-record or write an explanation of how you would help children in first grade understand rhythmic patterns and the use of repetition in dance. Select a nursery rhyme and teach the rhythmic pattern to a small group of first graders. For example, first clap the rhythmic pattern of the nursery rhyme. Next, one half of the group claps the pattern while the other half claps the underlying beat. Move to the pattern (with simple locomotor movements) as you recite the rhyme. Select, practice, and repeat favorite movements. End with a still shape. Do you recognize a pattern? What movements did we repeat?

Designing Phrases and Making Curved Pathways

3 or 4 lessons

FOCUS Designing phrases of traveling and turning, making curved aerial and floor pathways in 3/4 time

MOTOR CONTENT

Selected from Theme 3—Introduction to Space and Theme 6—Instrumental Use of the Body

Body

Activities of the body—traveling while turning; turning jumps; traveling jumps; gestures while traveling and staying in place

Space

Pathways—air, floor; straight, curved

OBJECTIVES

In this unit, children will (or should be willing to try to) meet these objectives:

* Link several movement ideas together to form a sequence in 3/4 time, then perform, observe, and discuss movements confidently (reflects National Standards in Dance 1h and 2a).
* Understand and demonstrate how straight and curved pathways are traced in the air and on the floor as the body moves through space (reflects National Standard in Dance 1e).
* Understand that a 3/4 meter has three beats per measure and is commonly known as a *waltz meter*.
* Create a dance based on their own artwork or writing that demonstrates an understanding of curved lines and pattern repetition; explain connections between dance and artwork (reflects National Standards in Dance 2b and 7b).

EQUIPMENT AND MATERIALS

Drum. Musical selections: Selection A—lively waltz music, such as "Fiddlers Three"; Selection B—"Waltz" by Tchaikovsky; Selection C—"Emperor Waltz," "Roses From the South," or "Voices of Spring" waltzes by Johann Strauss; Selection D—recorded folk dances, such as "Chiapenecas" (Mexican waltz) or "Spanish Circle Waltz"; Selection E—slower waltzes, such as "I Ride an Old Paint" or "Goodnight, Irene" (see piano music).

LEARNING EXPERIENCES

1.0 [Demonstrate a curved pathway by having children write their names in the air with a hand using cursive. Use visual aids to further illustrate curved lines, for example, a photo of vapor trails from airplanes; or art prints with strong shapes defined by curved lines, and the like.] Watch the imaginary path your hand makes as it moves through space. Explore all the space around you. Make curved pathways in front of you, behind you, to the right-left, up, down. .

1.1 Hold an imaginary paintbrush in your hand and make *large*, sweeping movements through space . . . now small squiggly movements. Cover all the space around you with curvy lines.

1.2 Make curved pathways with different body parts. [Elbows, shoulders, head, hips, knees, arms, legs.] Which body parts make shorter paths? Longer trails?

1.3 Make really long, curved pathways in the air by swinging or sweeping your arms and legs through space. [Tap a three-beat rhythm on the drum, accenting the first beat.] *And*, 'Swing, two, three; swing, two, three; swing, two, three.' Let different body parts give away to gravity. Feel the wind rush by!

1.4 Select the curved pathway you like best and practice it. Work hard to keep the edges rounded. Add a second curved line—it can be short or long—using a different body part. Add a third pathway until you have designed a whole movement sentence. [Move among children, questioning them and observing their work.]

QUESTIONING AND OBSERVING

What body part begins your movement sentence? Goes next? Ends your sequence? Practice repeating your sequence exactly the same way. (The teacher and students observe for accurate repetition.)

2.0 [Travel, designing a curved floor pattern.] Notice how I am making a curved pathway on the floor with my feet. Everyone, design [cut] a long, curvy trail or path with your feet. Travel all about the room. [Use imagery of skiing or skating, if you wish.]

2.1 Make all the edges rounded as you travel. Think of your design and work hard to round out the turns in your pathway. Feel your body lean to one side, then to the other. *Swoosh* through space!

2.2 See if you can create a spiral design on the floor that goes around you in bigger and bigger circles. The design becomes larger and larger as you circle farther and farther away from your starting point. Take care not to bump into anyone. Let us know when you arrive at the end of your spiral. Make a period with your feet with invisible ink.

2.3 Let your feet write your name or a secret message in cursive as you travel. Leave imaginary letters on the floor wherever you go!

2.4 Explore different ways of traveling in curved pathways—walking, running, hopping, skipping, sliding.

2.5 Imagine you are taking a sightseeing tour. Visit as many sights as you can, leaving behind curved pathways with your feet. Take a trip up a winding mountain or walk along the seashore where waves chase your feet. [Elicit ideas of places children might travel. If you wish, integrate learning experiences 2.0

Travel carefully in circles around your home base. Imagine making a spiral design like that of a snail or seashell.

Keep making bigger circles until you are far from your home base, then travel back home on the same curved pathway.

to 2.8 with creative writing in the classroom (in the form of stories about travels) or with an art project on shapes bound by curvilinear lines and repetition of patterns.]

2.6 Draw curved pathways in the air with different body parts as you take your trip [or trace lines of your artwork]. Sometimes leap or jump from one foot to the other over imaginary objects. Think of how the top of your head makes a curved pathway, too.

2.7 Choose some stopping places on the way. Show how you can bend, twist, stretch, or turn in place to create curved pathways in the air. [Allow children adequate time to explore a variety of locomotor and nonlocomotor activities. Play any waltz music.]

2.8 Share your dance with a partner. Show how you designed floor patterns and created interesting pathways in the air. Discuss the connections between your artwork [or creative writing] and dance. [Play music softly.]

3.0 Imagine you have chalk dust on your feet. Travel in a straight pathway and then *jump*, turning in the air. Here we go: 'Walk, walk, walk, *jump* and *turn*!' [Repeat a few times.] Land softly and travel without stopping. See if you

Choose several lines from your art print and draw them on the floor with your feet. Vary the size of your movement to create interesting patterns in space.
Artwork by Nate, age 8.

can leave straight pathways of imaginary chalk dust on the floor with your feet and spirals in the air with the top of your head.

3.1 Find more ways to make straight and curved pathways on the floor and in the air. Show clear differences in these two types of pathways. [Have children invent and repeat a variety of step-*jump* combinations.] Be careful of others as you travel.

3.2 Take a slow, smooth walk, rising and sinking as you travel. Imagine your head and shoulders tracing smooth curves or waves in the air. 'Up, up, up; down, down, down.' [Repeat several times.]

3.3 [Tap a 3/4 meter on drum, accenting the first beat and saying, "*One, two, three.*"] As you travel, accent your first step by bending your knees on count one, then rise up on the balls of your feet for the next two beats. In dance, we call this pattern a triplet. '*Down,* up, up; *down,* up, up.' [Repeat several times.] How many beats are in each measure? [Three.]

3.4 [Tap a 3/4 meter or play any waltz music.] As you travel in curved pathways, allow your arms to open and reach out, then close [drop] to your sides. Make wide, sweeping, curved pathways with your arms. '*Down,* up, up; *open* and close.' [Repeat. You may vary 3.3 and 3.4 by using the swing of arms to help students feel the accent.]

3.5 Keep traveling and when you are ready to *jump* and *turn* in the air, swing your arms up and bring them in close to your waist or chest to help you make the turn. Hold arms tight to your body at the moment you are turning. Push off hard with your feet and stretch your legs long! [Continue drumbeat or music.] Feel those arms wrap up the air around your torso to *jump* and *turn*!

3.6 Make your movement exciting! Travel slowly in curved pathways, then take a quick, sudden turn on the spot or a jump and turn in the air! [No accompaniment.]

3.7 Let's make up a 'curved pathway dance' with traveling and turning. Travel in curved pathways for nine counts [three measures], then show three surprise turns for three counts [one measure; or one big turn that lasts three counts]. Each phrase in our dance has 12 counts. Here we go: '*Travel,* 2, 3; 4, 5, 6; 7,

ASSESSMENT: PORTFOLIO

Document children's dancework (process and product) by videotaping or photographing. Include a video segment or photo(s) in each child's portfolio, along with a copy of their artwork or creative writing.

8, 9; *turn, turn, turn!*' [Tap the first beat of each measure stronger in 3/4 time and say counts aloud. Repeat many times. Alternatively, have students work in pairs to music, allowing them to decide when and where to turn or jump. Partners refine their favorite jumps and turns, performing simultaneously or alternating.]

4.0 [Accompany learning experiences 4.0 to 4.4 with any waltz music.] As I play the music, travel in curved pathways and let your arms draw curved pathways in space. Be careful of others.

4.1 Round out your edges and sharp corners as you travel. Make both floor and air pathways very round and curved.

4.2 Sometimes allow your feet to push you up into the air for a big turning jump! In dance, we call this a *tour en l'air*. See if you can accent [make stronger] the first count of every six [the "one"] by pushing high into the air to turn. '*Jump* [and turn], 4, 5, 6; *jump* [and turn], 4, 5, 6.' [Repeat phrase several times with music, tapping a strong first drumbeat.]

4.3 Let's make up a dance that has two parts. In part *A*, travel in curved pathways for six counts [two measures]; in part *B*, stop traveling and make curved pathways in the air with different body parts for the next six counts [two measures]. Here we go: '*Travel,* 2, 3, 4, 5, 6; *on* the spot, 4, 5, 6.' [Repeat many times with music. Challenge some classes to vary their traveling.] '*Jump* [and turn], 4, 5, 6; *on* the spot, 4, 5, 6.'

4.4 [Divide the class into two groups to perform. Play waltz music and say counts aloud initially, "*Travel,* travel, travel, 4, 5, 6; *on* the spot, 4, 5, 6."] Everyone in this group, show us your *A* phrase of traveling, then go immediately into your *B* phrase. Repeat your phrases several times so we, the audience, can clearly see movements in curved pathways on the floor and in the air. When your dance is finished, hold very still.

[Variation one: Partners teach each other their phrases. Both perform partner number one's phrases *A* and *B*, then partner number two's phrases *A* and *B*. To end, both perform their own phrases simultaneously. Variation two: Children make up a dance showing both curved floor and air pathways. Partner number one travels in curved floor pathways around partner number two who creates curved aerial pathways on the spot by bending, stretching, twisting, and swinging in place. Exchange roles after several measures.]

ASSESSING DANCE IMPROVEMENTS

Answer the following about your performance in this unit (or for dance in general):

1. **Compared to last year, I have improved the most in:**
2. **Three dance skills I do well are:**
3. **One dance skill I would like to improve is:**

Fourth Grade Games

Unit 1

Spiral Football Pass

4 to 6 lessons

FOCUS Introducing the spiral overhand pass with a football, emphasizing throwing and catching lead passes

MOTOR CONTENT

Selected from Theme 1—Introduction to Basic and Manipulative Control and Theme 5—Introduction to Basic Relationships

Body

Manipulative activities—spiral pass with a football

Relationships

Player placement—receiver moving to an open space
Ball placement—passing to a space in front of the receiver

OBJECTIVES

In this unit, children will (or should be willing to try to) meet these objectives:

- Modify their overhand throw pattern by gripping the football near one end with fingers spread across the laces of the ball and having their little finger side of the hand lead the throw, making the fingers be the last part of the hand to leave the ball (reflects National Standard in Physical Education 1).
- Develop momentum with a snapping, karate-chop motion of the lower arm and hand executed when the ball and hand pass above the dominant shoulder (reflects National Standards in Physical Education 1 and 2).
- Run quickly into open spaces to elude a defensive player, adjusting speed and stride to receive a pass (reflects National Standard in Physical Education 1).
- Judge the speed of a receiver when throwing the ball in front of the receiver so the receiver can catch the ball without breaking stride or changing direction (reflects National Standard in Physical Education 1).
- Have patience when a pass is incomplete, accepting mutual responsibility for completing passes as a receiver and as the passer (reflects National Standards in Physical Education 5 and 6).
- Design their own game or establish rules to make the game they are playing enjoyable for everyone (reflects National Standard in Physical Education 7).

EQUIPMENT AND MATERIALS

One junior size sponge football for every two students; four cones or jugs to mark goal lines for each group of six to eight students.

LEARNING EXPERIENCES

1.0 [If taught inside, have children aim at wall targets. Outside, you may be able to hang tires or hoops outside from goal posts.] Find a partner, get one football, and practice passing the ball at a target [back and forth to each other if no targets are available].

1.1 Try to release the ball when your throwing hand is high in the air above your shoulder because in football you need to throw the ball far.

1.2 Watch your neighbor. See if the ball is released when the front tip of the ball is pointing up at an angle and the throwing hand is still very high to help send the ball in a nice high arc. Balls traveling in a high arc give the receivers time to reposition to catch. Show your neighbors how high their hand was when they released the ball. [Change roles.]

1.3 Show opposition by stepping forward on the foot on the side opposite your throwing hand just like you do when you throw a softball. Don't let the foot on the same side of the body as your throwing arm do the stepping. [Have a child demonstrate.]

1.4 To make the ball spiral, try to throw the ball with the little finger side of your throwing hand facing your receiver, not the palm of your hand. [Demonstrate.]

1.5 Have you seen anyone break a board with the side of their hand? The action of your elbow and hand when you throw a football is similar to that karate chop. Snap your elbow and cut the space above your shoulder with the side of your hand as your throw the football.

1.6 Watch your receiver catch your pass. If they had to travel to the side to catch, pay close attention to your release. Point your hand right to your partner as you release the ball. If your partner travels toward you to catch, throw a little harder or release the ball a little higher. If your partner travels backward, you need to let up on your power. Try to throw the ball right to your receiver.

1.7 Remember, those karate experts can't break the board with the side of their hand unless they make that hand travel really fast. Speed up your throwing arm and elbow-snap and make your hand reach high as you throw.

2.0 Catchers, work on catching every pass. Be prepared to travel. Focus on the ball as your passer prepares to throw and, if necessary, run to catch it.

2.1 When catching, get both hands on the ball. Spread your fingers to make your hands big to give that ball room to land in your hands.

2.2 I'm coming around to ask you what you should do to keep the ball from bouncing out of your hands when it lands in your hands. [After observing, stop the class and let someone share the answer. If no student gave an answer relevant to absorbing force, review "giving" with the direction of the force to keep the ball from rebounding.]

2.3 Take pride in completing passes. Sometimes you see football players bringing the ball in toward their bodies when catching. How many completed passes can you and your partner make out of ten tries?

STRENGTH

Squeeze a small rubber ball 10 times with each hand. Squeeze the ball and try five downward arm swings toward the floor and out away from your shoulder, including a final wrist flick. To strengthen your grip and forearm, practice squeezing a ball hard at home while watching TV or when riding in a car.

2.4 Receivers, be ready to run to the ball if it isn't coming to you. Look at your passer. Be on the balls of your feet, ready to run.

2.5 See how many completed passes you can make without missing.

3.0 If you completed five or six passes out of ten tries, listen carefully. Remember those lead passes you made playing basketball? See if you can throw and catch lead passes with the football. The distance you throw a football is usually greater than a basketball, so the receivers will need to run faster and the passers will need to aim a little farther out in front of the receivers. Receivers, as the passer gets set to pass the ball, start a slow jog to one side. Passers, send the ball to the space ahead of the receiver. Try to make the ball and your receiver reach the same spot at the same time.

3.1 When practicing passing, work hard to throw the ball so the runner and the ball reach each other exactly at the same time without making the runner change speed or direction.

3.2 Receivers, be prepared to help your passer complete the pass by changing your speed or direction to get the ball. Remember, neither of you is a pro, yet, so be prepared to scamper to complete the pass.

3.3 Passers, plant that rear foot and then step forward on the opposite foot, pointing the toes of your stepping foot toward the spot where you want the ball to go. A firm footing will help you throw farther and more accurately.

3.4 Run a little faster if you are catching most of the passes. Passers, be prepared! When you see the receiver running faster, aim your throw to a spot farther ahead of the receiver.

3.5 [Organize the class into groups of three: one passer, one receiver, one defender. Explain and have them practice a two versus one situation, rotating positions after each pass: passer to defender, defender to receiver, receiver to passer.] Passers, pass in front of the receiver just at the moment you see the receiver break free. Defender, try to intercept the pass.

3.6 Receivers, you will have only one person defending the pass. Travel into an open space away from the defender to receive the pass.

3.7 Defenders, keep focused on the receiver and the ball if you can. Be ready to change your pathway when the receiver breaks free to intercept the pass.

3.8 Receivers, try hard to change your pathway quickly to create an open view between you and the passer.

4.0 [Do not wait until the last day to play the game. The game should be a part of several lessons to give children time to develop game strategy and to see how further skill development improves the quality of their game. Organize the class in groups of six or eight, dividing the groups into two teams of three or four each. Let each group decide on a few rules and start to play a game of No Contact Pass Football, where every play is a pass play. Have them get four cones or jugs to mark their goal lines.]

4.1 [Observe the games closely to make sure each child has an opportunity to be the receiver. Give this task when needed.] What kind of rule would help us give all players a chance to be the receiver? [Since there are no more than (four) on a team and one person is the passer, every player could have one turn. You may suggest more "downs," if children have difficulty sharing the role of the receiver or if their skill level is low.]

4.2 [Observe to make sure the children are sharing the role of the passer. Suggest the teams change passers each time a team regains possession of the ball.]

4.3 Receivers, run quickly and change your location so you have a clear space between you and your passer. Don't let your defender get her body between you and the passer.

4.4 Passers, throw your pass ahead of your running receiver. Remember to give everyone practice in catching the pass.

4.5 Receivers, always try to keep your eyes focused on the passer. If you turn your back to the passer as you run down field, try to look over your shoulder at your receiver or to get in line with the ball to intercept the pass

4.6 Defenders, be ready to change your path or speed to stay close to the receiver or get in line with the ball to intercept the pass.

4.7 Passers, throw the pass in front of your receiver the moment he changes pathways or look for an alternate receiver who is open.

NO CONTACT PASS FOOTBALL

Players — Two teams of 2 to 6 players

Area — 50 feet x 20 feet or larger depending on passing skill of the players

Object of the Game — To score touchdowns by catching passes when standing behind the opponent's goal line

The Game — Toss a coin or use an alternate method to decide which is the offensive and defensive team to start the game. Teams take their places on the field. The defense starts the game (and puts the ball in play after scoring a touchdown) by lining up midway in the field. One player passes the ball as far as he can toward the offensive team's goal line. The offensive team tries to catch the pass. If missed, both teams must let the ball come to rest. The offensive team gets possession of the ball where the passer was standing or at the spot where a team member caught the pass. They get four pass plays (downs) to score a goal by completing a pass to a teammate standing behind the opponent's goal line. Each down starts at the spot where the last pass was completed. The ball may not be advanced by running either by the offensive receiver or by a defensive team member after intercepting a pass. No body contact is permitted.

The defensive team gains possession of the ball: where the fourth play ends when the offensive team fails to score a touchdown, at the point where a pass is intercepted, or by receiving a pass from the opponents to resume play after a touchdown is scored.

Scoring — A touchdown is scored when the ball is caught behind the opponent's goal line.

Penalties — By offense: loss of yardage and down; by defense: offense gets one additional down

ASSESSING THROWING					
Class list	Grips across laces with fingers guiding.	Karate action used.	Ball released when hand is above shoulder.	Opposition used to produce force.	Times pass to receiver's speed.
Rodney	4	3	3	4	4
Yvonne	3	3	3	3	3

Scale: 5 = Consistently 4 = At least half the time 3 = Inconsistently

Forehand Strike

4 to 6 lessons

FOCUS Developing the forehand strike with a paddle or racquet, emphasizing selecting proper force and controlling the height of the ball

MOTOR CONTENT

Selected from Theme l—Introduction to Basic Body and Manipulative Control; Theme 2—Introduction to Space; and Theme 3—Introduction to Movement Quality (Effort)

Body

Manipulative activities—forehand strike with a paddle or racquet

Effort

Force—selecting proper force

Space

Levels—sending the ball to a medium level

OBJECTIVES

In this unit, children will (or should be willing to try to) meet these objectives:

- Adjust the body and feet to face the nonracquet side and shoulder toward the net or partner in preparation for the forehand stroke (reflects National Standard in Physical Education 2).
- Change the force of the hit to control the placement of the ball (reflects National Standard in Physical Education 2).
- Know that power for the forehand is developed by lengthening the backswing, stepping toward the ball with the opposite foot, turning the upper part of the body in the direction of the swing, and reaching for the ball out in front of them (reflects National Standard in Physical Education 2).
- Retrieve balls for others and ask for theirs politely when play on the court stops (reflects National Standard in Physical Education 5).
- Improve their skill and others' skills by maintaining a "with-it-ness" attitude, making every effort to return balls appropriately to extend rallies or score a point (reflects National Standards in Physical Education 1, 5, and 6).

EQUIPMENT AND MATERIALS

One racquet or paddle for each child; one 4" high density foam ball for each child; ropes, benches, or other barriers to serve as nets.

LEARNING EXPERIENCES

1.0 [Use a firm, flat, hand to teach these experiences in situations where paddles are unavailable, for students not willing to show concern for others, or those needing more practice in striking before compounding the task by adding the extra length of a racquet.] Trying hard not to let your ball disturb anyone else, see how you can drop the ball, letting it bounce, and then strike the ball toward the wall with your racquet. Continue to strike the ball to the wall as long as it is in your own space. If the ball doesn't come right to you, catch it, drop it, and strike it again. Get a racquet, a ball, find a space facing the side wall, and begin. [To maximize learning and safety, observe and adjust the spacing of students and remind them to hold racquets tightly. Caution them to look before retrieving a ball so no one gets hit with a racquet.]

1.1 See how many times you can strike the ball against the wall in your own space, letting it bounce each time before you strike it again.

1.2 Try to strike the ball when it is out in front of you. Don't let the ball get close to you or behind you before striking it.

1.3 Begin to pay close attention to how you are standing as you strike the ball. Check and be sure you have your racquet back and your whole nonracquet side pointed toward the wall so you can strike the ball out in front of you.

1.4 When practicing a forehand stroke in tennis, have your opposite shoulder facing the wall. Move your feet to get your entire racquet side turned away from the wall with your racquet back. Reach your arm and racquet out, keeping the face of the racquet pointing to the wall as you strike the ball.

1.5 Bend your knees as you step forward on your opposite foot.

1.6 Keep the head of your racquet up as you reach out, stroking firmly and smoothly through the ball to finish your hit. Keep your wrist firm so the top of the racquet doesn't drop toward the floor.

1.7 Bend your knees to keep the racquet handle parallel with [flat as] the floor as you contact the ball, straightening your knees as you swing. Think of a table just below the ball. Swing the racquet across the imaginary table top.

2.0 Let's watch the action of [Sheryl's] feet. Notice how she transfers her weight onto her rear foot, the foot away from the wall, as she takes her racquet back. Then, as she starts her forward swing, she bends her knees as she steps onto her front foot, pointing the front foot toward the wall. This weight shift and stepping in the direction you want the ball to go will give you more power and will really help you control and place the ball. Concentrate on that weight transference and stepping toward the wall.

2.1 Take care. Think about what is going on around you before retrieving your ball. A polite tennis player never goes onto someone else's court. When a ball lies unnoticed in someone else's space, say, 'help please' when their point is finished and 'thank you' as they hand the ball back.

2.2 You are improving your footwork. Work with the person next to you. Stand back and watch the other person's feet as he strikes the ball five or six times. Be the teacher. Let your partner know if weight shifted to the front foot as they contacted the ball. [Change roles.] Show your partner their teaching has helped you improve your weight transference.

2.3 Count how many times out of ten hits your partner can strike the ball when it is out in front of them while transferring their weight onto their opposite foot. [Change roles.]

2.4 Everyone see if you can break the record you set when your partner counted your hits. Think about bending your knees. Feel that weight shift. Catch the ball and start over again when you feel your weight getting stuck and not shifting.

2.5 If you improved your record, move away from the wall a step or two and see if you can equal your record as you strike the ball a little harder.

3.0 Pay attention to where your ball is hitting on the wall. Try to make it hit no higher than your shoulders. A high ball in tennis is really easy for your opponent to hit so you can't return it.

3.1 Purposely send the ball high against the wall. Pay attention to what you do with the face of your racquet to send the ball high. See if you can tell me what you did with the face of your racquet. [Ask several students. Later on, use their correct comments as coaching hints.]

3.2 If you feel ready, try to alternate the level of your hits. Send the ball first about waist high and the next time send it so it hits the wall about twice that high.

[Choose between 4.0 and 5.0 if space or time does not allow your students to do both. Either setting can result in a competitive situation rather than cooperative as written, if you or students desire.]

4.0 Let's make our working space bigger by joining with another person. One person will strike the ball against the wall while the other person lets it bounce, then hits it to the wall. Take turns hitting one ball. Get a partner, put away one ball, and begin.

4.1 After you hit, take care and back away from where you think the ball will bounce to give your partner room to strike the ball. Watch out for each others' racquets.

4.2 Each time you strike the ball, try to get that nonracquet shoulder and the foot on that side pointed toward your wall.

4.3 Watch your power. Try to send the ball so your partner can return it. See how many times you and your partner can send it against the wall. Are you thinking about keeping the ball out in front of you to enable you to contact it with the center of the racquet?

4.4 Your feet really have to be ready to move. Stay on the balls of your feet and keep your feet light and moving.

4.5 If you and your partner are getting good at alternating hits against the wall, you can begin to alter the force or height of your return to make your partner work harder to adjust her position to return the ball.

4.6 Count how many times you and your partner can alternate hits against the wall.

4.7 If you would like, get some ropes to mark off the sidelines of your court. Begin to make up a game that requires you to alternate striking the ball against the wall making the ball rebound in between your ropes. Devise a scoring method for your tennis game. You may want to include a serving line.

5.0 [Arrange ropes, benches, or other barriers about waist high to serve as nets. Court size need not be more than 10 to 12 feet wide but should be about 30 to 36 feet deep.] Let's see how the two of you can keep the ball going back and forth over the rope on your own court. [Use one versus two if space is limited.]

5.1 Practice your tennis etiquette. Stop, wait, and let the others finish their point before you ask for your ball.

Make up your own tennis game.

5.2 Receivers, watch your footwork. Step toward the net on the foot opposite your racquet hand as you strike the ball.

5.3 Control your power to make the ball bounce between the net and your partner. Take pride in having your partner be able to return the ball.

5.4 See how many times you and your partner can keep the ball going before having to catch or retrieve it.

5.5 Watch your partner strike the ball. Remind them, if they need help, to try to make their swing parallel with [flat as] the floor and hit the ball when it is out in front of them. Both of you remember to let the ball bounce.

5.6 You might like to challenge another set of partners to see which set can keep the rally going the longest.

ASSESSING KNOWLEDGE OF THE FOREHAND STROKE

Explain how you use one of the following ideas to help you perform the forehand stroke. If possible, describe any problems that you had (or still have) and how you solved the problem (or are working on the problem). The three performance cues (with the reasons for using each cue) are:

1. Preparing by taking weight on the back foot (allows weight transfer to the front leg).
2. Stepping and bending the opposite knee (allows weight transfer into the stroke).
3. Hitting in front of the body (allows racquet to travel farther and develops more weight transfer into the stroke).

Unit 3

Lead Passes, Offense and Defense

4 to 6 lessons

FOCUS Throwing lead passes to players who are repositioning, emphasizing shifting quickly from offense to defense and defense to offense

MOTOR CONTENT

Selected from Theme 5—Introduction to Basic Relationships and Theme 7—Introduction to Complex Relationships

Relationships

Player placement—changing from offense to defense and from defense to offense; repositioning nearer a goal; repositioning to create spaces
Ball placement—passing to a space ahead of a moving receiver

OBJECTIVES

In this unit, children will (or should be willing to try to) meet these objectives:

- Demonstrate repositioning nearer a goal during game or gamelike play while responding to the changing need for moving toward or away from the ball (reflects National Standards in Physical Education 1 and 2).
- Move away from offensive teammates to create empty spaces to open game play (reflects National Standards in Physical Education 1 and 2).
- Throw into the space ahead of the moving receiver so the receiver can catch without changing stride or speed (reflects National Standards in Physical Education 1 and 5).
- Adjust their stride and speed when receiving a ball to accommodate the throw, striving to complete all passes (reflects National Standards in Physical Education 1 and 5).
- Understand when two teams share the playing space with each other, each member of the team with the ball needs to reposition continually to move the ball nearer the goal to get into scoring position (reflects National Standards in Physical Education 1 and 2).
- Share the ball with classmates of different skill levels and gender during practice and game play, giving all participating an equal opportunity to practice, learn, and enjoy the game setting (reflects National Standards in Physical Education 5, 6, and 7).

EQUIPMENT AND MATERIALS

One 8-inch playground, vinyl, plastic, or foam ball or junior-size basketball for each two children.

LEARNING EXPERIENCES:

1.0 See how you can pass the ball back and forth to each other, running side by side about five steps apart. Travel across the room from one side wall to the other. Find a partner, get one ball for the two of you, and begin.

1.1 As you toss, try to send the passes about chest high so the receiver can run nice and tall to catch the ball. Remember, it is easier to catch the ball on the run if you don't have to bend over to catch it.

1.2 Before you start, both of you turn the whole front of your body to face the wall across the room from you. Now, as you toss and catch, running not sliding, keep the entire front of your body facing the wall in front of you. Turn your head to look at your partner but do not turn your body as you run.

1.3 Change speeds as you pass and travel across the room. Sometimes in a game, you may even have to stop because a guard cuts in front of you.

1.4 As soon as you pass the ball, run in a straight line toward the side wall, staying ready to receive the pass from your tosser at any time.

1.5 Tossers, make sure your receiver has run slightly past you. Toss the ball ahead of your receiver so you move the ball farther ahead of you.

2.0 When your receiver is running, should you pass to where the receiver is or must you throw to the space ahead of the receiver? That's right! Pass *ahead* of the receiver. Toss your passes slightly in front of your receivers so they can catch the ball without altering their stride.

Throw ahead of your receiver with a lead pass.

2.1 Receivers are stopping and waiting to catch. Keep your receivers running by throwing the ball slightly ahead of them.

2.2 Remember to keep the front of your body facing where you are going. If you face each other, you can't move fast because you are sliding and not running.

2.3 Sometimes you must slow down or speed up to complete every pass. Think! An incomplete pass can end up in your opponent's hands.

2.4 [Select two children who are staying close and throwing short, crisp passes.] Let's watch how accurately [Sarah and Min] are leading the passer as they cut across in front of each other. Try to cut across the space in front of the tosser, seeing how many completed lead passes you can make as you travel back and forth across the room. When you miss, sit down and observe three to five passes to see if the passes of others are leading the receiver a bit more accurately.

3.0 [Arrange children completing lead passes in groups of three or four. Give them this next task. (Some will benefit working with a partner longer. Move them into small groups when they seem ready.)] You're making great lead passes! Working as a team of four [three], practice passing and repositioning nearer a basket [target]. Everyone try to create a space between you and the others.

3.1 Passers, keep your passes up about shoulder high to make it easier for the recievers to catch. Receivers, as you move away from the ball and create spaces, don't turn your back to the ball. Keep your eyes on the ball.

3.2 Everyone must take responsibility for keeping open spaces between each other. You are easier to guard when everyone is clustered. It is also harder to move the ball toward the goal when you are close together.

3.3 Throw only to players running toward empty spaces.

3.4 Keep your body front facing the wall across the room so you can run fast to reposition to receive the ball. Don't slide sideways. You'll not be moving nearly as fast if you are sliding.

3.5 Take pride in completing five [six, seven] passes as you travel across your assigned area.

4.0 [Quietly call two groups together who are creating spaces and completing several lead passes.] Sit down in teams so you and the person you are to guard are facing each other. Put away all balls except one. You are ready to put creating space and lead passes into a game called 'End Ball.' To play 'End Ball,' one team starts play by passing the ball in from behind their goal line. They [the offensive team] try to move the ball down court while the defensive team tries to intercept the passes. Score one point each time a teammate standing behind the opponent's end line catches a pass. After each score, the defensive team restarts play by one member throwing the ball in from behind their end line. Decide which team starts the game and begin.

4.1 Organize others to play the game as their skills develop. Take pride in completing every pass. Passers, pass the ball to shoulder height so the receiver can catch the ball on the run. Receivers, be ready to change stride when necessary to catch. A missed ball is likely to go to the other team.

4.2 When your team has the ball, keep moving the ball toward your opponent's goal, trying to create spaces between you, your teammates, and the person guarding you. Pass the ball only to players traveling to empty spaces because the ball is easily intercepted when the receiver is standing still.

4.3 Receivers, don't turn your back to the ball. Keep an eye on the passer. This helps you to know when the pass will be coming to you.

AEROBIC

If you got tired during the lessons in this unit, you probably need to improve your ability to move for longer periods of time—your *aerobic* fitness. Running, biking, or jumping rope for 10 to 30 minutes will help you. Pace yourself so that you are able to talk with a friend during the activity.

4.4 Guards, watch carefully and be ready to fake, change speeds, and reposition in relation to the ball and to the location of the opponent you are guarding. Stay between the person you are guarding and the end line.

4.5 If you intercept, quickly change to offense and move to create open space. Offense, if you lose the ball, you must think and start immediately to defend, moving quickly to guard your opponent.

4.6 While long passes are exciting, they can cause problems. They are hard to control for accuracy, the defense has time to move and intercept or deflect them, and fewer teammates get to contribute. Can you think of a rule for your game that encourages more lead passes and eliminates long passes? [One solution might be requiring a set number of passes—three, four, or five.]

4.7 [Observe for children getting little opportunity to receive a pass. The next suggested step is for you and the children to analyze why. For example: Are the teams too large? Are the passers not able or willing to pass to teammates who are in the most advantageous position? Are some children not moving free from their guards? Then, you and (or) the children may design a solution or develop a rule which would give all children a chance to receive and pass the ball. For example:] Let's make a rule that every person on the team has to catch the ball at least once before a team can score a goal.

4.8 [Regroup the teams several times during the unit to provide opportunities for boys and girls to work together on the same team.]

ASSESSING REPOSITIONING STRATEGY				
Class list	Offense moves to open spaces.	Offense moves away from the ball to create space.	Defense moves to close, reduce space for offense.	Defense moves to block passing lanes.
Shanna Dye	3	2	2	3
Jeff Lewis	4	4	3	3

Scale: 5 = *Consistent* 4 = *Consistent but sometimes too slow* 3 = *Inconsistent and often too late* 2 = *Seldom; appears to be confused* 1 = *Rarely; emphasize skill learning, not strategy*

ASSESSING THE GAME END BALL				
Class list	Transitions fast to offense.	Transitions fast to defense.	Repositions to create space.	Knows value of transitioning when asked.	Willingly shares ball with both genders and differing-ability children.
Fred Star	3	3	4	3	3
Amy Lewis	5	5	5	4	5

Scale: 5 = *All the time* 4 = *3/4 or more of the time* 3 = *Half the time* 2 = *Very inconsistent* 1 = *Rarely if ever, does not know*

Overhead Volleyball Pass

Unit 4

5 or 6 lessons

FOCUS Introducing the overhead volleyball pass and repositioning to receive a pass

MOTOR CONTENT

Selected from Theme 1—Introduction to Basic Body and Manipulative Control; Theme 2—Introduction to Space; and Theme 5—Introduction to Basic Relationships

Body

Manipulative activities—introducing the overhead volleyball pass

Space

Pathways and levels—sending the ball in high, arcing pathways

Relationships

Ball placement—playing the overhead pass in front of and above the head
Body to ball—aligning the midline of the body to the ball

OBJECTIVES

In this unit, children will (or should be willing to try to) meet these objectives:

- Set the ball high in the air with the pads and second joints of the fingers, following through by completely extending the arms and hands up and out in the direction of the pass (reflects National Standards in Physical Education 1 and 2).
- Understand that when setting the ball high, they produce force by extending the knees and elbows quickly as pads of the fingers make contact with the ball (reflects National Standard in Physical Education 2).
- Reposition quickly to align the midline of the body with the ball (reflects National Standards in Physical Education 1 and 2).
- Improve "with-it-ness" for game play by always focusing on the ball and returning to the ready position quickly (reflects National Standard in Physical Education 2).

EQUIPMENT AND MATERIALS

One vinyl or foam ball for every two students; standards and nets or ropes set approximately six feet high for every eight students.

LEARNING EXPERIENCES

1.0 [Create the best organizational plan for your setting. Arrange children in two facing lines with partners opposite each other. You might have two groups of two lines each.] Sometimes it is fun to practice a skill you already know. Show me how much you remember about the forearm pass. I will give you one clue. Always be sure you have the middle of your body aligned [lined up] with the ball before the ball contacts your forearm. See how you can send the ball up in the air to each other with both forearms flat. (See Third Grade Games Unit 4 on the forearm pass.) Select a partner, get one ball for the two of you, and begin.

1.1 I've noticed many of you are remembering to put your forearms close together to make the hitting surface very flat; and you're keeping your fingers and thumbs pointed down as the ball contacts your forearms. Everyone concentrate on positioning your forearms to make the flat surface face the direction you want to send the ball. [Change roles often throughout unit.]

1.2 Does someone else have a clue to help us remember the forearm pass [bump]? Great, [Becky] said you should bend your knees, then straighten them as your arms contact the ball. Act like you are standing up after sitting in a straightback chair.

1.3 Send the ball in a high arc so it bounces in front of your receiver.

1.4 Everyone show me what you need to do after you pass the ball to help you quickly align the middle of your body with the ball. Great! You have remembered to stay forward on the balls of your feet and reposition as soon as you see the ball coming.

1.5 Try to create more force by straightening your knees and letting the ball rebound off your firm arms instead of swinging your arms upward.

1.6 Remember to point the toes of your forward foot toward the spot where you want the ball to drop. See how many times you and your partner can pass it back and forth with your forearms.

1.7 Some of you might like to join with two others and see how many passes the two sets of partners can make.

1.8 Now, no matter where the ball is landing in your space, you and your partner reposition quickly to practice alternating hits. After you send the ball, quickly step out of the way to let your partner return the next ball.

2.0 Those who are ready to try something different, have one person toss the ball softly in a high arc so it falls down above the forehead of the receiver. Receivers, catch the ball with the finger pads of both hands and toss it back to your tosser's forehead. Just practice tossing the ball to make it land above your partner's forehead.

2.1 When you are a tosser, you have a very important role in helping your partner become a good setter by carefully tossing the ball softly in a high arc, making the ball fall down in front of the receiver's forehead. [Check the distance between partners. Children tend to be too far apart, causing them to make the toss travel parallel to the floor.]

2.2 Setters, get your feet in a forward stride position like you did for the forearm pass. Put one foot back and one foot forward, giving you a stable base to make it easy for you to bend your knees and hips to help you move under the ball. Stretch and spread your fingers loosely, about ball-width apart, your palms almost facing each other, and your index fingers and thumbs forming an open window or triangle. Watch the ball through this window as you push it high, back to the tosser.

STRENGTH

Stand two to three feet from a wall and, leaning forward at your ankles, place your arms straight forward from your shoulders with your palms flat on the wall, fingers spread and pointed upward. Keep your body straight, if you can, and push slightly away from the wall using your finger pads. Catch your weight carefully with your hands or even your finger pads. Practice 20 to 40 pushes at home each of the next few days.

2.3 Make the front of your body and your finger pads face your partner as you return the ball.

2.4 Watch carefully where your ball is going to tell you if you had control of the ball. If you controlled the ball, the tossers will not have to move their feet to catch the ball.

2.5 Send the ball higher by bending your knees, hips, and elbows a little more as you wait for the ball and by extending them a little higher and quicker as you contact the ball. Remember, the ball should only touch your fingers and thumbs, not your palms.

2.6 See how many times each of you can send the ball back to the tosser without having the tosser move their feet.

3.0 Some setters are ready for a greater challenge. Tossers, instead of tossing the ball in an arc directly in front of the receiver, toss the ball in an arc a little to the side of the receiver to make the receiver reposition their feet and whole body to return the ball.

3.1 Setters, get your weight forward on the balls of your feet, ready to move under the ball. Move quickly to be waiting under the ball, with your elbows bent, looking through the window made by your fingers and thumbs.

3.2 Tossers, ask your partners which side is more difficult for them to receive the ball. Toss the ball to their difficult side so they get more practice.

3.3 Remember to bend and extend your knees and elbows as you contact the ball. Try to send the ball at least 10 feet into the air. The higher your pass, the more time the receiver has to move under the ball.

3.4 [Observe for children who can reposition and set the ball high in front of their partners.] When the ball is set high, it is fun to see how many times you can set it back and forth.

3.5 Those people who have the ball, stand still, and those without the ball, choose a new partner close to you. See if you can break the best record you had with your last partner.

3.6 Check very carefully how you contact the ball. Set it only with the pads of your fingers. The ball must never touch the palm of your hands.

3.7 Listen. See if you can hear palms slapping the ball. Set it softly with only the pads of your fingers. No one should hear your palms slapping the ball.

4.0 [Put up enough nets or ropes so all children have space to work. The nets (ropes) should be about six feet high.] Some of you might like to add a net. You may need to start with one person tossing and one person setting the ball back to the tosser. Both people need to try to send the ball in a high arc.

4.1 Bend your knees, hips, and elbows with your fingers and thumbs forming a window as you watch the ball. Follow through by straightening your knees and hips and stretching your arms and fingers high above your head in the direction of your pass.

4.2 When the setter returns the ball high over the net, you may try setting it back and forth to each other.

4.3 [You may choose to group children to achieve a special social or skill mix.] Some of you may like to enlarge your groups to four by joining with the players next to you. Continue to set the ball over the net, trying to follow through directly to where you want the ball to go. As you work with two on a side, you'll have a bigger court; therefore, you will need to be ready to move quickly to align the front of your body with the ball because it will be coming from different angles.

Proper hand position for a set.

4.4 Remember, you must have the midline of your body and the toes of your lead foot pointing directly toward your target.

4.5 We want to practice setting the ball so catch the ball if it is lower than your eyes. Move your feet quickly to get to the ball before the ball drops too low to pass it back.

5.0 Let's play a game called 'Keep It Up' in groups of four or six. Count how many times the four [or six] of you can pass the ball back and forth over the net, contacting the ball slightly above your forehead. If you catch the ball, fail to send it over the net, or do not contact it when it is above your head, you must start over. The higher you set the ball to another person, the easier it will be for them to make a good return. Start your game by tossing the ball in a high arc over the net to a receiver.

5.1 Some of you may want to see if you can keep the ball going longer by passing the ball with your forearms when the ball drops too low to return it with an overhead pass. If you add the forearm pass [bump], you may let the ball bounce once before you tap it. Think about getting your knees bent and your forearms flat, ready to pass the ball.

5.2 To help cover your whole court and share the ball, pretend there are lines that divide the court into areas. Each person is responsible for one of the areas. People responsible for areas near the net should stand close to the net. Those responsible for the back areas should stand near the middle of the court because balls going over your head will usually go out of bounds.

5.3 [Change the makeup of teams several times when working in 5.0 to 5.3.] Everyone on this side of the net move down one court to your right. The people on the last court will come down to the first court. [You can also create different teams by having the front line or back line players from both sides of the net move down one court.]

ASSESSING THE VOLLEYBALL SET					
Class list	Positions (aligns) under the ball, using the "window."	Extends arms to meet the ball above forehead.	Uses pads of fingers to push the ball high(er).	Assists with leg extension if needed.	Follows through with hands and arms to send ball high(er).
Keller, Vanio	3	4	3	4	3
Ronto, Craig	4	4	4	5	4

Scale: 5 = Almost always 4 = Successful 2/3 or more of tries 3 = Successful about half the time 2 = Successful about 1/3 of the time 1 = Never; needs major changes in task and/or equipment

Throwing and Catching Deck Tennis Rings

4 to 6 lessons

FOCUS Refining throwing and catching a deck tennis ring with either hand, sending the ring to empty spaces, and repositioning before and after the catch

MOTOR CONTENT

Selected from Theme 1—Introduction to Basic Body and Manipulative Control; Theme 6—Advanced Body and Manipulative Control; and Theme 5—Introduction to Basic Relationships

Body

Manipulative activities—refining the unilateral throw, and throwing with catching hand

Relationships

Player placement—pointing throwing side and shoulder toward their target; repositioning behind teammate receiving the ring
Ring placement—throwing ring into empty spaces away from opponents

OBJECTIVES

In this unit, children will (or should be willing to try to) meet these objectives:

- Stay forward on the balls of their feet with feet slightly apart and knees bent in a ready position, run quickly to catch and throw the ring with either hand, returning the ring with the catching hand (reflects National Standards in Physical Education 1 and 2).
- Reposition quickly to catch and throw the ring, to back up a receiver, and to return to their own area (reflects National Standard in Physical Education 2).
- Know that squaring the body to the ring is performed by turning the entire front of the body, the hips, feet, and shoulders to face the ring (reflects National Standard in Physical Education 2).
- Understand that controlling the placement of the ring in relation to the receiver when throwing to players with different level or skills results in making the ring easier or harder to catch (reflects National Standard in Physical Education 6).
- Accept personal responsibility for staying alert during the game, repositioning quickly so everyone can always experience the best possible learning situation (reflects National Standards in Physical Education 2, 5, and 6).

EQUIPMENT AND MATERIALS

One deck tennis ring for every two students; ropes or nets and standards for every two or four students. (To make improvised deck tennis rings, open two sheets of newspaper. Start at the bottom right hand corner and roll the paper tightly to the upper left-hand corner. Overlap the ends of the newspaper roll to form a small circle about 6.5 inches in diameter. Wrap masking or cloth adhesive tape around the entire ring.)

LEARNING EXPERIENCES

1.0 See how you can toss the ring and make it very catchable by making the ring travel high, rotating horizontally. [Demonstrate.] Partners, stand facing each other with backs toward the side walls. Get a partner, one ring for the two of you, and begin.

1.1 Remember to prepare your body before you throw by turning your feet and hips so your throwing shoulder is pointing to your receiver. Do not stand so that the front of your body faces your partner.

1.2 Watch your ring and try to make the ring spin horizontally, not travel upright like a tire.

1.3 Make the ring and your arm cross your body as you throw. Send the ring straight to your partner by making your arm and hand reach high, straight toward your partner, as you release the ring.

1.4 Catchers, remember where your fingers point when catching things low? [Toward the floor.] Where do they point when you catch something high? [Up toward the ceiling.] Work on remembering which way to point your fingers and try to catch one-handed.

1.5 Be patient with your throwers. Some may never have thrown a ring. Everyone can try to improve their aim by pointing the throwing hand high toward the catcher as they release the ring.

1.6 Catchers, stay ready to travel to the ring. Have your weight forward on the balls of your feet, knees bent, and eyes on the ring.

1.7 See how many times you and your partner can catch and toss the ring back and forth horizontally with one hand without missing.

2.0 Begin to intentionally make each other stretch into the spaces on different sides to catch the ring. Point your throwing hand slightly away from your catcher as your hand releases the ring. Catchers, keep your weight forward on the balls of your feet and knees bent, ready to stretch quickly to catch the ring.

2.1 Try not to switch hands to throw. When you catch with your left hand, throw with your left hand. When you catch with your right hand, throw with your right hand.

2.2 Tossers, be sure your partner can catch the ring. Catchers, stretch to reach the ring when it comes close to you and be ready to run to catch when the ring goes farther away.

2.3 Catchers, run to the ring quickly to see how high the ring can be when you catch it. It is easier to catch a ring when it is high rather than low.

2.4 See how quickly you can return the ring. Make it fun for each other by trying to catch every throw, returning the ring quickly. Make sure each toss is catchable!

2.5 Tossers, throw to different sides of your receiver to make your catchers have to practice catching and throwing, first with one hand and then with the other.

2.6 You are doing a great job of throwing and catching with the same hand. Always remember to turn your whole body so your throwing shoulder is pointing to your partner. Make your catch and your throw one smooth movement.

2.7 Count how many times the two of you can toss and catch while trying to give both your left and right hands a workout.

2.8 See if you can beat your record or challenge some other set of partners to see who can catch the ring the most times without missing.

3.0 [Look for students who are catching and throwing with either hand. Place two to five on each side of a net or rope.] See how many one-handed catches you can make while sending the ring back and forth over the net.

3.1 How do you determine the strength of a chain? [A chain is as strong as its weakest link.] Think of a team as being a chain and try to be the best link in that chain. Stay ready with knees slightly bent, weight forward on the balls of your feet, and your head and eyes in the game. We all have different skill abilities, but we can all work hard to be a good team member.

3.2 Every time the ring is thrown on either side of the court, each of you turn and square the whole front of your body to the ring. Everybody should shift their position every time the ring is thrown.

3.3 When playing net games, each player is responsible for a part of the court. Right now, glance around and check what part of the court is yours and what space belongs to your teammates. Share responsibilities and space by allowing others to practice catching rings going into their space.

3.4 Where does the ring land if it goes over the heads of the back line players, if the back line players are too close to the back line? [The ring goes out-of-bounds.] Everyone look where you are standing before each serve. The back line players stand a good full step or two in front of the back line. Front line players need to stand only about one step from the net because they are responsible for rings that come close to the net.

3.5 When a ring goes into another teammate's space, let them have a chance to return it. You can help in a very special way called *backing up*. To back up a player, you move quickly behind that person in case they miss the ring. Then if the player misses, you are in a great place to catch the ring. Try to have someone behind the receiver playing the backup position each time the ring is thrown.

3.6 When you play backup or move from the center of your own space to catch the ring, a good strategy is to always return to your home place in the center of your space. This keeps all players evenly spaced and responsible for their own area.

4.0 You can either have a *cooperative* game where both sides are working together to see how many catches they can make without missing, or you may play a *competitive* game where two sides decide how many points from 10 to 15 a team needs to win the game. Only the serving team can score. The serving team loses the serve when they fail to return the ring.

4.1 [Students lose their concentration on skill performance as they get excited in game play and often need help refocusing. Revisit earlier tasks focusing on refinement when warranted while in the game setting.]

4.2 Return the ring as soon as you catch it. Holding the ring after you catch it allows the other side time to return to their home spot.

4.3 You are staying alert, and your games are becoming really skillful and fun. Now try harder to throw the ring to an empty space to make the other side hustle to return it.

4.4 Receivers, stay alert! Be ready to run to the ring. Few rings will be coming right to you.

4.5 Intentionally mix up the placement of your throws; it's a good strategy to keep your opponents guessing. Sometimes send the ring to an empty space near the back line and the next time, very close to the net.

4.6 [Regroup students so everyone learns to work with all members of the class. You might choose to increase team size to five when students show real interest and skill in team play.]

ASSESSING THE PLACEMENT OF RING AND BACKING UP A RECEIVER

Name	Throws ring to empty spaces about a receiver.		Run to catch a ring thrown to an empty space.		Moves quickly behind a teammate to back up the throw	
	Scale	Date	Scale	Date	Scale	Date
Keller, Vanio	3	12/9/96	3	12/9/96	3	12/9/96
Ronto, Craig	4	12/9/96	4	12/9/96	4	12/9/96

Scale: 5 = *Always* 4 = *Very frequently* 3 = *Sometimes* 2 = *Rarely* 1 = *Never*

Unit 6

Offensive and Defensive Repositioning

5 or 6 lessons

FOCUS Developing and refining offensive repositioning in soccer to create options for the passer and introducing defensive positioning to block the passing lane

MOTOR CONTENT

Selected from Theme 7—Introduction to Complex Relationships

Relationships

Player placement—offensive: repositioning to give options to the person with the ball; defensive: staying between the ball and the goal

OBJECTIVES

In this unit, children will (or should be willing to try to) meet these objectives:

- Reposition to new spaces nearer the goal when playing offense to give options to the teammate with the ball; reposition quickly to stay between the ball and the goal when playing defense (reflects National Standards in Physical Education 1 and 2).
- Know that the person with the ball has the responsibility for looking for two options for passing and the responsibility of the other teammates, the minute the ball is received by a teammate, is to establish a triangle with another teammate and the person with the ball to give two options for passing (reflects National Standard in Physical Education 2).
- Be supportive of all team members by sending a pass they would like to receive, allowing others to play their positions without interfering, and developing an attitude that everyone on the team plays an important role— not just the person who has the ball or scores the goal (reflects National Standards in Physical Education 5, 6, and 7).

EQUIPMENT AND MATERIALS

Four cones, rubber discs, or beanbags for space markers; one soccer, foam, or playground ball for every three to four children.

LEARNING EXPERIENCES

1.0 [Set up squares with four cones, beanbags, or rubber discs about 10 to

15 feet apart for every three students in the class.] Today, we are going to work on repositioning or running to an open space to receive a soccer pass. [Jose], please get a ball and stand by one cone. [Lisa] and [Matt], stand by two other cones. [Jose] may either pass the ball to [Lisa] or [Matt]. The player who does not receive the pass should run quickly to the open cone to get ready to receive the next pass. Good, did you notice how quickly [Matt] started running to the open cone after he saw the pass going to [Lisa]? [Comment on several more passes, pointing out the need for giving everyone many chances to be the receiver.] Let's see how all of you can pass the ball with your feet to a player while the person not receiving the pass runs quickly to an open cone. Get into groups of three, one person get a ball, go to a square made with four cones, and begin.

1.1 Keep watching the ball and be on your toes, ready to run to the open cone when you do not see the pass coming to you.

1.2 Passers, make rolling passes by directing the ball with the inside or outside of your foot so the receiver can stop it easily and pass it quickly. Receivers, be ready to move to get one foot in front of the ball to collect or trap the ball, then pass it quickly to the teammate not passing the ball to you.

1.3 Passers, try to feel the ball touch below your ankle as you pass to a new receiver. Keep your ankle firm as you contact the ball.

1.4 Receivers, stay on the balls of your feet, ready to trap or collect the ball with one foot and pass it with the other. Touch the ball only two times. Say to yourself, 'trap and pass.'

1.5 Passers, give both feet and both sides of your feet practice in stopping and passing the ball.

1.6 Stay on the balls of your feet as you are passing the ball, waiting to receive a pass or getting ready to reposition to the new space. Keep those feet alive and bouncy, not dead on the floor [ground].

1.7 Let's see how skillful you are at passing and repositioning. Count the number of completed passes you make while I time you for 15 seconds. Ready? Begin.

1.8 Has anyone noticed what shape the three of you are creating each time you reposition? Yes, it is a triangle. Every time two teammates make an open triangle with the passer, it always gives the passer two choices of receivers. Passers, each time you pass the ball, look for two receivers creating the triangle. Receivers, position in relation to each other and the passer to form a triangle so the passer always has two choices.

1.9 Remove the cones when you feel you can reposition to form a big triangle on your own. Keep passing and repositioning. I am going to look for those big triangles.

2.0 [Have one group demonstrate while the others sit and watch.] We are going to add a defensive person to see if you can continue to pass the ball accurately when a defender is trying to block a passing lane. Defenders, as three people are passing the ball, you run to a spot between two of the cones. By running to this spot between the two cones, you block one of the passing lanes and take away one of the options of the passer. The passer then has no choice of receivers but must pass the ball to the only open person. After each pass, the offensive player who did not receive the pass runs to the open cone as the defender runs across the middle of the playing area between two other cones to block off another passing lane. [Change roles after five passes.]

2.1 The offensive strategy is to reposition to create passing space. If you are the pass receiver who has been blocked by the defender, run quickly to the empty cone to give the passer a new option. Know where you are going and dash there fast.

2.2 Passers, be sure you are contacting the ball in the center to keep the ball rolling on the floor to make it easy for your teammate to receive.

2.3 Passers, look for the triangle before you pass. Can you see it? Which person is open to receive the pass? [Stop the groups and question the players to see if they understand the triangle formation and if they are fully aware of an open passing lane. You may want to diagram this on a blackboard if the students are not understanding the concept.]

2.4 Defenders, as the receiver gets the pass, reposition quickly so the passer has to reposition quickly to give the new passer an open receiver.

2.5 Offensive players, see how many passes you can complete in 30 seconds without letting the ball go out of your space. Only the passes that are trapped by the receiver count. Begin.

2.6 [Give this to groups showing the ability to give options to the passer.] The defensive strategy is to confuse the offense by varying what you do. Defenders become a little more aggressive. Try to take the ball away.

2.7 In soccer, the offensive team is called the attacking team. Let's see if the attacking team can complete four consecutive passes before the defender gets the ball. When the defender intercepts the pass, the passer trades places and becomes the defender, and play begins again.

3.0 [Set up a playing area for each group of four children that has one goal and gives the children plenty of room to pass the ball.] Now let's try working with a goal. Three of you will be the attacking team repositioning to form triangles to give the passer two choices. One person will be the defender trying to intercept the pass. The attacking team has to complete three passes before trying for a goal. The defender changes places with the passer each time he intercepts a pass or with the player who scored a goal. [Throughout the tasks and lessons, change teammates often to help everyone on the team see that they have an important job to do.]

3.1 Defenders, your main job right now is to cut off one passing option of the passer. If you get a chance to gain possession of the ball, take it. Trade places with the passer after you get the ball.

3.2 You need to keep your eyes on the ball as you move to open spaces toward the goal to form your triangle. Look at the ball and be ready to receive the pass at any time.

3.3 Passers, send the ball quickly ahead of your receiver, then run and reposition to form a new triangle.

3.4 The two attackers without the ball should try to go to very different spots nearer the goal so the passer can see two different passing options. Create an open passing lane. Don't stay behind the defender because your passing lane is now blocked by the defender and you won't get the pass.

3.5 Let's see if you can begin to pass the ball more quickly. If you complete four passes, the person nearest the goal—away from the defender—can try a shot on goal.

3.6 Try not to touch the ball with your feet more than three times before you pass the ball to another person. Say to yourself, *touch, touch, touch*, pass and move to an open space away from the defender.

3.7 Really show a team effort by making sure all three attackers have touched the ball at least once before anyone kicks for a goal.

3.8 [Observe for those who are giving the passer many options. You may choose to challenge these children by having them play three on two.]

4.0 [Organize the class to work two on three, or three on three for those who are ready, with one goal and a goalie. When a goal is scored, the scorer trades places with the goalie and the scoring team becomes the defenders kicking the ball to the other team.] Begin to work the ball down the field with short passes that lead the receiver toward the goal line. Defenders, try to block the passing lanes, repositioning to stay between the ball and the goal line.

4.1 Defenders, stay in front of your opponent to block a passing lane. If the passer passes the ball and runs to receive a pass, try to get to the spot ahead of them where the ball may be returned.

4.2 Attackers, keep repositioning to create spaces and make your passes short and quick. This will keep your defenders changing positions and on the run.

4.3 Defenders, try to close up the space by blocking the most direct passing lane.

4.4 Watch where you are passing the ball. Make sure you have picked a place in front of your receiver to aim your pass so the receiver can get to the pass without breaking stride or changing direction. Keep the passes on the ground.

4.5 [Bring this rule in if a team tends to exclude certain players.] Let's add a new rule to our game. Everyone on the team must pass the ball at least one time before anyone can kick for a goal.

4.6 [Some children may benefit from playing a game on a shorter field with goals at each end. Combine two groups of five and keep the distance between the goals short—about 60 feet.]

Staying alert to block a passing lane.

Unit 7

Developing Defensive Relationships in Baseball

5 or 6 lessons

FOCUS Developing defensive relationships of positioning in relation to the base to protect space and emphasizing extending to catch

MOTOR CONTENT

Selected from Theme 5—Introduction to Basic Relationships and Theme 6—Advanced Body and Manipulative Control

Body

Nonlocomotor activities—extending to catch the ball, keeping a foot in contact with a base

Relationships

Player placement—basemen repositioning to the side of the base charging the ball at an angle
Ball placement—throwing the ball to the base ahead of the runner

OBJECTIVES

In this unit, children will (or should be willing to try to) meet these objectives:

- Position away from the base to protect more space to keep balls from leaving the infield (reflects National Standard in Physical Education 2).
- Field a rolling or fly ball, throwing it accurately to the appropriate teammate (reflects National Standard in Physical Education 1).
- Stretch toward the ball to catch while keeping one foot on the base (reflects National Standard in Physical Education 1).
- Accept responsibility for improving their throwing and catching ability needed to make team play rewarding both to them and to others (reflects National Standards in Physical Education 2, 5, and 7).
- Explain their first responsibility as basemen is to protect as much of the infield space around the base as they are capable of covering by positioning outside of the baseline adjacent to their base in the field of play (reflects National Standard in Physical Education 2).

EQUIPMENT AND MATERIALS

One 5-inch funball or "mush" softball; four bases; one batting tee; one plastic or foam covered bat for every four children.

LEARNING EXPERIENCES

1.0 To start, loosen up your arm and see how accurately you and a partner can throw ground balls overhand to each other and practice fielding ground balls. Work up to moving about 30 steps away from each other [more if skill warrants]. [Throughout the unit, observe and help individuals with aspects of the overhand throw, such as (1) bending the throwing arm at the elbow out to the side to form a right angle with the throwing arm and shoulder, (2) transferring weight back onto the foot on the same side as the throwing arm, (3) stepping forward onto the foot opposite the throwing arm to release the ball, and (4) leading the forward movement of the throw by rotating the trunk forward.]

1.1 Make the ball land several steps in front of your receiver so everyone gets practice charging the ball quickly to field a rolling ball.

1.2 As you field the ball, try to go from your catch right to throwing a grounder back to your partner. The quicker you throw, the more you have to stay alert.

1.3 One of you continue to throw grounders, and the fielder of the ground ball throws the ball back on the fly as if throwing it to a baseman. Basemen, try to catch the fly ball while keeping one foot on an imaginary base. [Change roles several times.]

1.4 Both begin to throw fly balls to each other. Step and stretch to catch the ball as far out away from the base as you can, still keeping one foot on the base. Stretching to catch the ball as soon as you can will help get runners out when we are playing a game.

1.5 Throw harder or try to release the ball a little higher if your throw is not getting to the baseman on a fly. [Some may need to move a little closer.]

2.0 Join with two others to form a square with all four of you standing near a base. The person at home plate throws the ball to the first baseman, who throws to second, second throws to third, and third throws back to the catcher. If you aren't getting the ball to the baseman on the fly, move your bases a little closer. [Practice throwing in reverse order.]

2.1 Take aim and try to release the ball straight at your receiver because every throw made to a baseman needs to be easy to catch.

2.2 When receiving a throw from a teammate, travel to the ball to catch it if you see that it is thrown too far from you to keep one foot touching the base as you catch it.

2.3 Basemen, after you get the ball and touch your foot to the base, quickly throw the ball to the next baseman. Think of your receiver as you throw the ball. You may need to take some of the speed off your throw.

2.4 Check to see how accurately you can throw and how well you can catch by counting how many basemen catch the ball before the ball touches the ground. Does anyone know what throwing the ball around all the four bases is called? Good, [Geoffrey], it's called *around the horn.*

2.5 The ball players on first, second, and third bases show me where you should stand in relation to your base to keep the ball from getting past you and going out into the field. [First baseman stands to the right of the base, out toward right field; second baseman usually stands to the left side of the base; and third baseman stands to the left.] Great, now the catchers are going to each throw a grounder that has to land in the space between them and their basemen. The baseman nearest the ball charges the ball, collects it, and runs back and tags her base, then throws the ball on to the next baseman, who steps on their base and completes throwing the ball around the horn. [When the catcher has

COOLDOWN AND FLEXIBILITY

It's good to jog and slow down after the game. Now, let's sit and stretch. What muscles did you use the most? When muscles have been used a lot and are warm and a little tired, it is a good idea to cool down and then stretch slowly. Hold the stretches until you count slowly to 15. This can improve flexibility, too. Do this at home after a good game too. It helps when we make a habit of these fitness practices.

Catcher
☐

First Base   Third Base
☐   ☐

☐
Second Base

Infield space to be protected by each baseman (see tasks 2.5 and 2.6).

thrown two grounders to each of the basemen, rotate positions with the catcher moving out to take third base, third to second, second to first, and first coming in to be the catcher.]

2.6 Basemen, first check to see if you are positioned to the side of your base to protect the space in the infield near your base. Then get in your ready position, weight forward on the balls of your feet, knees and hips bent slightly with both hands hanging down in front of you, ready to move in any direction to field the ball.

Basemen, stand to the side of the base in your ready position.

2.7 Catchers, mix up your throws. Fake. Sometimes act like you are going to throw it to one place and then throw to another. Basemen, stay ready with your weight on the balls of your feet. Don't be fooled by fakes.

2.8 Basemen, make each throw catchable. Work on trying to make each throw go right to the next baseman by throwing hard enough to reach the baseman on a fly, trying to aim your release right at your baseman.

3.0 [Join two groups together to play the game of "Beatball" (see details on page 110) with two additional students becoming batters and two playing short-stop or short-left and right field.] Catchers, place a ball on the tee and take three or four steps back to stand behind home plate so you do not get hit with the bat. Basemen and fielders, be ready to field the ball and throw it quickly to first base and each of the bases, including home. All basemen have to touch their base with a foot before throwing the ball to the next base. The batters will score one point for each base they reach ahead of the ball.

3.1 Batters, check to see if your nonthrowing side is facing second base and stand far enough away from the tee so the middle of the fat part of your bat crosses the tee when you swing.

3.2 Basemen, not letting a ball get past you is your most important responsibility. When the batter is preparing to hit, always stand away from your base to protect your territory. Be prepared to move quickly at an angle to align yourself to the ball if it comes into your area or to run back to your base to receive a throw from a teammate.

BEATBALL

The game of "Beatball" is designed to develop and use beginning fielding skills for infield players. Specifically, the game focuses on the defensive relationships of the basemen to their bases and the adjacent space each is to cover, improving their abilities to field a ball quickly and to throw accurately so the ball can be caught. To start play, a player throws or bats the ball off a tee. The runner runs the bases, trying to touch each one in order ahead of the ball. The defensive team fields the ball, throws it to first, then to each subsequent base. The runner is out when the ball is caught at a base in front of the runner. The runner scores one point for each base reached ahead of the ball.

Fielding strategies to be included as coaching hints as students practice in 2.0 through 2.8 and during game play:
- positioning away from the base to cover the field;
- throwing quickly after fielding the ball; and
- staying out of the runner's path, touching edge of base only.

Batting and base running strategies include
- hitting to the largest open field area;
- running fast, not watching fielders; and
- touching inside corners of bases.

ASSESSING KNOWLEDGE OF SOFTBALL

Students draw or bring pictures to illustrate at least one of the following:
- Fielders positioning to provide best coverage of space.
- Batter adjusting position to place hit or send the ball to the most open area.
- Player positioning to catch a ball when a runner approaches.
- Catcher stretching to catch a ball and help the thrower.
- Baseman's foot touching the edge of the base away from the runner.

(Title the pictures and post so all may benefit from the examples.)

Fourth Grade Gymnastics

Unit 1

Creating and Performing Matching Sequences

4 or 5 lessons

FOCUS Changing speed and relationships of body parts to create and perform matching sequences

MOTOR CONTENT

Selected from Theme 1—Introduction to the Body; Theme 3—Introduction to Time; Theme 4—Introduction to Relationships of Body Parts; and Theme 7—Awareness of Relationships to Others

Body

Nonlocomotor activities—weight bearing, balancing

Effort

Time—varying speed

Relationships

Of body parts to each other—matching movements with others

OBJECTIVES

In this unit, children will (or should be willing to try to) meet these objectives:

- Increase flexibility and develop a variety of balances on different bases of support as they intentionally change speed when arriving into and traveling out of balanced positions and when changing relationships of body parts while balanced (reflects National Standards in Physical Education 1, 2, and 4).
- Change the bases of support continuously by intentionally going to extremes when twisting, stretching, and curling to place new body surfaces or parts in different places on the floor to form new bases of support (reflects National Standards in Physical Education 1 and 2).
- Apply movement concepts to make different body shapes in the air while traveling by supporting themselves with different body parts, by changing the relationship of one body part to others, or when balancing by involving the actions of the body (twist, stretch, curl, swing) (reflects National Standards in Physical Education 2).
- Match all aspects of movement (body, space, effort, and relationships) with others so all perform identically (reflects National Standards in Physical Education 1, 2, and 5).

• Accept responsibility for improving the range and variety of their movements by doing their best work, trying to intentionally place body parts on the floor (reflects National Standards in Physical Education 2 and 5).

EQUIPMENT AND MATERIALS

Enough mats for all children to be able to work continuously. (The children can work on the floor without mats. If you don't have enough mats, plan to rotate groups to divide time between work on the floor and on a mat.)

LEARNING EXPERIENCES

1.0 Take a balance position you can hold that is comfortable but challenging. Then, without moving your base of support, see how you can take a free body part you're not already using as part of your base near to the floor and then far away from the floor without losing your balance.

1.1 As you balance, see how far you can take that free body part away from the floor in all different places about your body. Keeping your balance, take that body part high and low to the spaces in back of you, in front, and to the sides.

1.2 As you move your free body parts in a gymnastic way, exaggerate the lines you are making with various parts of your body. Fully extend when making long, straight lines, bending sharply at joints to create clear angles and rounding body parts when curling.

1.3 You are beginning to show clear lines as you create different shapes with free body parts. As you experiment, keep changing your base of support until you can hold a balance very still with both feet up in the air.

1.4 See how many different relationships you can make with your feet in the air without moving your base of support. [Remind them that they can take their feet wide apart to the side; one in front, one behind; both close together, ankles touching; both together, heels touching; and so on.]

1.5 Steady your balance with both feet in the air. Carefully place both knees down onto the floor and go into another still balance. Exaggerate the straight lines, angles, and curves you are creating with different parts of your body.

Exaggerate the lines you are making with your body. Show stretched parts and curved parts.

1.6 Keep coming out of your balance by placing your feet or knees in different places about your base. Control the placement of your knees [feet] so you go right into a new balance. Do not give up and collapse. [Look for two or three students who are holding a balance and carefully placing their knees or feet on the floor to form a new balance. Have them share their response with the class, as illustrated in 1.7.]

1.7 Observe [Mary Alice's] balance very carefully. Remember her balance and where she places her knees [feet]. Everyone try to copy [Mary Alice's] balance. [Call on one or two others to serve as models to copy.]

2.0 Start with a balance on one hand, a knee, and its lower leg. Carefully twist and curl to see if you can get your shoulders or your back to become your base. When you get your shoulders or your back to become the base, hold your balance there for a moment, then carefully move onto a new base, hold your balance, and then stand up. Start your first balance again on one hand, knee, and lower leg and come out of it again into a different balance.

2.1 On your own, choose your base of support and keep twisting, stretching, and curling to constantly place different body parts on the floor to serve as your base of support.

2.2 As you twist, curl, and stretch onto new bases of support, regain your balance on each new base of support and make the lines and shapes you are making with different parts of your body very clear.

2.3 Sometimes as you twist, stretch, or curl to change relationships of free body parts, pick one of your changes and speed up your movement. The speed can help take you onto a new base of support.

2.4 Intentionally make a curl, twist, or stretch help you produce that little sudden burst of speed to take you to a new base of support—but take care—be ready to freeze a balance on your new base.

2.5 Remember one of your starting balances and every twist, curl, and stretch you did. Try to repeat your performance exactly.

2.6 Those of you who have your series memorized, begin to make the changes in your base of support very smooth—without stops. Sharpen the lines you make with your different body parts.

2.7 Focus on the shapes you are making with your body as you repeat your sequence and exaggerate each shape. Get as fully twisted, stretched, or curled as you possibly can but keep your sequence flowing with no stops—except at the beginning and end.

3.0 As you work on curling, stretching, and twisting while changing your base of support, show definite changes in level. Extend different body parts as high and as far away from your base as possible.

3.1 Include rounded shapes, twisted shapes, and wide or long, fully stretched shapes to help you place different body parts on the floor to become your new base.

3.2 Include a variation in speed. Show both a very slow, gradual change in body shape onto a new base, and then sometimes make the change in shape and base of support very fast. Prepare your base for your fast movement so you catch your balance and don't fall.

3.3 Begin to remember the order, speed, and levels of your shapes and see if you can copy your performance exactly.

Match each other's shapes so you look exactly alike.

3.4 Share your series of changes with the person next to you. One of you be an observer and watch the performance of the other person very carefully. Then let the observer show their series while the other person observes.

3.5 Sit and discuss for a moment which of the two series will be the easiest for both of you to perform at the same time in exactly the same way. Select one series and begin to work together on performing that series.

3.6 As you work on matching, take care to make your base of supports identical. You must perform your shapes at the same time, at the same speed. You are trying to look exactly alike.

4.0 Remember your matching series you did with a partner? Now join with another pair, change partners, and teach each other your series. Try very hard to get your new partner to perform your series as smoothly as your original partner. [Intersperse feedback throughout 4.1 to 4.4. Sometimes you might have to remind the children to match their partner's speed, sometimes the base of support, sometimes the body shape.]

4.1 [Observe closely and, when the work of the two new sets of partners begins to show understanding for both series, suggest the four begin to try matching each other doing series number one.

4.2 [If four children can perform one series simultaneously, suggest they try to perfect the matching of series number two.] If you are able to match one series, the four of you work on matching the second series.

4.3 [Once any four children can match series one and series two as separate series, suggest the four children put the two series together into a single matching sequence without stopping in between the two series.] If you are being successful in matching the first and second series separately, put the two series together to make one long series.

4.4 [Give all of the children an opportunity to share their sequences, even if they only mastered matching one series in a group of four. In some cases some of the children may be still working on matching one series with one partner.]

4.5 Let's watch our groups now. As we observe, let's watch for [any of the following.] Are all performers using the same body part for the base of support? Are the performers making matching body shapes? Is the speed of the group matching? If so, they will move exactly at the same time.

SELF-EVALUATION ANALYZING VIDEOTAPE TO IMPROVE GYMNASTICS

Videotape partner series. While others continue to work, partners view their videotape portion to evaluate the following: (1) changes in speed moving into and out of balances; (2) variety of balances; and (3) use of extremes of twisting, stretching, and curling. After using this analysis to modify their sequence, the partners describe, in writing or orally, what they changed or kept the same and their reasons for their decisions.

Unit 2

Muscle Tension and Extension of Nonsupporting Body Parts

4 to 6 lessons

FOCUS Maintaining muscle tension and extension of nonsupporting body parts to refine performance

MOTOR CONTENT

Selected from Theme 1—Introduction to the Body and Theme 5—Introduction to Weight

Body

Activities of the body—stretching and extending; and others selected by the children

Effort

Force—tense, strong, tight, firm; weak, loose, relaxed

OBJECTIVES

In this unit, children will (or should be willing to try to) meet these objectives:

- Improve the performance quality of the entire body by firming muscles, stretching nonsupporting body parts to increase tension, ridding the body of any loose, heavy feelings (reflects National Standard in Physical Education 2).
- Select and combine their favorite gymnastic activities in a repeatable sequence, showing an alert, lifted posture to begin and end their sequences (reflects National Standards in Physical Education 1 and 7).
- Help to develop and maintain a working atmosphere in their group by critiquing the performance of others, by incorporating suggestions made by classmates to improve their performance, and by remaining attentive to the tasks (reflects National Standards in Physical Education 2 and 5).
- Discern the difference between full extension and firmness and body parts lacking firmness and full extension (reflects National Standard in Physical Education 2).

EQUIPMENT AND MATERIALS

Select and arrange apparatus, or allow the children to help; a tumbling mat for each 4-6 children and one rubber band for each child.

LEARNING EXPERIENCES

1.0 [To make this analogy more vivid, distribute rubber bands to the children and have them place them on the floor. When you are ready, they can stretch and relax their rubber band as you demonstrate with yours.] Notice how the rubber band becomes longer and tighter, when we stretch it. Now look how loose and limp the rubber band becomes when we quit pulling. Think of your muscles as the 'rubber bands' in your body. You can stretch them, and when they are stretched, they become tighter. And, just like the rubber band, when you relax them, they become limp and loose. Stretch and then relax the rubber band several times, thinking about the pull you have to put on the rubber band to stretch it. Now give me your rubber band and think about the effort you have to make as you stretch one leg while you balance on your other foot. The muscles in your leg will not stretch on their own. You have to stretch them by extending your toes as far as they can possibly go. Now stretch your other leg. Stretch your knee, your ankle, and your toes until they make one nice, straight line. Feel the tension in your body created by your stretching effort.

1.1 Keep changing the foot on which you are balancing. Stretch your free leg and ankle. Can you feel the muscles grow strong, tight, and firm? Relax the muscles and feel the difference. Keep telling yourself the muscles can't create a tight feeling by themselves. They need you and your brain to send them the message to tighten up.

1.2 Think, right now are your muscles really tight or are they rather loose and relaxed? Sit down a moment. Are your muscles really tight and stretched or are they easy and relaxed? Right, most of the time in almost every position you get into during the day, you are not stretching your muscles to their fullest. Stretching our muscles and developing the feeling for the effort required to make them firm, strong, and stretched takes practice because these actions are not a natural part of our lives. Developing this fully stretched feeling and making your body strong is what is needed to make an athlete or any performer really look in charge of their body.

1.3 Think a moment and select one gymnastic stunt or movement you feel you can do very well. With [one to five others], get a mat. See if you can perform that action, making your muscles show you are clearly in charge of them.

1.4 Don't forget to take complete control of your starting and ending positions. Make your whole body look alert by stretching all the way up to the base of your head. Remember, the rubber band did not stretch on its own. You had to work to stretch it.

1.5 Perform your selection twice each time it is your turn. First perform it with your brain sending a stretching message to your muscles. The second time do it in a very relaxed way, still looking pretty good but without the stretched, firm feeling. Feel the difference needed to be stretched and firm and being relaxed and loose.

1.6 Select a very different gymnastic movement, continuing to contrast the stretched, firm feeling with the relaxed, loose feeling. Exaggerate the stretch to create and feel a big difference.

1.7 With the people at the same mat [or near them], take turns performing one of your favorite gymnastic movements, showing a definite relaxed or a definite stretched feeling in your body. The rest of you, sit and tell the performer if their body looked firm and stretched or more relaxed and loose. Show a big difference in your performance by controlling the firmness of your muscles.

2.0 Put two, three, or four gymnastic movements together, trying to keep the message of 'firm and stretched' flowing from your brain to your muscles.

2.1 Watch the performance attitude you have before you start. Think greatness! Think of how proud members of the marching band look when they wear the uniform of their school. If you can start with a firm, lifted feeling, it will help you keep that feeling as you do your short sequence.

2.2 As you finish one movement and go into the next one, don't completely relax that rubber-band feeling you have in your body. Keep a tight, compact feeling throughout the movement when you move from one stunt or activity to another.

2.3 In your sequence, include at least one roll and one place where you transfer your weight from your feet to your hands to your feet. Make your body firm up as you roll and as you stretch to reach as you transfer your weight from your hands back to your feet.

2.4 In your group, begin to play Follow the Leader. Leaders, show a full stretch and [or] a tight, compact body as you combine three or four of your favorite gymnastic movements. Followers, copy the sharp look the leaders create.

2.5 Leaders, at the beginning and end of your sequence, hold your best performing posture while you count to five. Help your followers develop that beautifully lifted, tall standing position. Remember, how you start and end are just as important to your performance as the nice things you put into your sequence. [Look for sequences showing clear body lines and alert starting and ending postures.]

2.6 [Derek], please do your sequence and include that tall, lifted feeling when you begin and end your sequence. Everyone, carefully observe his alert starting and finishing posture. [Call on two or three children to present a model deserving to be copied.]

2.7 Everyone go back and improve the alert, lifted feeling needed to begin and end your sequence. See if you can look like [Derek].

3.0 You can select and set up one or two pieces of apparatus to help bring out your best gymnastic performance. [Select the apparatus and/or designate arrangement of apparatus, basing your decisions on safety or special content considerations.] See how you can put some of your favorite gymnastic work together. Let's see if you can keep that stretched or compact feeling throughout your performance. Those waiting a turn, stand back away from the performers to give them the free working space they need to take that lifted, performing posture.

3.1 Work to maintain that nice stretched or compact feeling as you mount or go over the apparatus. Don't give up and let your body become relaxed while you're in the air.

3.2 Guard against collapsing in your landing. Land with that nice 'in control' feeling, going right into your next action on the mat.

3.3 Take a moment to think about what you can do to show greater variety in your sequence. You might want to include weight on hands, change the direction of a roll, or add a balance on top of the apparatus.

3.4 Some of your sequences are too short. Some are too long, maybe causing you to lose concentration and good performance. Decide whether you need to add to your sequence or shorten it—but don't lose that super performance posture.

3.5 Rid your sequence of any unplanned movement. Think about what your plan is as you move from one part of your sequence to another. Plan your next base of support far enough ahead.

3.6 In your group, take turns performing your sequence for each other. Sit down a moment after performing while the observers tell which parts of your sequence seemed to be sharpest, tightest, and most fully stretched so you know which parts to polish.

3.7 Remember where your groups told you your performance was tightest, firmest, and the most stretched. Repeat your sequence. See if you can feel yourself stretching and firming up in other places too in your sequence. Maintain that feeling throughout your whole sequence.

4.0 Choose some of these ways to change your sequence: Put your balance in a different place; change how you mount or dismount; perform several moves on top of the apparatus; add more rolls; or change your direction or speed when working on the mat. Change enough things so you feel you are developing a new sequence but don't forget that rubber-band feeling. The most important thing is to create that sharp, proud feeling by tightening muscles and stretching fully.

4.1 to 4.5 [Repeat tasks 3.1 to 3.5 to modify 4.0.]

4.6 Let's share this feeling for controlling firmness developed through stretching or making your body compact. Notice how sharp the performers look now. Observers, notice the improvement everyone has made in controlling their muscles, the 'rubber bands' of their bodies. [Have one performer from each group demonstrate. Repeat the task several times throughout the unit, giving all a chance to demonstrate.]

4.7 Demonstrators, really show you learned to make your 'rubber bands' work. Stretch your free body parts, making straight lines when you mean for them to be straight and rounded ones when you want the lines of your body to be curved.

Show how you've learned to control the "rubber bands" of your body.

Unit 3

Developing Phrases With a Partner

4 to 6 lessons

FOCUS Developing short gymnastic phrases with a partner, emphasizing copying movement

MOTOR CONTENT

Selected from Theme 7—Awareness of Relationships to Others

Relationships

To individuals—copying part or all of a partner's sequence

OBJECTIVES

In this unit, children will (or should be willing to try to) meet these objectives:

- Share ideas, selecting from them moves they can copy, adapting movements when necessary to work together effectively (reflects National Standards in Physical Education 1 and 5).
- Value accuracy in their own performances, making their actions clear so their partners can more easily copy their moves exactly (reflects National Standard in Physical Education 2).
- Observe carefully and copy the actions of a partner, developing interdependence (reflects National Standard in Physical Education 5).
- Develop skill in rhythm, timing, and spacing to be able to move at the same pace and cover the same space as another (reflects National Standards in Physical Education 1 and 5).

EQUIPMENT AND MATERIALS

Tumbling mats and landing mats where necessary to protect landing areas. *Optional:* Other equipment could be added but not necessary.

LEARNING EXPERIENCES

1.0 Working in twos, one will be the leader and slowly perform their best gymnastic movement making tracks about the room in zigzag lines, loops, straight lines, and circular pathways. Make your pathway very clear so your partner can follow you exactly. [Change roles. Use this task and 1.1, 1.2 briefly.]

1.1 Remember, in copying, only one person moves at a time. The leader moves, and the partner observes carefully, then copies the leader's pathway.

1.2 Leader continue to make a very clear pathway as you travel but change what you do as you are traveling.

STRENGTH AND ENDURANCE

We have mostly been using our legs in this unit. Arms need work, too. Hanging from a chinning bar or rope and pulling yourself up, even if just a little, is a good way to improve your strength and endurance. It's fun, too! Some children lay a metal pipe or bar safely across two chairs and pull up to this low bar. Ask your parents if there's a bar at home secure enough to hold your weight. If so, try to do some pull-ups regularly each week.

2.0 Leaders, make a short zigzag pathway with two or three lines as you travel with weight on hands and feet. Observers, watch and then carefully copy the movement and the pathway. [Change roles.]

2.1 Leaders, keep repeating the same sequence, making your moves clear [with clarity], repeating exactly the same movement you did before.

2.2 Followers, be sure you copy the placement of the hands and feet of your leader, making your actions exactly like theirs.

2.3 As you are working, see if it takes the same amount of time for both the leader and the copier to complete the sequence. If one of you is moving faster than the other, your movement is not exactly alike.

2.4 Work on being a moving photocopy. Leaders, observe your copier and help them copy your movement exactly.

3.0 You did a beautiful job with copying a pathway and an action. Let's see if we can make it more challenging by increasing the number of actions. [If students need more guidance, work on a sequence that includes a run, jump, and roll.] Decide who will lead first and who will watch and copy exactly.

3.1 Keep your sequence short and simple so you can make it more exact.

3.2 Sit a moment and discuss the parts of the sequence that are hardest to duplicate. Then go back to work and be more exact as you copy the actions *and* the timing of the actions *and* the amount of space the leader covers in each part of the sequence.

3.3 Leaders be sure you give your partner very clear, still starting and ending positions to copy.

3.4 [Reverse roles and repeat 3.0 to 3.3.]

4.0 Do you have your sequence clearly memorized? Can the follower copy where and how the leader begins and ends the pathway as well as copy the leader's timing and spacing? If so, see if you can work together so that, when the leader begins, instead of waiting for the leader to perform the whole sequence, the copier begins as soon as the pathway is clear. This way some of the time you both will be moving and some of the time one will be holding a still position while the other performs.

4.1 You will have to know exactly where your partner is both in amount of time spent moving and where the action is going so that you *echo* their movement. In echoing, you still copy your partner's movement, but you don't wait until their sequence is finished before you start to copy.

4.2 Measure the distance between you so that you can maintain that same spatial relationship [amount of space] at the end. [Allow them to add to their sequence or have them continue to work on perfecting what they have already developed. Allow the children to share their work at the end of the unit, an excellent opportunity to share not only with classmates but also with the classroom teacher, principal, and parents.]

Echo your partner's movement, keeping the same amount of space between you all the time.

ASSESSMENT: HELPING OTHERS COPY SEQUENCES

Pairs observe each others' sequences and give feedback, both reinforcing and corrective, about rhythm, timing, and spacing. After trying to use the feedback received, partners write two or three sentences that evaluate the quality of the feedback they received and exactly how they used it in their routines or why they choose not to use the feedback.

Twisting and Turning Into and Out of Balances

4 or 5 lessons

FOCUS — Twisting and turning into and out of balances with planned movements that can be stopped and held or are free and ongoing

MOTOR CONTENT

Selected from Theme 1—Introduction to the Body; Theme 2—Introduction to Space; Theme 3—Introduction to Time; and Theme 6—Flow and Continuity in Movement

Body

Locomotor activities—traveling into and out of balances on preselected body parts
Nonlocomotor activities—twisting and turning

Effort

Flow— ongoing, free; planned, momentary pauses

Space

Directions—traveling out of balances in different directions

OBJECTIVES

In this unit, children will (or should be willing to try to) meet these objectives:

- Develop a movement sequence that clearly demonstrates (a) a performance posture, (b) twisting out of balances in different directions, and (c) a planned flow of movement, linking several skills together, stopping only in planned, practiced balances (reflects National Standard in Physical Education 1).
- Twist to come out of the same balance in different directions and onto the same or different body parts (reflects National Standard in Physical Education 1).
- Know that twisting free body parts not included in the base of support creates different balances on that base and makes it possible both to transfer weight to a greater variety of body parts and to travel out of the balance in different directions (reflects National Standard in Physical Education 2).
- Develop and refine a smooth sequence of ongoing transitions by deliberately planning the order of the movements and by eliminating unplanned stops and actions (reflects National Standards in Physical Education 1, 2, and 5).

- Maintain a working atmosphere in their group at all times, always sharing the working space and practice time equally with the other members of their group (reflects National Standard in Physical Education 5).

EQUIPMENT AND MATERIALS

Tumbling mats; a selection of apparatus and landing mats to protect landing surfaces.

LEARNING EXPERIENCES

1.0 Today, start by taking an inverted [feet and legs in the air] balance you can hold without wobbling. [You may wish to designate the type of inverted balance, such as a shoulder stand.] Come out of the balance exactly the same way as you arrived into the balance. In groups of four, place a mat in a large semicircle with the long sides of the mat facing into the center of the circle, and begin to work.

1.1 Before you go into your balance, look where your feet are. See if you can balance and bring your feet back down in that same place.

1.2 Go into your balance, holding it just briefly. Carefully come out of it just like you went into it. See if you can bring those feet down in exactly the same spot where they left the mat. Check where your feet landed and see if you can bring them even closer to their takeoff point the next time you balance.

1.3 To make your feet touch in a very different spot when you come out of your balance, carefully turn the part of your body that is up off the mat so your

Take an inverted balance—there are a variety of solutions you can try.

STRENGTH

It takes strength, especially in the arms, to hold positions when you are inverted. Remember to hang, swing, push, and pull almost every day. Using the playground bars and gym apparatus is a good idea, even if only for a short time.

hips twist. Then try to bring your feet down on the mat away from your takeoff spot and stand up. Once you stand up, quietly take your balance, practice your twist, then come out of the balance again.

1.4 Really tighten your muscles, especially in your stomach and free body parts to control the speed coming down. Place those body parts on the mat. Don't let gravity do the work coming down and just let them fall! Control the speed coming down.

1.5 Sit a moment off of the mats and look at the muscle tension of this group. Notice how their entire bodies look strong and tight. When they twist, they don't lose that tightness, making it possible to place their body parts on the mat carefully. They stay constantly in charge of every body part.

1.6 Let's all feel the contrast between firm, strong muscles that are in charge and can bring your body parts down on the mat softly and weak, not-working muscles that let the body part fall on the mat. Perform your balance two times. The first time, have lazy muscles and see how they let you fall out of your balance. The second time, feel your muscles take charge. Notice that firm and strong muscles help you plan and control the placement of each body part on the mat.

1.7 Feel your muscles tighten to be in control, take a balance, then twist toward the other side so you can come out of the same balance in different directions. Twisting to both sides gives you much more variety in your gymnastic work. Remember to stand up briefly each time you come out of your balance.

1.8 Each time you twist, select a different body part to be the first part to take your weight coming out of your balance.

2.0 See if you can go into a new balance by trying extra hard to be in charge of balancing, twisting, and placing the body part down when coming out of your first balance so you can go immediately into your second balance. Be prepared to hold your second balance for just a moment. Stay in charge, twist and come out of it and stand tall.

2.1 Before you come out of your first balance, plan your second base of support. Use the body parts that touch the mat first for your new base. Prepare the base for your second balance carefully so you make no adjustments to your base. Practice performing your two different balances one after the other without one single unplanned movement.

2.2 [Talk them through the series of three balances several times. Pace your directions to accommodate those least able to hold balances.] Everyone stand up tall, facing your mat, ready to take your balance, as I talk you through your balances. See if you can stay right with me. Ready? Carefully, with tight muscles, go into your first balance. Hold your balance. Now twist and think about your new base, placing your body parts down on the mat. Go into your second balance and hold. Twist, plan your new base, then go into a third balance and hold. Now carefully come out of this balance, stand tall, and hold.

2.3 See if you can repeat going into and out of three or four balances at your own speed, trying to keep that performance tension all of the time. End standing tall each time you complete the three or four balances so you develop the feeling of finishing your work and being in charge of every muscle of your body.

2.4 Sit back away from the mat and, one at a time, show each other your entire sequence. Observers, check to see if everyone in your group performs with that alert look in their body that muscle tension and being in charge creates.

2.5 [Challenge classes or individuals having success so far to see if they can develop a similar sequence of three or four balances traveling onto and off of apparatus, balancing sometimes on the apparatus, sometimes on the mat.]

2.6 [Repeat tasks 2.1 to 2.4 when students start to work on apparatus because the transition from the mat to apparatus often causes regression in their performances.]

3.0 As you plan your new base of support, travel in a different direction when you come out of each balance. Make your sequence more exciting!

3.1 Before you start, think! Do you always twist to the same side? Are you traveling out of every balance in a different direction? Twist so you travel out of your balances in two or three different directions.

3.2 Concentrate on making a smooth transition [change] as you move from one balance to another. Exaggerate the smoothness when going from one base of support to the next. Stop only when you hold your next balance.

4.0 [Students can benefit from further work on the apparatus. If they have been successful in their work in 2.5 and 2.6, this task can be very rewarding for them and you.] Now, let's see how you can develop a gymnastic sequence where you travel into and out of balances both on the mat and on the apparatus. Your sequence must include twisting to travel out of your balances in different directions.

4.1 Take time with your starting position. Think performance! Be in charge from the very moment you start. Show firm muscle tension.

4.2 Do two or three balances, twisting to come out of each one as you dismount. You may have to travel briefly before going into your next balance. Plan and remember every movement as you travel. Make each movement represent your best gymnastic work. Don't select easy gymnastic skills if you can perform something harder safely and with good control.

Travel into and out of balances on the apparatus.

4.3 Finish what you are doing. Then watch [Ronnie's] sequence. Notice there are no extra movements because of planning ahead. When you start working, remember planning ahead and eliminating unplanned movements improve gymnastic performances tremendously.

4.4 Your sequences are looking much more like performances because you are eliminating some unplanned movements. [David] has been showing the other quality we have been working on. Watch for something special and tell me what really makes his performance skillful. That's right! He looks in charge all the time. He never loses his performance posture or attitude. Go again, [David]. Notice, from the time he starts standing tall until he finishes standing tall, he never stops being firm and lifted in his movements. He never lets his muscles give up. All of you do your routine again, see if you can keep your mind on that performance posture as you work.

4.5 Take turns, having one person from each mat perform. Let's watch for maintaining a performance posture and planned flow of movement traveling into and out of your sequence of balances.

ASSESSING TWISTING AND TURNING IN A SEQUENCE OF BALANCES				
Performs with a posture that is "tall" and uplifted.	Links movements so that an ongoing flow is evident.	Uses twists of free body parts to vary the same balances.	Uses twisting movements to move out of balances in different directions.	Deliberately tries to eliminate unplanned stops or actions in sequences.
Bland, R. Comte, T. Cowan, M.	Baer, T. Bland, R.	Fox, J. Dav, D.	Bland, R.	Bland, R

Scale: Under each column, write names of those who have limited success or great difficulty.

Unit 5

Transferring Weight Between Feet and Hands

5 or 6 lessons

FOCUS Transferring weight from feet to hands, back to feet on the floor, along and off apparatus

MOTOR CONTENT

Selected from Theme 1—Introduction to the Body; Theme 3—Introduction to Time; and Theme 4—Introduction to Relationships of Body Parts

Body

Locomotor activities—flight, rolling, stepping, including roundoff and cartwheel

Relationships

Of body parts—near, far; apart, together

OBJECTIVES

In this unit, children will (or should be willing to try to) meet these objectives:

- Refine wheeling actions by traveling in a straight line, keeping free body parts straight, slowing down their actions, and placing each supporting body part deliberately on the floor (reflects National Standards in Physical Education 1 and 2).
- Transfer their weight over and on top of apparatus while controlling and changing the relationships of their hands and feet (reflects National Standards in Physical Education 1 and 3).
- Complete an entire wheeling action on top of the apparatus or complete the recovery phase of the wheeling action on the floor (reflects National Standard in Physical Education 1).
- Incorporate a hurdle step in the approach to achieve flight while performing a cartwheel-type action over a bench or box (reflects National Standard in Physical Education 2).
- Know that they need more muscle tension in slower movements to hold the body shape and to maintain balance (reflects National Standard in Physical Education 2).
- Create a safe environment by moving away from others, checking the location of others before beginning a turn (reflects National Standard in Physical Education 5).

EQUIPMENT AND MATERIALS

A selection of apparatus for students to travel over, onto, off of, and along, such as benches, boxes, planks, tumbling mats, ropes or newspaper rolls. (Arrange apparatus to encourage variety in approaches and responses.)

LEARNING EXPERIENCES

1.0 [Students should be confident in transferring weight from feet to hands, back to feet on the floor before attempting an entire sequence on top of the apparatus. By allowing students time to develop confidence working on the floor and accepting a wide variety of responses, more students will be successful.] Practice on the floor along a line to make sure your hands and feet are traveling in a straight line before you attempt to transfer your weight from your feet to your hands to your feet on the bench. Take care to absorb [cushion] the force of your landing carefully. Find many ways to travel from feet to hands to feet as you travel over, along, or off the benches, planks, or boxes.

1.1 Starting on top of the bench, find ways to come off of the bench by placing your hands on the bench and taking your feet into the air, landing on the floor together [simultaneously] or with one foot following the other. Be prepared to land softly with your back and hips over your feet.

1.2 Travel across the bench by gripping with one hand on either side or by placing both hands on top. Lift your hips over your hands and land on your feet on the other side of the bench. Give in your hips, knees, and ankles to make your landing soft. Stretch your upper body so you land standing very tall.

1.3 Finish with a bouncy landing and a pop-up.

Stretch your body as you go over the bench so you land standing very tall.

2.0 Feel comfortable performing part of the stepping action on the floor [mat] and part on the bench. Keep working on stretching fully. Some of you may be ready to try your stepping action [inchworm, cartwheel, walkover, and the like] on top of the bench. Remember to place each body part carefully near the center of the bench as you travel.

2.1 Practice your stepping actions on your hands and feet on the floor, along a line [or plank] lying on the floor, until you can place your foot near to your hand, in the middle of the line [or plank].

2.2 Whether you are on the bench or the floor, you need to stretch and stay tall throughout your entire action to stay balanced and traveling along a straight line.

2.3 As you place a foot down, bend the ankle, knee, and hip if needed to help you regain a stable base.

2.4 When you feel ready, add a second action, such as a roll along or off of the bench, making a short movement phrase.

2.5 Take time to practice your rolls. Include different kinds to lengthen your phrase or sequence. Many of you are capable of including a backward or shoulder roll.

3.0 Those of you traveling over the bench, begin to change the relationship of your hands and arms to each other and to the bench as you travel over it.

3.1 Place your hands side by side on top of the bench as you travel sideways, sending your legs high in the air to land on the other side of the bench.

3.2 Reach and place your hands on the far side of the bench as you travel over it.

3.3 Select a roll and add it after you land coming off the bench.

4.0 Many of you have developed short movement phrases as you have traveled on, along, and over the benches or planks. Begin to link two or three of these phrases together into a gymnastic sequence.

4.1 Your sequence may take you away from your equipment and then back to the equipment. Plan the order of your actions and the path you will follow carefully to make your sequence interesting.

4.2 Since we have been working mostly on traveling on hands and feet, you might find it necessary or exciting to include balancing and rolling actions to link the sequence together and to give your arms a rest.

4.3 Work to eliminate all extra movements. Make every movement an important, planned part of your sequence.

4.4 As you polish your sequence, think about how the movement flows together. Feel each action lead you right into the next. Make each action smooth and your body parts alert and tight. Try to remember a nicely stretched ending.

4.5 Let's share our sequences. [Have groups share while others observe for full extension, firm body parts, the sequence flowing smoothly from one base of support to another, and a nicely stretched ending.]

ASSESSING WEIGHT TRANSFERENCE USING APPARATUS

At the conclusion of this fourth grade unit, write in the child's portfolio (or the longitudinal anecdotal record, if used) two or three sentences, describing the child's use of the hurdle step and wheeling action to produce height and force. If possible, relate performance in this unit to other gymnastics units this year as well as to those in the previous year.

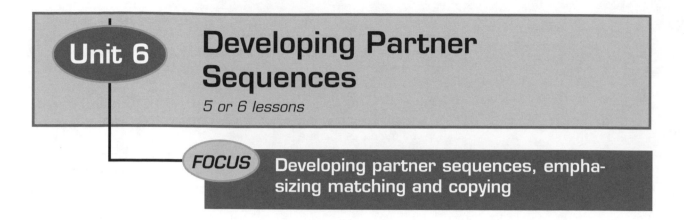

Unit 6

Developing Partner Sequences

5 or 6 lessons

FOCUS Developing partner sequences, emphasizing matching and copying

MOTOR CONTENT

Selected from Theme 7—Awareness of relationships to Others

Relationships

Of individuals—matching and copying

OBJECTIVES

In this unit, children will (or should be willing to try to) meet these objectives:

- Develop a partner sequence with no unplanned movements that includes matching and copying (reflects National Standards in Physical Education 1 and 5).
- Know that matching means performing the same action simultaneously with another person and copying means to duplicate precisely actions previously performed (reflects National Standard in Physical Education 2).
- Make adjustments to accommodate their partner's abilities and limitations when selecting actions for sequences (reflects National Standards in Physical Education 6 and 7).

EQUIPMENT AND MATERIALS

For every two to four children: mats, a selection of apparatus.

LEARNING EXPERIENCES

1.0 Today, find a partner and each of you combine three or four gymnastic movements without stopping to make a short sequence. Share a mat and the surrounding floor space with your partner.

1.1 Rearrange your actions to make them flow smoothly from one to the next. Some actions blend more smoothly than others. It may be, for example, easier to go from a headstand into a roll than from a headstand into a cartwheel. [Give children time to select, rearrange, and refine their sequences.]

1.2 Exaggerate each shape by extending or tucking body parts. Make each action as clear as you can by firming up your muscles to make the exact shape you want your body to show.

1.3 Plan where you need to place your next supporting body part as you finish one action and prepare to go into the next. Place each body part at the end of one action exactly where you need it to perform the next action. Make one action flow into another with no unplanned movements.

1.4 When you worked on twisting and turning into and out of balances, you concentrated on placing each body part carefully. Now, as you place each body part carefully, make each body part strong and firm so it can support you.

1.5 This half of the class, sit and watch the others perform their sequences several times. Look carefully for someone performing gymnastic activities similar to those you selected. [After awhile, have the performers sit also.] Observers, go over and sit by a person whose sequence had actions similar to yours. If your actions were different from everyone else, please sit with someone without a partner who has about the same gymnastic ability as you. Then, take turns demonstrating your sequences for each other.

1.6 Discuss with each other what part of your sequence is the easiest for you and what is the hardest. Select three or four moves you both can do from your two sequences. Combine these to make a new, simple sequence. Give special thought to the beginning and ending of your sequence.

1.7 Perform your sequence at the same time. Look like twins. Match every movement.

1.8 As you practice your sequence, cue [signal] each other. You both should perform each part at the same time in exactly the same way.

2.0 Decide who is 'one' and who is 'two.' The ones will perform the sequence first and hold the ending position. Then the twos will perform the sequence, copying it exactly. [Do this several times, encouraging everyone to rid their sequences of unplanned movements.]

2.1 This time, twos are the leaders, and the ones are the copiers. To copy, you need to watch for details. Look at the exact placement of the body parts on the mat. Notice the relationships of different body parts and the speed of the movements.

2.2 Go through your copying sequence two times with ones leading first and twos leading second.

2.3 Watch the speed of your leader as each action is performed. Duplicate each change in speed.

2.4 Let's all do our sequences together. Ones, take your beginning position and make them very clear. Twos, take the same beginning positions and hold that position very still until the ones have completed the sequence. Ones, hold your ending position until after the twos have completed the sequence and are holding the ending, too. [Reverse roles.]

3.0 Now see if the two of you can perform your sequence together, matching each movement. Perform each movement at the same time and make every action look exactly alike as you move.

3.1 If you are having trouble matching your sequence, practice each part of your sequence separately. Take the part of the sequence that you find hardest to match and cue [signal] each other all the way through the action to help synchronize [match] your movement. [Encourage children to concentrate on matching speed and to make supporting body parts strong.]

3.2 Let's share some of your matching sequences with the class. Performers, make your sequence look as sharp as you can by controlling the muscle tension from your starting position to your ending position. Plan a starting cue so you start together. Observers, see if the performers look like gymnasts and are matching each other exactly. Remember the part where the partners matched each other the closest so we can discuss the good parts of the sequences. [Have four or five pairs of partners demonstrate. Discuss.]

3.3 Both perform your sequence matching each other as closely as you can. Then repeat it with one of you copying the other. Remember to hold a still, lifted, alert gymnastic pose when you are not performing and at the end like gymnasts do to show they have finished.

3.4 Some of you may be able to make a longer sequence by matching each other the first time and copying the second time. End by matching each other again. Remember to always hold a very still pose when waiting for your partner to move and at the end.

4.0 Choose two pieces of apparatus the two of you would like to work on. Develop a short matching or copying sequence, performing part of it on the floor and part on the apparatus. [If apparatus is limited:] Practice the floor parts of your sequence while waiting for the apparatus.

4.1 Discuss and plan where will you begin and end the sequence in relation to the apparatus and each other.

4.2 If you both plan to be on or go over your apparatus at the same time, plan your mounting and dismounting carefully. Work on this until you can safely match and copy each other's movements.

4.3 Depending on your piece of apparatus, you can add many things such as spins, balances, rolls, weight on hands, as well as mounting and dismounting.

4.4 Work hard to perform together during the matching part of your sequence. Pay particular attention to your speed so both of you move at the exact same pace.

4.5 The most difficult thing to match in a sequence is the body parts not supporting you. Check each other carefully to make sure your free body parts are in the same position as your partners.

4.6 When you copy or match your partner's actions, look at what the other does with each body part—what their hands, feet, legs, body, and head are doing. If you copy the movement of each body part closely, you should look like twins.

4.7 Work to rid your sequence of unplanned pauses or movements. Make your transition on and off the apparatus very precise, exact, and smooth. Practice until you can perform your whole apparatus sequence without spoken cues.

4.8 The parts of your sequences are really beginning to blend into a regular gymnastic performance. Let's watch [Jack and Shane] and see what is special about their performance. Right! They maintained a performing attitude throughout their sequence. Their muscles were always working to be strong and in control. Let's see if you can keep the same performing attitude as you perform your sequences. Start and finish with the tall, upright posture of a skilled gymnast.

5.0 [Divide the observers into groups and have each group observe some special aspect of the performance. For example, those who held very still as the other person moved, which set(s) maintained the performance attitude, whose sequence blended smoothly from one phase to the other, which pair timed their movement identically, and who had the smoothest transitions on and off the apparatus.] Now that you have your sequences polished for the Olympics, let's enjoy sharing them. When you observe, give the performers your undivided attention. Choose different groups each time you include this task.

Fourth Grade Dance

Combining Weight and Time Qualities

4 or 5 lessons

Combining weight and time qualities while traveling, pausing, and gesturing

MOTOR CONTENT

Selected from Theme 2—Introduction to Weight and Time; Theme 5—Introduction to Relationships; Theme 6—Instrumental Use of the Body; and Theme 7—The Basic Effort Actions

Body

Activities of the body—gestures and locomotion; sequences of activities

Effort

Weight-time combinations—strong-sustained; light-sustained; light-sudden; strong-sudden

Relationships

Interpersonal—meeting, parting; leading, following

OBJECTIVES

In this unit, children will (or should be willing to try to) meet these objectives:

- Sensitize the body to changes in force and speed by exploring a full range of weight-time combinations (reflects National Standard in Dance 1g).
- Develop and perform movement phrases and sequences, incorporating changes in weight-time qualities, both with and without rhythmic accompaniment (reflects National Standards in Dance 2a and 2d).
- Recognize that in most dances changes in weight-time elements result in rhythmic changes.
- Use improvisation to discover or invent movement phrases and sequences and to solve movement problems (reflects National Standard in Dance 2c).
- Share ideas and work effectively with a partner while designing dance phrases and sequences (reflects National Standard in Dance 2e).
- Respond to dance using another art form; explain or demonstrate connections between dance, music, theater, and visual arts (reflects National Standard in Dance 7b).

EQUIPMENT AND MATERIALS

Drum or other percussive instrument(s) capable of producing sudden and/or sustained sounds, such as castanets, tambourine, or maracas; musical selections with a variety of strong-sustained, light-sustained, light-sudden, and strong-sudden qualities such as Kraftwerk's *The Man Machine* or *Computer World*, Lacksman's *Deep Forest* or *Desert Walk*, Cusco's *Apurimac II—Return to Ancient America*, or Nakai and Eaton's *Ancestral Voices*.

LEARNING EXPERIENCES

1.0 [Accompany tasks with strong-sustained music or percussion and state cues in a strong, slow voice.] Let's select different body parts to extend away from our torsos, one at a time. As you move each body part very slowly, feel those strong muscles pressing or pushing body parts into space. Ready? Begin, 'One part away, away, away, with strength, and back in, in, in, near the torso. Now another body part, out, out, out, strongly, and pull in, in, in.' [Repeat many times.]

1.1 On your own, keep selecting different body parts to move slowly and strongly [hands, feet, hips, shoulders, back, and so on]. *Push* each part away—*pull* it back.

Students' paintings provide landscape images with strong, sustained movement. Words and phrases derived from landscapes, geography, and topology are rich in movement vocabulary and may be used to initiate or guide learning experiences: "mountains pressing against the sky," "valleys extending," "rivers and streams flowing." (Painting by Andrea, age 10.)

1.2 As each body part extends slowly with tremendous tension in the muscles, concentrate on feelings of strength. *Push*, press, extend, and lift body parts—out, up, away. [Optional: As children move, project images exuding strength and power on wall or backdrop, e.g., volcanoes, mountain peaks, steep rock sculptures, art scupltures, or landscape paintings (use slide projector or computer panel connected to overhead projector, or a laser beam projector).]

1.3 Imagine before you an incredibly heavy, enormous boulder. It weighs 20 tons! *Push* that boulder away from you. Show me the strain in those muscles. Drip with sweat each step of the way! Now *pull* it back. Pull smoothly. It is too big and heavy to make jerky movements. Your movement is sustained [continuous] as you struggle.

1.4 Hoist a heavy object up onto your body. Carry the object a distance. Lift, carry, then sink to the ground as your strength wears out. Keep changing the body parts that lift, support, and carry your object.

1.5 The distance you must travel is very far—50 miles through burning desert in blazing heat at high noon! Every body part is strong and involved in your struggle. With each attempt, travel a little further.

1.6 Lift and carry a heavy object with the help of a partner. Find someone, decide what type and size of object the two of you will carry, and begin.

1.7 Cooperate with your partner to move that heavy object from its place. When it becomes too difficult to lift and carry, both of you *push*! No voices—just strong muscles! When you reach your destination, find another object to move of different size and weight. [Pairs of children perform movement phrases for each other. Observers guess imaginary objects. Give muscles a rest by introducing tasks 2.0 to 2.4. Revisit strong-sustained movement in tasks 1.8 to 1.14.]

1.8 [Post a list of action words to suggest *strong-sustained* movements: compressing, condensing, contracting, creeping, hauling, heaving, knotting, loading, lowering, pressing, pulling, pushing, slithering, squeezing, tightening, turning, twisting, wringing, (and so on).] With a partner, select and demonstrate three action words. Include both traveling and moving on the spot as you explore forceful, sustained movements.

1.9 Make different body parts lead each action. Arms can stretch high, loading or hauling. Elbows lead movement away from and toward the body while twisting, wringing, squeezing, tightening. Hips and knees bend or feet step, *compressing* [pushing] weight down toward [or into] the ground. Where is your movement going? [Up, away, down, toward, into, and so on.] Look there and lead!

1.10 Are body parts far apart or close together? [Have partners demonstrate their actions: "Arms, legs extend outward toward space (as in turning), or pull inward (slithering)."]

1.11 Find ways you can travel away from your partner [pulling, heaving], then back together [hauling, compressing]. Explore each action fully. Compress, using hands, arms, shoulders, back, hips, knees, and heels.

1.12 Can your whole body move in firm, sustained ways? Show this in one of your actions. Feel the resistance as your muscles work together!

1.13 Pause from time to time to hold a still position. Feel a gripping action in your lower torso.

1.14 Demonstrate your three actions [e.g., loading, tightening, knotting] for another set of partners. Observers, watch for firm-sustained movement—an attitude of power or force.

2.0 [Play slow, quiet music or lightly tap a triangle (gong, cymbal, wind chime), stating tasks softly.] Imagine all the tension in your body evaporating slowly. Every cell in your body is filling with air. You are becoming lighter—almost weightless—as you travel quietly, effortlessly through the empty space.

2.1 Begin traveling at a low level and gradually rise as you go. Once you have reached a high level, slowly and softly travel and sink. Descend to the ground, allowing many body parts to carefully and lightly absorb your weight. Without pausing, rise again to travel. [Repeat.] Try manipulating a hoop as you travel. Keep it airborne and in constant motion.

2.2 Imagine you are passing a large helium-filled balloon back and forth to a partner using different body parts. Every movement is light and soft. Find a partner and begin.

2.3 What other buoyant object could be passed high overhead? Use your whole body to send and receive this form back and forth carefully with slow, smooth movements.

2.4 Make your light-sustained actions last a long time. Feel your whole body float, gliding along with the object as you toss and catch. Fill empty space with your movements of sending and receiving.

2.5 Let's make up a partner dance about meeting and parting. Beginning at a low level, gradually rise and travel slowly toward your partner. Meet at a high level, circle around each other, separate, then slowly sink to the ground. In this dance, there are no specific counts. You and your partner decide how long to spend on each part.

2.6 [Post a list of action words that suggest light-sustained movement qualities or attitudes: drifting, encircling, expanding, floating, flying, gliding, hanging in the air, hovering, lifting, rising, rocking, rolling, rotating, revolving, slow running, skimming, sliding, slinking, soaring, spreading, swaying, swinging, tossing, turning, undulating, weaving, (and so on).] Select action words and improvise or invent movements as you go. Work alone or with a partner.

2.7 Remember as you move lightly, there is barely enough muscular tension to support you, resist [fight] gravity, or produce force. Think 'light' to get that feeling of lightness as you and your partner change directions, levels, and pathways. Add pauses to make your dance more interesting.

3.0 [Fast, light music accompanies these tasks, or shake hand castanets (tambourine, maracas).] With a feeling of very light tension in your body and an awareness of the need for safety, travel quickly through the empty space. Put wings on your feet and whiz through space.

3.1 Show fast starts and stops, traveling quietly on your feet. Be ready to move quickly in any direction. 'Look, travel . . . and pause.' [Repeat many times.] Keep a sense of lightness as you travel by lifting through the chest and leaning forward slightly.

3.2 Even as you pause, work to maintain a sense of lightness or lift in your entire body. Feel the air in your torso. Don't slump. Instead, imagine something catches your ear [pause], you are very alert! *Shhhhh!* What is it? Travel quickly . . . .

3.3 With our fast, light music [or hand castanets], make quick, light gesturing movements with different body parts. See if you can move eight different body parts to make a light, quick dance on the spot.

3.4 Let's combine our traveling, pausing, and gestures, remembering to keep a sense of poise [control] and lift in the torso at all times. This is important for a fast takeoff! We'll travel for eight counts, pause for eight, then make quick, light gestures for eight. Ready? Begin, 'Travel, two, three, four, five, six, seven, eight;

pause, lifting in the torso, [count eight beats]; gesture in place, [count eight beats].' [Repeat three times.]

3.5 [Vary this dance by exploring different *light-sudden* movements while traveling, pausing, and gesturing. Have children make up their own movements or choose action words from a list: agitating, bouncing, darting, disturbing, fidgeting, flapping, fleeing, flicking, fluttering, galloping, hopping, jumping, leaping, oscillating, pattering, puttering, quivering, rushing, shaking, scrambling, scratching, shivering, shuddering, skipping, sputtering, tapping, turning, trembling, twitching, vibrating, wobbling, (and so on).]

4.0 [Accompany tasks with sudden, powerful music or strong drumbeats.] As I play the music [or drum], listen to its strength and power. We will combine sudden time with strong tension. [Form partners, trios, or quartets.] Let's work on traveling very quickly with power in our muscles. When you hear the strong music [drumbeats], one person will lead the other[s] by traveling to wide, open spaces. Be ready to follow behind with your own strong-sudden movement! [Change leaders often. Children also enjoy playing their own rhythm instrument while leading their partner or group.]

4.1 Leaders, challenge your followers with big, turning jumps in the air; stamping, clapping, beating rhythms; lunging, thrusting gestures. [Divide class in half to provide space for free, spontaneous traveling and to take turns sharing ideas.]

4.2 Followers, be ready to move quickly in any direction. Watch your leader closely.

4.3 Begin some distance from your partner or group. Travel quickly and strongly to meet, then circle around each other. Pause. Suddenly, you part with a vigorous stamping and jumping turn [no voices], and travel away.

4.4 Make your entire dance strong and sudden! Lots of tension and strength makes very forceful movement.

4.5 What other actions and gestures could your group perform when meeting, circling, and parting? [Explore strong-sudden action words: clapping, exploding, erupting, flinging, hurling, jolting, jumping, lunging, piercing, pounding, propelling, punching, shoving, slashing, spinning, stamping, swirling, throwing, thrusting, whirling, whipping around, (and so on). Share dances and discuss their movement qualities and attitudes.]

4.6 This partner [group] dance has two sections: *A* is movement on the spot and *B* is traveling. Right where you are, make four gigantic, fast, strong movements you can put together in a sequence. Rehearse your on-the-spot phrase [part *A*], then add fast, strong, traveling actions for four counts [part *B*].

4.7 Let's try our eight-count combination: '*Gigantic* [one], movements [two], on the [three], spot [four]; now travel, six, seven, eight.' [Repeat phrase three times, accompanied by strong-sudden drumbeats.] Decide with your partner [group], who will meet, part, follow, and lead during part *B*.

5.0 [Direct the scenario initially or have students suggest dramatic ideas to express the full range of weight-time combinations.] Let's combine all the weight and time factors into one dance. Beginning at a low level, imagine you are trying to snooze, but some buzzing insect disturbs you. After a few light, quick gestures [light-sudden], you finally awaken fully and give a strong, *slow* stretch [strong-sustained]. Suddenly, you notice a huge beast above you, ready to pounce! Travel away with incredibly strong, fast movement [strong-sudden]. Finally, you are safe, and you softly, slowly sink down to resume your snooze [light-sustained].

5.1 [Combine and contrast movement qualities as you explore interdisciplinary themes, such as "Fascinating Creatures of Earth and Space." Children write and produce original stories in the classroom, then draw or construct imaginary creatures in visual arts. In music, have children create sound scores to accompany dance improvisations, contrasting the four weight-time qualities: Explore isolated actions of body parts and segmented movement (strong-sustained); qualities of flying, encircling, hovering, scattering, gathering, searching, collecting (light-sustained); attitudes of agitating, disturbing, flickering, fluttering, darting, whizzing through space, creating chemical trails or pathways (light-sudden); filling the air with motion, whirling, whipping up space, piercing, pointing (strong-sudden).]

5.2 Make up your own dance with a partner or small group combining all four weight-time qualities. Decide what story your dance is telling or what attitude your movement will express. [Children enjoy translating stories or poems written in the classroom into movement.]

5.3 [Translate sounds of onomatopoeia using synthesizer or vocalizations into weight-time qualities. Consult a music teacher, if necessary.] Listen to our sounds [voices]. What kind of movement attitude does each phrase or line suggest? Practice your movements with a partner, then we will perform the verse together. See example below.]

Synthesizer/voice	Movement quality
Crash, slam, bang!	Strong-sudden
Click, click, click, click-clink	Light-sudden
CLANK!	Strong-sudden
Crrrrrrreeeeeeeeeeeeeeek	Strong-sustained
Sluuuuuuuuuurrrrrrp	Light-sustained
Fizz . . . bubble, bubble . . . hisssss	Light-sustained
Pop, pop, POP, POP, POP, EXPLODE!	Strong-sudden

ASSESSING WEIGHT AND TIME IN DANCE

Draw a graph to indicate how your sequence changes for strong and light, and also for fast and slow. Place these graphs one over the other to show how both time and weight change in the sequence.

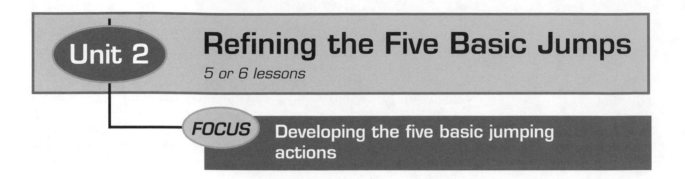

Unit 2 — Refining the Five Basic Jumps

5 or 6 lessons

FOCUS Developing the five basic jumping actions

MOTOR CONTENT

Selected from Theme 6—Instrumental Use of the Body and Theme 7—The Basic Effort Actions

Body

Five basic jumping actions—one foot to the same foot (hop); one foot to the other foot (leap); one foot to two feet (jump); two feet to two feet (jump); two feet to one foot (jump).

Other combinations—turning jumps, gestures during jumps, traveling jumps, step-jump rhythms

Effort

Time—fast, slow
Force—strong, light
Space—direct, flexible

OBJECTIVES

In this unit, children will (or should be willing to try to) meet these objectives:

- Identify and accurately demonstrate the five basic jumps (reflects National Standard in Dance 1b).
- Design a repeatable movement sequence (with and without rhythmic accompaniment) that combines the five basic jumps with traveling and turning activities (reflects National Standards in Dance 2a and 2b).
- Understand that (a) a strong extending action of the hips, knees, and ankles during takeoff achieves greater height in jumps; and (b) to cushion landings, the weight of the body should be transferred through the balls of the feet, to the heels, bending the ankles, knees, and hips.
- Work to improve jumping skill by positioning shoulders over hips during takeoff and landings, avoiding tilting the shoulders backward or forward to maintain balance.
- Explain how healthy practices such as nutrition and exercise enhance their ability to dance (reflects National Standard in Dance 6b).

EQUIPMENT AND MATERIALS

Drum or wood block; one tambourine or shaker for each child; lively folkdance music, such as "Tarantella" or "Sicilian Tarantella."

LEARNING EXPERIENCES

1.0 [Lightly tap a drum at a steady walking pace.] Travel through the empty spaces with soft, quiet steps. Place each foot carefully, paying close attention to how softly and quietly your feet touch the floor. Stop quickly when the drum stops. Ready? Begin, 'Travel—quiet feet . . . and stop.' [Repeat many times.] Take important steps without making a sound.

1.1 Stretch and extend your leg with each step. Feel your foot lengthening and stretching, too. We are warming up our feet for running and jumping.

1.2 Take *longer* but faster steps. Cover some distance, still placing the feet carefully as you step. Watch out for others as you travel.

1.3 [Increase tempo of taps on the drum.] Run lightly now, pushing off from one foot to the other. Spring into the air with each running step. Push off and feel that forward, upward action!

1.4 Still concentrate on placing the foot carefully with each running step. Bend your knees for light, soft, quiet landings.

1.5 Keep looking for empty spaces. Be ready to move quickly in any direc-tion—right, left, backward, forward.

1.6 Travel, and *every* time you hear a loud tap on the drum, carefully shoot [pop or jump] up into the air, land softly, and travel again. Make each jump a *surprise!* Here we go. [Tap a sequence of seven light taps with a louder beat on count eight.] 'Travel, two, three, four, five, six, seven, *eight!* And travel, two, three, four, five, six, seven, *eight!*' [When children demonstrate understanding of the sequence, tap a loud beat on count six or four. "Tap, two, three, four, five, *six!* Or—tap, two, three, *four!*"]

2.0 [Tap a variety of rhythms; see examples below.] Listen to the rhythm of the drum and try to match that rhythm with your feet as you travel. Remember to *extend* through your hips, knees, and ankles as you take off and to *bend* when you land.

2.1 You have just performed a variety of different steps and jumps created by the way you take off and land. Now push off from one foot and landing on that same foot—a hop on the right [left]. [In dance, we may call it a *temps levé* (tahn luh-*vay*).] See if you can spring into the air from one foot and land on the same

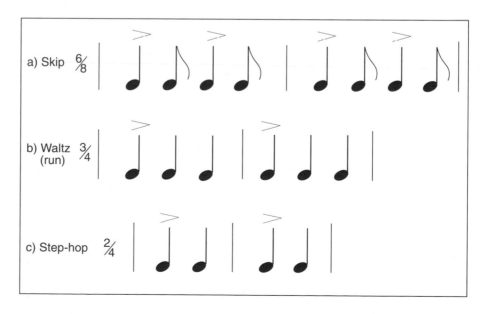

foot with each tap of the drum. 'One foot to the same foot, [tap] hop, [tap] hop, [tap] hop.' [Play even drumbeats at a moderate tempo, observing for extension in the hip, knee, and ankle of the hopping foot on takeoff.] After several tries, hop on your other foot. [Change feet several times.]

2.2 Let's travel forward while hopping. As you push off, swing your free, working leg up. Lift the body, '[Tap:] Up, [tap] up, [tap] up!' [See if the free leg swings up, lifting or leading the takeoff.

2.3 Remember to land softly with each jump [hop] by first landing on the ball of the foot, getting your heel down, too, then cushioning your weight by bending the knee and ankle.

2.4 Let's make up a short combination of eight hops on the spot and eight traveling jumps. Here we go: 'Hop on the right, two, three, four, now the left, six, seven, eight; now travel right, two, three, four, travel left, six, seven, eight.' [Repeat.]

2.5 Some of you might like to add a turn as you hop in place. Show your own variation of hopping. [For example, "Hop (turning) to the right, two, three, four, now to the left, two, three, four; and travel, two, three, four, five, six, seven, eight." Repeat many times.]

2.6 As you hop this time, place the free [working] leg and foot in different places around you—in front, behind, to the side, in the air. [For example, "Tap your free foot in front of you. Hop, tap, tap, tap, to the front [change feet]; hop, tap, tap, tap, to the front."]

2.7 Design a short dance of 16 counts in which you jump [hop] on the spot from one foot to the same foot, changing feet at least once, and take your free leg to different places around you. Some of you might also like to add turns. [Provide time to choreograph; accompany with music, played softly. If possible, give each student a tambourine.]

2.8 Let's perform our dances in groups of six. Audience, as each group performs, watch for jumps [hops] that take off from one foot and land softly on the same foot, with at least one change to the other foot. Also, look for different ways of gesturing with the free leg. Did anyone include a turn in their dance? [Play music to accompany dances.]

3.0 As you travel, concentrate on taking off strongly from one foot and landing on the other foot. This type of jumping action is called a leap. [In dance, we call it a *jete* (zhuh-*tay*), and if we go very high in the air or very far in distance, we call it a *grand jete*.] Here we go. [Tap a slower, stronger pace on the drum to elicit leaps. If space is limited, divide class and alternate turns so the children can experience freedom of flight.] 'Run, run, run, run; [now slower] and *leap*, and *leap*, and *leap*, and *leap*!'

3.1 Remember to take one large running step per beat. When the tempo is slower, make your leaps higher and longer. Spend more time in the air!

3.2 Let's combine our running and leaping another way. Listen to the drum. The beat says, 'Run, run, *leap*; run, run, *leap*.' The leap comes from the third running step. [Tap a rhythm, "soft, soft, *loud*!" (accent in air). Repeat several times.]

3.3 Now try the opposite: '*Leap*, run, run; *leap*, run, run; [and so on].' [Tap "*loud*, soft, soft."] When you hear the *loud* tap, *push off* strongly into a leap!

3.4 Reach forward with your lead foot as you leap through open spaces. Stretch your landing leg hard! [Emphasize covering distance first, then gradually increase height of leaps.]

3.5 What can you do to leap higher? Right! Bend your knees and *push off*, extending [straightening] the knees and feet very hard as you push! Jump high, lifting through the chest, and pause a moment in the air. Feel height achieved! [Repeat a variety of even tempos for running and leaping.]

3.6 As you push into the air to leap, swing your opposite hand forward to add height to your jump and to maintain your balance when you're landing. [Stress arm action after children show good leg extensions during takeoff.]

3.7 We have learned two different types of jumping actions—hop and leap. Let's make up a short dance combining the two.

Part 1:   Hop in place for 16 counts. Change feet at least once.

Part 2:   Travel by running and leaping for another 16 counts. Change directions at least once.

Tap or shake your tambourine to accompany the music and some of your jumps.

4.0 Right where you are, jump lightly from two feet to two feet. Let ankles and knees give so your whole foot settles to the floor before jumping again. Here we go: 'Lightly two and two, and two, and two.' [Repeat many times.] Try hard to feel those ankles give, heels touch the floor, and take off with both feet at the same time. This is a third type of jumping action.

4.1 Let's try again with four counts of rest between every four jumps. Don't work for height—just keep those ankles oiled and easy. [Tap even drumbeats at moderate tempo.] 'Jump, two, three, four, rest two, three, four; [and so on].'

4.2 Let's practice jumping 'two feet to two feet' in slow motion [no drum], gradually increasing the height of our jumps. Land softly on the balls of your feet, touch down heels next, and ride that landing for a brief moment before *pushing off!* [Repeat with stronger jumps.]

4.3 Some of you may be able to change direction on one of your landings. As I tap the drum, jump two feet to two feet and turn to your right or left. Remember to turn while you are in the air and land facing that new direction [focus on wall or another spot]. [Initially, design a sequence such as "jump, jump, jump, turn." Practice, then have children reorganize the jumps and turns, demonstrating their own sequences.]

4.4 Let's travel a little with each jump 'two feet to two feet' as we try a longer sequence. 'Jump, and travel, two, three, four, five, six, seven, eight; now pause, two, three, four, five, six, seven, eight.' [Repeat.] Take care. Stay with the beat. Don't try for distance. Work for soft, complete landings, letting the heels settle down to the floor. Don't land on heels—land on the balls of the feet first.

4.5 It is important to keep your shoulders over your hips when you jump to help you maintain your balance and a lifted posture. Try not to lean too far forward when you land. [Repeat sequence in 4.4.]

4.6 Let's make up a dance using our three types of jumping actions:

Part 1:   Hop [one foot to the same foot], gesturing with your free leg for 16 counts.

Part 2:   Run and leap [one foot to the other foot] for 16 counts. Cover distance in your leaps.

Part 3:   Jump [two feet to two feet] on the spot and while traveling for 16 counts. Add turns for interest.

As you design your sequences, I will play music and call out the different parts. [Use tambourines, if you wish.]

4.7 Remember, you are showing the audience three distinct types of jumps, so make each jumping action clear. Show precise takeoffs and landings.

4.8 Repeat your dances and concentrate on a lifted posture and soft, springy landings. Feel free to add arm movements or leg gestures.

4.9 Let's have this third of the class perform part 1, this group perform part 2, and the last group do part 3. Hold very still until it is your turn in the music. [For an additional performing experience, have children form trios with each person dancing one of the parts. Rotate roles, if you wish, so everyone can perform all three sections.]

5.0 There are two other types of jumping actions we can work on to vary our dances. One is a jump that takes off from two feet and lands on one foot. [In dance, we call this type of jump a *sissone* (see-son).] The other jump takes off on one foot and assembles the feet in the air to land on two feet. [We call this an *assemble* (ah-sahn-*blay*): Feet separate in the air, then are brought together quickly to land.] Show your own variations of these two jumps. First, we'll jump 'two to one, two to one.' Now let's try 'one to two, one to two.' [Provide practice time for both types of jumps. Play even drumbeats at a moderate tempo or play music so children can sense moving in time with a musical beat and along with others.]

5.1 As you try these jumping actions, work hard to show differences in your takeoffs and landings. Really push off with either one foot or both feet. Will you land on one foot or two?

Design a group shape in the air. Show precise take-offs and think about how your body shape relates to your partners' shapes.

5.2 As you jump, make a clear shape with the free, gesturing leg. Swing it high in the air or to the side or bend the knee. Think of designing the shape of your entire body as you jump in the air. [Observe for sharp, focused shapes.]

5.3 Teach your favorite shape[s] to a partner. See if both of you can perform shapes in the air at exactly the same time in exactly the same way. Show precise takeoffs and landings. Suspend each shape in the air!

5.4 Let's design a dance to music that has all five jumping actions. Allow 16 counts for each part. Some of you may want to follow this order:

Part 1:   Jump [hop] from one foot to the same foot, changing feet at least once.

Part 2:   Jump [leap] from one foot to the other while traveling.

Part 3:   Jump from two feet to two feet on the spot while turning.

Part 4:   Jump from one foot to two feet.

Part 5:   Jump from two feet to one foot.

[Post the order of jumps for reference. Practice without, then with, music.]

5.5 As you design your jumping dance, remember to land softly. Bend and give in your ankles, knees, and hips. Are you landing on the balls of the feet? Do your heels touch down softly with each jump? Have a partner watch and check your jumps.

5.6 As you take off, *extend* through your legs and point your toes hard. Maximize your jumps! Show higher, stronger jumps. Spend a longer time in the air! Tell your partner how much space there is between the floor and your partner's feet when they jump.

5.7 As you perform your dances, remember the audience wants to see all five jumping actions. Make each takeoff and landing precise since this is what makes each jump different. [Play music. Children may accompany their dances with a tambourine.]

6.0 [Children enjoy practicing various step-jump combinations adapted from folkdances. The following version of "Sicilian Tarantella" was taught to fourth graders at Janney Elementary School, Washington D.C. by Santa Giardina and Kathleen MacPeak, student teachers at the Catholic University of America. According to legend, this dance from Taranto, Italy was first performed in the 14th century by men and women who, when bitten by a tarantula spider, danced rapidly to sweat out the poison.]

Part 1:   [Tap tambourine to accompany children's movements, snaps, and claps. Dancers begin facing a partner several steps away.] Step and swing the right foot across the left [hop left]; repeat on the other side to hop right [four counts]. Take four running steps in place, snapping fingers or clapping hands [four counts]. [Repeat three times.]

Part 2:   Run four steps toward partner and bow [four counts] and run back four steps [four counts]. Repeat this three times, snapping fingers, clapping, or playing tambourine.

Part 3:   Run toward partner, hook right elbows, and skip around, then travel back to places [eight counts]. [Repeat, hooking left elbows. Repeat part 3.]

Part 4: Jump in place any way you wish, snapping fingers or clapping hands. Watch your partner at all times [eight counts]. [Accompany with tambourine.]

Part 5: Jump or skip all about the room, taking turns leading and following each other [eight counts].

Part 6: On the spot, reach up with one hand to point at a star with your partner, touching fingertips. Skip eight steps around [eight counts]. Repeat going the other way around [shaking tambourine].

Group Shapes and Movement Sequences

3 or 4 lessons

FOCUS Contrasting changes in level to design group shapes and movement sequences

MOTOR CONTENT

Selected from Theme 3—Introduction to Space; Theme 5—Introduction to Relationships; and Theme 6—Instrumental Use of the Body

Body

Body shapes—a variety of different shapes

Space

Levels—high, middle, low (deep)

Relationships

Group formations—trios forming giant group shapes

OBJECTIVES

In this unit, children will (or should be willing to try to) meet these objectives:

- Experience changes in level while traveling, turning, and creating body shapes.
- Demonstrate kinesthetic awareness, concentration, and focus when performing (reflects National Standard in Dance 1g).
- Apply their knowledge of levels to movement improvisations and the design of simple, repeatable movement sequences, alone and in small groups (reflects National Standards in Dance 2a and 2c).
- Recall that levels define and describe where a movement occurs in space: near the floor (low); around the torso between low and high (middle); above the head or high above the floor (high).
- Observe group dances and discuss similarities and differences in body shapes held (stillness), levels used, and the like (reflects National Standard in Dance 4b).
- Work cooperatively with others while designing and performing group dances (reflects National Standard in Dance 2e).
- Identify at least three personal goals to improve themselves as dancers (reflects National Standard in Dance 6a).

EQUIPMENT AND MATERIALS

Drum. *Optional:* Musical Selection A—popular music with a strong, steady beat; Selection B—music specifically composed with a variety of levels such as "Levelance" or "Plink, Plank, Plunk."

LEARNING EXPERIENCES

1.0 Let's review how much you have already learned about levels. With each tap of the drum, make your whole body change levels on the spot. '[Tap:] Move to a high, medium, or low level; [tap] change to a completely different level; [tap] change your level again—hold that shape; [tap] change to a new level.'

1.1 With each level change, make a totally new shape with your body. Change your base of support to create interesting shapes at different levels. [Designate changes by tapping drum. See fitness box.]

1.2 Watch carefully what level I move to, then make a shape with your body at a *completely different* level. [Repeat several times, each child working in own space.]

1.3 This time, your leader will make a shape at a high, middle, or low [deep] level. Followers, try very hard to make a shape at the *same* level. Let's form groups of three or four, with one of you leading. Follow your leader closely! [Rotate the leadership role frequently.]

1.4 Now leaders, make unusual shapes at specific levels. Followers, try hard to copy the *same* shape but make your shape at a *different* level.

1.5 Leaders, challenge your group by making unique shapes but be sure each shape can be performed at different levels.

1.6 Followers, notice the obvious features of your leader's shape and show those same features at a new level. Make each shape look special at your own level! [Change leaders every three or four turns.]

2.0 Listen as I tap the drum softly for four beats, then *louder* for four. Each phrase has eight taps. Travel lightly on your feet during the four soft taps, then make a *strong* body shape you can hold on the *loud* taps. 'Travel, two, three, four, *make a different shape* and *hold,* eight.' [Repeat phrase several times, observing for stillness of body shapes and variety in traveling.]

2.1 Most of you traveled on your feet at a medium level. See if you can travel in different ways at high and low levels—jumping, leaping, rolling, sliding, shuffling, skipping. [Maintain the same length of travel time for several repetitions, then vary the duration of traveling to 16, 12, 6, or 4 beats.]

2.2 This time, make your shape at the *same* level as your traveling phrase. Let's try this to 16 counts of traveling: [16 soft taps:] 'Travel at a low level [count to 16]; [four loud taps] make a *low* shape; travel at a high level [count to 16]; take a *high* shape [count to 4].' [After a few repetitions, vary the tempo or rhythm by tapping fast drumbeats to elicit running or leaping; slow beats to walk; uneven beats to gallop, skip, or shuffle.]

2.3 Use *all* the traveling time of 16 counts before striking your fabulous pose. See how much empty space you can cover! Add large arm gestures or wide sweeping turns as you travel—maybe big traveling jumps or leaps. [Practice with and without counts.]

2.4 Challenge yourself! When you hear one *loud* tap, quickly make your shape at a totally *different* level than your traveling phrase. We'll begin with 11 counts of traveling. [Soft taps:] 'Travel [count to 11]; [loud tap] *fast*—change your level or shape [12].' [Repeat several times. Vary phrase by traveling for 7 counts and striking a shape on count 8.]

MUSCULAR STRENGTH AND ENDURANCE

Tighten or *contract* your stomach [abdominal] muscles to help make your base of support strong and stable. Feel how much muscle tension you need to hold each shape firm. Can you make increasingly difficult shapes, using just the right amount of tension to hold each shape? Lift through your chest, tighten your abdominals. Suspend each shape in the air!

2.5 Be clear about how you travel and what your body shapes look like. Try to sharpen the lines of each shape. [Observe for stillness and clarity of position as children show increased awareness and kinesthetic sense of details in body shapes.]

2.6 As you travel, think ahead, 'Where and how will I stop and make a shape?' Plan to make a different-looking body shape than the ones you have made before. Will your shape be straight, wide, round, twisted, angular, or a combination of these?

2.7 Design a movement sequence demonstrating different levels while traveling and holding still shapes. As you work, select your favorite ways of traveling and creating body shapes at different levels. Ready? Begin: 'Travel [eight counts]; shape at level number one, hold, hold, hold; travel again [eight counts]; shape at level number two, and hold [four counts]; travel [eight counts]; last level change, and hold four counts!' [This dance consists of 36 counts.]

2.8 Can you remember the whole sequence or pattern? Try repeating your traveling and shapes in the same order.

2.9 Count out your own sequence as you refine your dance. Show contrasts at different levels. This dance expresses how well you can define the space around you while traveling and on the spot.

2.10 Let's perform our sequences in groups of five or six. Audience, watch for changes in level while traveling and on the spot with clearly defined body shapes.

3.0 Let's *improvise* a dance with three different levels. To *improvise* means we make it up as we go along. [Select three children for demonstration.] Working as a trio, number one takes a level [high, middle, or deep]. Number two travels, attaching at a different level to number one. Number three joins the group at a third level. Notice how you end up forming one giant shape! Find a group of three and repeat this sequence several times to form different giant shapes. Each shape should show three levels.

Students work together to form multi-level, giant group shapes.

3.1 Let's add traveling to our giant group shapes to create a dance with specific counts. [Tap slow, even drumbeats as you cue.] 'Person number one, travel for four counts and take your shape at a special level. Dancer number two, travel to join number one for the next four counts, ending at a different level. Now, dancer number three, travel four counts to join number one and number two and take a completely different level. Everyone, hold your giant shape for four more counts, then begin again.' This sequence has 16 counts.

3.2 To start again, see if number one can travel far away from the group so number two and number three also have to cover ground to meet number one. Make your traveling large, energetic, exciting. Spring or leap toward a new point! Jump, hop, or skip to open spaces, turning as you travel!

3.3 Person number one, hold very still while making group shapes so the followers can attach themselves safely. Often in dance, you must hold positions very strong and still, either supporting or being supported by another person's weight. [Use terms "attach, join, fasten, bond, link, and connect" interchangeably.]

Students revisit this unit by creating architectural structures of the "dome," "arch," and "flying buttress." See learning experience 3.10 on page 151.

3.4 Don't collapse out of your shape, number two and number three. Tighten muscles and hold a firm shape until it's your turn to travel away. Feel those abdominals [stomach muscles] working.

3.5 Practice building your giant shapes, then we'll show our level dances to the class. Repeat your 16-count sequence three times, but vary the way you travel each time and show different giant group shapes.

3.6 Count out your own sequences as you refine your dances. Also think about showing great contrast in levels. [Give the children time to design three solid group shapes.]

3.7 As you rehearse, take care to move out of your giant shapes slowly, carefully, and without causing others to lose their balance. Be aware and considerate of other's positions.

3.8 [Divide class in half with several trios performing at once to a 16-count sequence. Repeat three times, holding the final group shape for 4 counts.]

3.9 [Revisit 3.1 to 3.8.] As you design your sequence for your performance, feel free to change the counts for your traveling and stillness sections. Decide in your group how long the leader and followers travel and how long to pause. Maybe rearrange the order of your traveling; give number two and number three a chance to lead.

3.10 [Revisit 3.0 to 3.9 in fourth, fifth, or sixth grade by building group shapes at the same or different levels with two to six people. Consult the visual arts or classroom teacher as to how to integrate movement experiences with model building in which students actively explore architectural structures of the arch, dome, tunnel, and the like (see Abhau, 1986; Salvadori, 1990). Compare building principles with mechanical principles involved in creating group shapes.]

4.0 [This dance is designed for music Selection B—"Levelance."] Listen to the different levels in this selection of music. It has high-, low-, and middle-toned music. Decide who will dance to each tone, then move when your music tells you, connecting in multileveled, giant group shapes [as before].

4.1 As you design your sequence for performance, feel free to change the counts of your traveling and pausing sections. Decide with your group how long the leaders and followers travel and how long to pause.

4.2 As you rehearse your dances, work together to carefully move out of your group shapes. Slowly and with great concentration, release your muscles without disturbing the group shape that remains.

4.3 Work hard to rid your sequence of all unplanned movement. Eliminate actions like brushing hair out of your eyes, tugging at your clothes, and other unplanned movement. Stay focused and committed to each planned movement so the audience won't be distracted by extra movement. This shows a 'performance attitude.'

4.4 As we watch our group dances, let's look for three different levels, how still dancers hold their giant shapes, and how safely the group shapes dissolve. Does each group demonstrate concentration and a performance attitude?

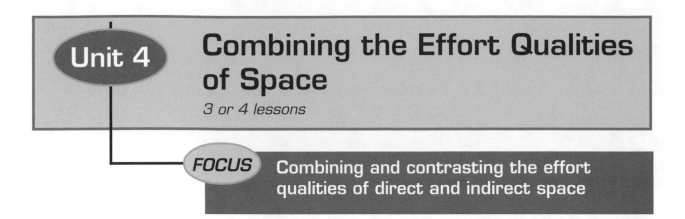

Unit 4

Combining the Effort Qualities of Space

3 or 4 lessons

FOCUS Combining and contrasting the effort qualities of direct and indirect space

MOTOR CONTENT

Selected from Theme 4—The Flow of Movement; Theme 6—Instrumental Use of the Body; Theme 8—Everyday and Occupational Rhythms

Body

Combinations of body activities—gestures and stepping; gestures and locomotion; sequences of activities; miming actions, activities, or gestures in pairs or small groups

Effort

Space qualities—direct (straight) and indirect (flexible)

OBJECTIVES

In this unit, children will (or should be willing to try to) meet these objectives:

- Design, refine, and perform a movement phrase and sequence (with and without accompaniment) that compares and contrasts the use of direct and flexible space; identify parts of their dances and confidently discuss the choices they made and the meanings they intended (reflects National Standards in Dance 2a, 3c, and 4a).
- Define and maintain personal space by moving carefully on the spot and through empty spaces (reflects National Standard in Dance 1d).
- Understand that effort qualities are determined in part by the amount of space used to perform movement: Direct movement conserves the amount of space needed to perform a movement; flexible movement increases the amount of space needed.
- Create, repeat, and vary dance phrases to increase skillfulness in movement and sensitivity toward using space as a means of changing expression in movement (reflects National Standard in Dance 2d).

EQUIPMENT AND MATERIALS

Rhythm instrument(s) capable of producing sudden, sharp sounds (drum, wood or tone block, claves, or tambourine) and lingering sustained sounds (gong, cymbal, wind chime, tambourine, triangle, or rainstick). *Optional:* Music Selection A—popular or ethnic music with strong beats or accented phrases such as Kraftwerk's *The Man Machine*, Mendes' *Brasileiro*, or Cusco's *Apurimac II*; Selection B—dreamlike, gentle piano by Winston or Chappell; Selection C—environmental sound recordings of the sea, thunderstorms, and so on, or new age music such as Rowland's *Fairy Ring* or Evenson's *Forest Rain*.

LEARNING EXPERIENCES

1.0 Right where you are, without moving your feet, reach one hand straight outward into space. Keep reaching your hand directly to several different places—up, down, in front, behind. Change hands, exploring all the space around you.

1.1 Plan in advance where you will move your hand. Show very straight, direct movements, right to the point. Don't waste any space. [Play sharp sounds on instrument to elicit quick, straight movement.] Faster now. Keep each movement clean and direct.

1.2 Use fingertips, fist, or sides of the hand to make each action straight and direct. Show several ways, staying in your own space. [Divide class in half to demonstrate and observe gestures.] What names would you give these gestures? [Jot a word list entitled "Direct Actions," challenging children to expand the list.]

1.3 Choose different body parts to indicate [show] places around you. '[Tap: Foot up, [tap] elbow down, [tap] knee to the side, [tap] a different body part.' Keep changing body parts, finding new places. Take a step to the right [left, forward, backward] to extend your reach.

1.4 Select a molecule in space a short distance from you. Travel directly there, pointing out one specific molecule. Don't disturb any others. Find another one, and another, close to you. [Initially, provide verbal cues, "Go and point! And go." Repeat.]

1.5 Think where to travel before you go. Move directly there. Plan your trip in advance! Go to a place and point; another place—reach out. Go directly. Travel efficiently from place to place. Astound the audience with your preplanned destinations!

1.6 Show direct, precise movement as you discover new molecules. Point, pierce, and shoot different body parts outward into space—toes, heel, fist, head, shoulder, knee, sole of the foot. [Name body parts used or suggest parts.]

1.7 Challenge yourself to point out molecules that are hard to reach. Select a few spots so high you have to *jump* to touch them. Put these in as surprise movements as you travel to open spaces.

1.8 Choose two spots very near, close enough to reach without traveling, and one spot very far away that forces you to travel. Let's make up a rhythmic pattern. 'Close [jab], close [jab to another nearby spot], and travel far; jab, jab, and travel.' [Add specific counts or music Selection A. For example, jab on count one, jab on count two, then travel for six counts to make an eight-count phrase; repeat many times.] Show clean, direct jabbing movements on the spot. Surprise us with quick, straight jumps as you travel!

2.0 With each tap of the gong [or other instrument producing sustained sound, letting each sound linger before tapping again], allow your hand to meander [wander] through all the space around you. Fill the space with wavy, roundabout movement that builds up and spills over without any hard edges. [Repeat 1.0 with other body parts or combinations of body parts.]

A jump, jolt, or jab! Try leading with different body parts—the hip, head, shoulder, or knee.

2.1 These flexible, indirect movements have no certain beginning place or ending, they just keep going. [Accompany movements with slow, soft taps on gong.] Listen to how long each sound lingers and try to make your flexible movements last just as long. [Name or describe indirect gestures as in 1.2.]

2.2 Work deliberately and consciously now to move a different body part indirectly with each tap on the gong. Meander your knee [elbow, shoulder, back, head, arm, hip, foot] all about your personal space. When we move indirectly, we say we are *indulging* in the space.

2.3 Keep selecting different body parts and move each part in flexible ways, using a lot of space, indulging in the space. The audience should never know for certain where you are going next with the body part. Keep moving.

2.4 Travel about the room in indirect ways . . . enjoy all the empty, open spaces! Gallop, skip, and turn, drawing curvy pathways in the air . . . on the floor . . . with your arms and legs. Make every single molecule in the room move as you travel!

2.5 Keep looking for and moving into open spaces safely. Change the way you travel with each tap of the gong.

2.6 As you travel this time, look as if you are going several different places at once by filling our dancing space with your movement. Change the body parts moving, your direction, and your level and allow your focus to move all at once. [Allow movement to arouse children's interpretations and imagery: traveling down a winding footpath or rocky trail with obstacles and unexpected turns and twists; riding ocean waves of different sizes and shapes, moving in various directions.]

2.7 Select two spots close to you and one spot farther away. Move in flexible, indirect ways to each of these places. [Maintain the pattern by repeating, "Close, close, *far*," tapping gong softly for short distance, then loudly for long distance. Or perhaps play tambourine with a "tap, tap, *shake*."]

2.8 As you travel far, allow your movements to build or grow. [Give examples, if necessary: Imagine climbing, jumping, leaping over large obstacles; or riding waves that travel faster and faster, forming groups of long, smooth swells.] Some of you may wish to join a partner to work on your movement idea. [Accompany with music selections B or C, if you wish.]

3.0 [Post or project a list of action words on wall. Select from sports-related actions, ordinary gestures, or everyday body activities (see example below).] Choose one or two movement[s] from our word list. Demonstrate your movement[s] in front of a partner. Can your partner guess the action, gesture, or activity you have chosen?

3.1 Mime or imitate each movement as accurately as possible. Pay attention [for example] to how the hand is cupped to hold an imaginary baseball [sports action]; how the wrist moves as you write or draw in the air [gesture]; how the upper torso moves in a carefree, roundabout manner when strolling [body activity].

3.2 With a partner [or small group], select one movement you especially like. Perform the movement, over and over again, until you feel a pulse or rhythm in the action. [Observe and help pairs or groups move exactly the same way, at the same speed.]

3.3 Allow the rhythm to grow or build by making your movement larger. Really exaggerate the action, gesture, or activity.

3.4 Is the movement direct or indirect? Be clear in your performance. Direct movements are straight, lean, and clean-looking. Indirect movements have a wavy, roundabout, squiggly, or *throwaway* quality.

3.5 What sounds might accompany your direct [or indirect] movement? [Children may add vocal sounds as they move. For example, "Uh oh," "Yes," "Totally cool," or use nonsensical words. Partners or small groups could accompany each other by combining a myriad of rhythm instruments to make sounds that match the movement to create group music-making.]

3.6 Let your movement really take you through space . . . travel with it! In what directions can you take the movement? [Allow time to explore and extend the movement.] Show the audience a certain attitude or feeling toward space by how much or how little space you use. [Share these movement studies with the class.]

ACTION WORDS		
Sports-related actions	Ordinary gestures	Body activities
Baseball pitch	Writing/drawing in air	Walking/strolling/capering
Basketball shot	Standing up/folding arms/waving	Marching/strutting/striding
Baton twirl	Reading a book/blinking eyes	Stumbling/slipping/falling
Bowling roll	Sitting down/typing on a computer	Pushing/shoving/pulling
Golf swing	Shivering/trembling/tapping	Tumbling/crawling/creeping
Hockey drive	Putting on/taking off hat	Running/dashing/rambling
Soccer kick	Plucking flowers/picking fruit	Whirling/turning/twisting
Swimming stroke	Eating food/drinking milk	Drifting/gliding/sliding
Surfboard rider	Brushing teeth/combing hair	
Tennis serve		

3.7 Let's create a longer sequence. Select three action words [actions, gestures, or activities] and perform these in a specific order. Your movement sequence, like a sentence, should demonstrate a definite beginning, middle, and end.

3.8 Pay special attention to how you perform each movement. Show a certain quality or attitude toward space and time. How much space will you need? Are your movements direct or flexible? How fast or slow will you perform each movement? With what body parts? In which directions? [Rotate among pairs or small groups, reinforcing cues in 3.1 to 3.4 and the questions here in 3.8.]

3.9 Move carefully on the spot and through open spaces. Keep a safe, working distance from others. [Observe if children maintain personal space.]

3.10 Decide if you want to accompany your movement sequence with sound, vocalization, or music. [If possible, ask the music teacher to help children compose musical scores that fit their movement sequences.]

3.11 [If possible, enlist the cooperation of the visual arts teacher.] In visual arts class, you manipulated wire to create a sculpture that occupies space and reflects one of your action words. By placing your sculpture on an overhead projector screen, we can produce oversized images on the wall [scrim]. Your artwork sets the mood or scene for movement and becomes an important part of your dance. [Alternatively, project photos of artwork using a computer connected to an overhead projector.]

ASSESSMENT: DEMONSTRATION AND DISCUSSION

Demonstrate your sequence of action words and confidently discuss your movement choices, solutions to questions, and attitudes toward space and time.

The Polka Step

Unit 5

2 to 4 lessons

FOCUS Extending the foot pattern of a gallop and slide into the polka step

MOTOR CONTENT

Selected from Theme 5—Introduction to Relationships and Theme 6—Instrumental Use of the Body

Body

Locomotor activities—step-jump rhythms (polka); turning

Relationships

Partners—mirroring

OBJECTIVES

In this unit, children will (or should be willing to try to) meet these objectives:

- Respond accurately to an uneven rhythm pattern (short-long, short-long) by clapping, moving body parts, or traveling (reflects National Standard in Dance 1f).
- Mirror accurately the step pattern of sliding and turning (a-slide and skip) with a partner, face-to-face and back-to-back, to learn the polka step (reflects National Standards in Dance 1b and 2f).
- Concentrate on moving to a musical beat in unison with a partner or group to create life, sparkle, and joy in their dances (reflects National Standard in Dance 2e).
- Recognize that they are creating dances as they repeat step-jump combinations to form dance phrases; then vary phrases by changing direction, adding gestures, and so forth (reflects National Standard in Dance 2d).
- Research dances of Colonial America to identify and discuss: What dances were performed, why, and in what settings? (reflects National Standard in Dance 5c).

EQUIPMENT AND MATERIALS

Drum or rhythm sticks; any musical recording in 2/4 or 4/4 time with a buoyant, spirited quality, preferably a polka, see Strauss' *Pizzicato Polka* (or see Third Grade Dance Unit 2 Equipment and Materials for polkas), Denver's "Grandmother's Feather Bed" from *Back Home Again*, or traditional folk and country dance music such as "Greensleeves."

LEARNING EXPERIENCES

1.0 [Play music.] Listen to this lively music and clap to the underlying beat or move a body part in time with the beat. What is an underlying beat? [The steady, continuous beat or pulse of a rhythmic pattern or movement (see example below).]

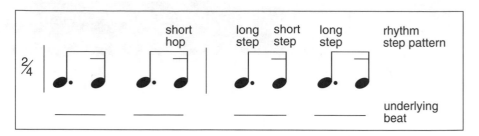

1.1 As you softly clap or gesture to the beat, you might hear another rhythm that has an exciting, bouncy feeling: 'Short-long, short-long.' Let's try clapping [gesturing] to this uneven rhythm. Say the words with me.

1.2 Begin to tap these rhythms on the floor with your hands [or feet]. First, let's do the underlying beat [repeat the four-part pattern in example above several times], then change to the uneven rhythmic pattern, 'Short-long, short-long.'

1.3 Join with a partner. One person clap [tap] the underlying beat, counting four beats. The other clap the uneven rhythm, 'Short-long, short-long,' repeating these words softly. See if both of you can stay with the music. [Change roles. To simplify, have children clap the underlying beat while you clap or tap the uneven rhythm; change.]

2.0 Let's try traveling to the music, keeping your movement lively and bouncy. I see many of you galloping, skipping, sliding, and dabbing the air [gesturing]— all of these activities and actions fit well with the music.

2.1 Let your traveling take you in different directions—forward, backward, and sideways. Make a definite change in your direction on the first beat of each four-count phrase. 'Travel, two, three, four; and change, two, three, four.' [Repeat, accompanying on drum.]

2.2 This time, gallop forward and see if you can change your lead foot every eight counts. 'Gallop [eight counts]; and change feet [eight counts].' [Repeat, galloping four and changing, then galloping two and changing.]

2.3 Who can repeat the same pattern, but gallop sideways? [Child demonstrates.] What do we call this activity? Yes, a slide! Reach out sideways with your lead foot, *glide*, and glide, and glide.

2.4 See if you can change what you do with your feet each time you hear a new set of eight [four, two] counts. [Initially cue, "Change."]

3.0 Without holding hands, show how quickly and quietly you can make three large circles, one inside the other, with everyone facing the center of the room. [Use floor lines for inner circle.] Spread out so you will be able to travel to your right [counterclockwise] freely, without touching anyone. Now, facing the center of the circle, begin to move sideways to your right, trying to stay with my verbal [spoken] cues. Ready? 'Step sideways with your right foot, bring your left foot next to it, and step right again [slide right].' We'll slide several times counterclockwise. Keep going.

3.1 Now you are getting it. 'Let's slide and slide and slide—a little faster.' [Increase speed gradually until the whole class feels themselves sliding rhythmically in unison, eventually getting a little lift as the weight is transferred, "Glide step, cut, step (slide)."]

3.2 You are facing the center as you slide. Without changing the rhythm or your direction, turn and continue sliding with your back to the center. You are now traveling counterclockwise.

3.3 Make a half-turn every time you hear me say, 'Turn,' and try to keep your circles big. Start by facing in toward the center. Here we go: 'And slide, and slide, and slide, and slide, and slide, and slide, and slide, and slide, and ready, and turn, and two, and three, and four, and five, and six, and seven, and ready, and turn, and two, [and so on].' [Repeat counting and giving verbal cues until the class can change the direction they are facing, still traveling counterclockwise in the circle.]

3.4 Feel the right foot and the right side of your body lead you when you are facing the center of the room. Feel the left foot and left side of your body lead you when you are facing the outside of the room. Let's take it again. [Play music, saying, "Right side lead," "Left side lead."]

3.5 Try to turn every four slides [then every two slides]. Practice on your own, showing me you can keep your spacing as you make your turns.

3.6 Super job! Be ready, and I will start with four counts facing in and four facing out. Then listen carefully: I will change it to two in and two out. Ready? 'Face in, and two, and three, and ready, face out, and two, and three, and ready, and in, and two, and out, and two.' [Keep counting in twos until class is changing the direction they are facing every two slides.]

3.7 See if you can make your turn lift you off the ground each time you change direction. Lift up, leading the action with your knee. [Children hop as they turn—the beginning of the polka step— "hop, step, together, step."]

3.8 Some of you may not know it, but you have just been doing the polka. Listen and see if your slide can match the rhythm of the music. [May be done freely about the room, disregarding the circular group pattern. As you travel say, "A-gallop and skip," or, "A-slide and skip," and "Turning as you skip."]

4.0 Join with a partner. Just as we worked by ourselves traveling counterclockwise around the room, two slides with faces to center and two slides with backs to center, face your partner so one of you starts with the left side leading and the other starts with the right side leading. Mirror the action of your partner.

4.1 Listen to the music and see if you can keep repeating two slides facing, then turn away from your partner and do two slides with your back toward your partner. Here we go: 'Facing front, two, back, two, front, two, back, two.' [Repeat cues.]

4.2 Join both hands when you are facing, then drop the hands on your leading side as you turn to go back-to-back so that your arms and joined hands can swing around and lead as you travel back-to-back. [Help one pair of partners demonstrate.]

4.3 Practice on your own until you and your partner can feel the same rhythm as you travel together.

4.4 Try to mirror the size of your partner's steps. This is important if you both are going to be feeling the same rhythm. Also, try to think ahead: Be ready for the turn, anticipating your next movement.

4.5 Reduce the size of your steps, and let's see if you can make your feet lighter. This will help you turn quickly and keep sparkle in your steps!

ASSESSMENT: PARTNER SELF-EVALUATION

Raise your hand to show how well you and your partner are able to mirror your steps and move in synchrony: A fist held high means satisfactory to outstanding; a wave means needs improvement or help.

4.6 You have just learned the polka! Change partners and see if you are just as good at doing the polka with a new partner.

5.0 Remain facing your partner and find ways that you can mirror each other, either with gesturing actions or sounds, such as clapping or slapping one or both hands.

5.1 Snapping fingers, clapping hands, bumping hips, tapping shoulders, and bending down to pat the floor are all gestures you could mirror. See if you can practice several of these, trying to keep the eight-count rhythm pattern.

5.2 As you select actions, intentionally choose some that make you change levels, change the direction you are facing, or change your base of support. Work at keeping joy and life in your movement! Make us wonder what will happen next. [Observe for lively, spirited movement quality.]

5.3 Make sure you know the number of counts for each action so that your phrase fits into the eight-count rhythm pattern.

5.4 I will put on the music, and you practice by repeating your phrase several times so you really are moving together.

6.0 Let's combine eight polka steps with our in-place gesturing and sound pattern for another eight counts. [Play music, count aloud, and cue if needed.] 'Polka, two, three, four, five, six, seven, eight; gesture, two, three, four, five, six, seven, eight.'

6.1 Keep repeating the two parts and try to go from your polka right to clapping or gesturing, without missing a beat.

6.2 Have a seat. Let's watch [Kevin and Drew] and see how well they blend the gesturing [clapping] with their polka. [Have several students demonstrate.]

6.3 When you start again, remember to keep your polka step light, buoyant, and the same size as your partner's.

6.4 Change partners and show your eight-count gesturing pattern to each other. Select the best actions and put them together. Practice your gestures and show how the two of you can blend these into your dance by combining gestures with polka steps. [Practice awhile, then stop to briefly discuss aerobic benefits of dancing.]

7.0 We have learned and practiced two parts to our dance. Some of you may want to add a third part. We have worked on traveling alone and traveling together, so you may want to select a way to meet and part and add that to your dance. Those of you who choose to keep a two-part dance, continue trying to work on making your feet lighter and blending your gestures with your polka.

7.1 Whatever you have selected as your third part, try hard to fit into the eight-count rhythm pattern.

7.2 You may want to try it with one partner moving in place and one partner traveling, then switch.

7.3 Those of you who have developed a third part, work to go from one part to another very smoothly without missing a beat.

7.4 Everyone, as you repeat your dance, whether it is a two-part or a three-part dance, try to match your partner exactly and lift through your upper torso.

7.5 Try to make your dance a little longer by choosing one part of your dance and repeating it more than once.

7.6 Practice your dance, and both of you work to remember the order of the parts in your dance. Don't forget the beginning and ending.

AEROBIC ACTIVITY

Muscular endurance means muscles are able to continue longer and longer without becoming tired. *Aerobic endurance* means your heart and blood system are pumping blood to the body more easily. Dance is an excellent way to build aerobic endurance if it lasts a long time and makes your exercise heart rate higher than your resting heart rate.

Appendixes

APPENDIX A: CONTENT STANDARDS IN PHYSICAL EDUCATION

A physically educated person

1. Demonstrates competency in many movement forms and proficiency in a few movement forms.

2. Applies movement concepts and principles to the learning and development of motor skills.

3. Exhibits a physically active lifestyle.

4. Achieves and maintains a health-enhancing level of physical fitness.

5. Demonstrates responsible personal and social behavior in physical activity settings.

6. Demonstrates understanding and respect for differences among people in physical activity settings.

7. Understands that physical activity provides opportunities for enjoyment, challenge, self-expression, and social interaction.

Reprinted from Moving into the future: National standards for physical education, 1995, with permission from the National Association for Sport and Physical Education (NASPE). Requests for permission to reprint can be sent to NASPE, 1900 Association Drive, Reston, VA 20191. [This source provides an introduction to the rationale underlying National Standards, descriptions of content standards, sample benchmarks, and assessment examples for Kindergarten through Grade 12.]

APPENDIX B: CONTENT STANDARDS IN DANCE (FOR CHILDREN IN GRADES K-4)

The National Standards for Arts Education are a statement of what every young American should know and be able to do in four arts disciplines—dance, music, theatre, and the visual arts (p. 131). Two different types of standards are used to guide assessment of student learning and program goals: (p. 18).

- Content standards specify what students should know and be able to do in the arts disciplines.
- Achievement standards specify understandings and levels of achievement that students are expected to attain in the competencies, for each of the arts, at the completion of grades 4, 8, and 12.

1. Content Standard: Identifying and demonstrating movement elements and skills in performing dance
2. Content Standard: Understanding choreographic principles, processes, and structures
3. Content Standard: Understanding dance as a way to create and communicate meaning
4. Content Standard: Applying and demonstrating critical and creative thinking skills in dance
5. Content Standard: Demonstrating and understanding dance in various cultures and historical periods
6. Content Standard: Making connections between dance and healthful living
7. Content Standard: Making connections between dance and other disciplines

Reprinted with permission of the National Dance Association from: Consortium of National Arts Education Associations (1994). *National Standards for Arts Education: What Every Young American Should Know and Be Able to Do in the Arts. Dance, Music, Theatre, Visual Arts.* Reston, VA: Music Educators National Conference, pp. 23-25. (For a rationale, description, and clarification of the National Standards in Dance, including Achievement Standards "a" through "h," write the National Dance Association, 1900 Association Drive, Reston, Virginia 20191).

References

These references are for the Preface and Introduction only.

Consortium of National Arts Education Associations. (1994). *National standards for arts education: What every young american should know and be able to do in the arts (dance, music, theater, visual arts).* Reston, VA: Music Educators National Conference (MENC).

McGee, R. (1984). Evaluation of processes and products. In B. J. Logsdon, K. R. Barrett, M. Ammons, M.R. Broer, L. E. Halverson, R. McGee & M. A. Roberton, *Physical education for children* (2nd ed., pp. 356-421). Philadelphia, PA: Lea & Febiger.

National Association for Sport and Physical Education (NASPE) Standards and Assessment Task Force. (1995). *Moving into the future: National physical education standards: A guide to content and assessment.* St. Louis: Mosby.

National Dance Association (NDA). (1994). *National standards for dance education.* Reston, VA: American Alliance for Health, Physical Education, Recreation & Dance (AAHPERD).

SUGGESTED READINGS

Allison, P. (Ed.). (1994). *Echoes II: Influences in elementary physical education.* Reston, VA: American Alliance for Health, Physical Education, Recreation & Dance (AAHPERD).

Bloom, B. (1956). *Taxonomy of educational objectives. Handbook I: The cognitive domain.* New York: David McKay.

Council on Physical Education for Children (COPEC). (1992). *Developmentally appropriate physical education practices for children.* [Position paper]. Reston, VA: National Association for Sport and Physical Education (NASPE).

Harrow, A. J. (1972). *A taxonomy of the psychomotor domain: A guide for developing behavioral objectives.* New York: David McKay.

Hennessey, B. F. (1996). *Physical Education Sourcebook.* Champaign, IL: Human Kinetics.

Hopple, C. J. (1995). *Teaching for outcomes in elementary physical education: A guide for curriculum and assessment.* Reston, VA: American Alliance for Health, Physical Education, Recreation & Dance (AAHPERD).

Jewett, A. E., Bain, L.L., & Ennis, C. D. (1995). *The curriculum process in physical education.* Dubuque, IA: Brown and Benchmark.

Krathwohl, D. R., Bloom, B., & Masiz, B. (1964). *Taxonomy of educational objectives, Handbook II: Affective domain.* New York: David McKay.

Lambert, L. (1996). Goals and Outcomes. In S. J. Silverman & C. D. Ennis, *Student learning in physical education: Applying research to enhance instruction* (pp. 149-169). Champaign, IL: Human Kinetics.

Melagrano, V. J. (1996). *Designing the physical education curriculum* (3rd ed.). Champaign, IL: Human Kinetics.

National Association for Sport and Physical Education (NASPE) Motor Development Task Force. (1994). *Looking at physical education from a developmental perspective: A guide for teaching.* [Position paper]. Reston, VA: NASPE & American Alliance for Physical Education, Recreation & Dance (AAHPERD).

RESOURCES FOR UNIT PLANS

Readings

Abhau, M. (1986). *Architecture in education: A resource of imaginative ideas and tested activities* (see #48. Acting out structures, p. 57). Philadelphia, PA: Foundation for Architecture. (A poster on structures in architecture is available from the Foundation for Architecture, 1 Penn Center, Suite 1165, Philadelphia, PA 19103 Tel 1-215-569-3187)

Belka, D. (1994). *Teaching children games: Becoming a master teacher.* Champaign, IL: Human Kinetics.

Bennett, J. P., & Riemer, P. C. (1995). *Rhythmic activities and dance.* Champaign, IL: Human Kinetics.

Bond, K. E. (1994). How 'wild things' tamed gender distinctions. *JOHPERD, The Journal of Physical Education, Recreation & Dance, 65* (2), 28 to 33.

Buschner, C. A. (1994). *Teaching children movement concepts and skills.* Champaign, IL: Human Kinetics.

Diamondstein, G. (1971). *Children dance in the classroom.* New York: The Macmillan Company.

Engel, B. S. (1995). *Considering children's art: Why and how to value their works.* Washington, D. C.: National Association for the Education of Young Children (NAEYC).

Gilbert, S. G. (1992). *Creative dance for all ages.* Reston, VA: American Alliance for Health, Physical Education, Recreation, and Dance (AAHPERD).

Graham, G., Holt/Hale, S., & Parker, M. (1993). *Children moving: A reflective approach to teaching physical education* (3rd ed.). Mountain View, CA: Mayfield.

Grant, J. M. (1995). *Shake, rattle, and learn: Classroom-tested ideas that use movement for active learning.* York, Maine: Stenhouse.

Hellison, D. (1995). *Teaching responsibility through physical activity.* Champaign, IL: Human Kinetics.

Hopper, C., Munoz, K., & Fisher, B. (1996). *Health-related fitness for grades 3 and 4.* Champaign, IL: Human Kinetics.

Kirchner, G. & Fishburne, G. J. (1995). *Physical education for elementary school children* (9th ed.). Dubuque, IA: WM C. Brown, Publisher.

Mauldon, E., & Redfern, H. B. (1969). *Games teaching: A new approach for the primary school.* London: Macdonald & Evans Ltd.

McCaslin, N. (1996). Movement and rhythms. In N. McCaslin, *Creative drama in the classroom and beyond* (2nd ed., pp. 53-71). White Plains, NY: Longman.

Meeks, L., & Heit, P. (1996). *Comprehensive school health education: Totally awesome strategies for teaching health* (2nd ed., pp. 245-252). Blacklick, OH: MeeksHeit.

Millar, J. F. (1990). *Country dances of colonial america.* Williamsburg, VA: Thirteen Colonies Press (259 dances with instructions and authentic melodies for violin or flute). [Recorded music for various dances is available from the Country Dance and Song Society, 17 New South St., Northhampton, MA 01060].

Mouzaki, Rozanna. (1981). *Greek dances for americans* (trans. from the Greek by Athena G. Dallas-Damis, pp. 78-103). Garden City, New York: Doubleday & Company.

Purcell, T. (1994). *Teaching children dance: Becoming a master teacher.* Champaign, IL: Human Kinetics.

Ratliffe, R., & Ratliffe, L. M. (1994). *Teaching children fitness: Becoming a master teacher.* Champaign, IL: Human Kinetics.

Rowen, B. (1994). *Dance and grow: Developmental dance activities for three through eight-year-olds.* Pennington, NJ: Princeton Book Company, Publishers.

Russell, J. (1975). *Creative movement and dance for children.* Boston: Plays.

Salvadori, M. (1990). *The art of construction.* Chicago, IL: Chicago Review Press.

Stinson, S. (1988). *Dance for young children: Finding the magic in movement* (p. 130). Reston, VA: American Alliance for Health, Physical Education, Recreation & Dance (AAHPERD).

Ward, P. (1996). *Teaching tumbling.* Champaign, IL: Human Kinetics.

Wall, J., & Murray, N. (1994). *Children and movement: Physical education in the elementary school.* Madison: Brown & Benchmark.

Young, J., Klesius, S., & Hoffman, H. (1994). *Meaningful movement: a developmental theme approach to physical education for children.* Madison, WI: Brown & Benchmark.

Piano Music

Listed by composer, musician, or song title.

"Goodnight, Irene." In K. Krull (collected and arr. for piano and guitar), *Gonna Sing My Head Off* (1992, pp. 48-49). New York: Alfred A. Knopf. (Also [Recorded by Leadbelly]. On *Goodnight, Irene* [CD] TCD-1006 (1996). Salem, MA: Tradition.)

"I Ride An Old Paint" (a western dance waltz). In K. Krull (collected and arr. for piano and guitar), *Gonna Sing My Head Off* (1992, pp. 52-53). New York: Alfred A. Knopf.

Kabalevsky, D. "Polka." In W. & C. Noona, *Noona Basic Piano 5* (KM 127, p. 11). Dayton, OH: The Heritage Music Press. (Available widely on piano sheet music).

"Marching Through Georgia." In Lloyd, R., & Lloyd, N. (Eds.), *The American Heritage Songbook* (1969, pp. 130-131). New York: American Heritage Publishing Co.

"Polly Put the Kettle On." In A. Appleby, P. Pickow (arranged for piano and guitar) & L. S. Byrum (Ed.), *The Library of Children's Song Classics* (1993, p.75). New York, London, and Sydney: AMSCO.

Recorded Music

Listed by composer, musician or title.

Cajun Spice [Recorded by various artists]. On *Cajun Spice: A Collection of South Louisianna Dance Music* "Sixty Plus" [CD] 11550 or [CS] 11550 (1989). Cambridge, MA: Rounder Records.

"Chiapenecas" (Mexican waltz). On [45-rpm record] Catalogue No. 1483. Available: Folkraft Records, P. O. Box 404, Florham Park, N.J. 07932 Tel 1-201-377-1885.

Cusco. (Various selections—soft to strong drum rhythms). On *Apurimac II—Return to Ancient America* [CD] HOMC-7067 or [CS] 7067 (1994). Los Angeles, CA: Higher Octave Music.

Chappell, J. Various piano selections. On *Living the Northern Summer* [CD] RM-0133 or [CS] RM-0133 (1992). Sausalito, CA: Real Music.

Denver, J. "Grandmother's Feather Bed." On *Back Home Again* [CD] RCA 5193-2-R or [CS] 7624-4-R (1988 reissue). New York, NY: RCA Victor, distr. by BMG. (Original work on [LP] RCA Victor CPL1-0548)

Evenson, D. (Various selections). On *Forest Rain* [CD] SP-7150-CD or [CS] SP-7150-CA. Tucson, AZ: Soundings of the Planet.

"Fiddlers' Three." On *Music for Creative Dance—Contrast and Continuum, Vol. 1* [CD] Catalogue No. 30510072 (1994). Available: AAHPERD Publications, P.O. Box 385 Oxen Hill, Waldorf, MD 20750 Phone: 1-800-321-0789.

Floran, Myron. "Chitty Chitty Bang Bang." On *Great Polka Hits* [CS] RC-8047 or [LP] RLP 8047; also on *22 Great Polka Hits* [CS] RC 7005 or [LP] RLP 7005 Santa Monica, CA: Ranwood, dist. by Welk Music Group.

"Greensleeves." On [45-rpm record] Catalogue No. 6175; also on *Folk Dances for Beginners #2* from *Young People's Folk Dance Library* [LP or CS]. Available: Folkraft Records, P. O. Box 404, Florham Park, N.J. 07932 Tel 1-201-377-1885. (Also available on [CS] Catalogue No. MAV 1042C from Wagon Wheel Records and Books, 17191 Corbina Lane #203, Huntington Beach, CA 92649 Tel 1-714-846-8169)

Handel, G. F. Menuet in G major [Recorded by Le Concert des Nations/Jordi Savall]. On *The Water Music* [CD] Astree Auvidis E8512 (1994). Gentilly Dedex, France: Auvidis. (Also on [CD] Phillips 434-122-2PH [1993]; and on [CD] Erato 4509-91716-2 [1994]. (Numerous additional recordings are available)

King, B. T., & Casillas, E. Native American selections. On *Hunting Magic* [CD] TT122D (1994). (Write for a free Southwestern music catalogue from Talking Taco Music, Inc., P.O. Box 781211, San Antonio, TX 78278)

Kraftwerk. Various selections. On *Computerworld* [CD] Elektra 3549-2 or [CS] 3549-4 (reissue 1988). New York: Electra Entertainment.

Kraftwerk. Various selections. On *The Man Machine* [CD] CLEO 5877 (1993 reissue). Sun Valley, CA: Cleopatra, distr. by Caroline Records.

Lacksman, D. "Deep Forest" and "Desert Walk." On Celine Music/Synsound 550 Music/epic [CD] BK 57840 (1992). New York, NY: Sony Music Entertainment.

Levelance. On *Music for Creative Dance: Contrast and Continuum, Vol. 1* [CD] Catalogue No. 30510072 (1994). Available: AAHPERD Publications, P.O. Box 385 Oxen Hill, Waldorf, MD 20750 Tel 1-800-321-0789.

"Marching Through Georgia." On [45-rpm record] Catalogue No. 1135. Available: Folkraft Records and Tapes, P. O. Box 404, Florham Park, N.J. 07932 Tel 1-201-377-1885.

Mendes, S. Various selections. On *Brasileiro* [CD] Elektra 61315-2 or [CS] 61315-4 (1992). Rockefeller Plaza, NY: Elektra Entertainment.

Nakai, C. R., and Eaton, W., with the Black Lodge Singers. Contemporary Native American flute music. On *Ancestral Voices* [CD] CR-7010 (1992). Phenix, AZ: Canyon Records Productions.

*"Patty Cake Polka" and "Heel and Toe Polka." On [45-rpm records] Catalogue No. #1260 and #1484, respectively. Available: Folkraft Records and Tapes, P. O. Box 404, Florham Park, N.J. 07932 Tel 1-201-377-1885)

"Plink, Plank, Plunk." [Performed by Boston Pops Orchestra/Arthur Fieldler]. On *LeRoy Anderson: Greatest Hits* [CD] Catalogue No. 31615 or [CS] Catalogue No. 31614 (1992).

"Riverdance" and other selections [Recorded by Bill Whelan]. On *Riverdance* [CD]82816-2 (1995). Burbank, CA: Celtic Heartbeat, dist. by Atlantic/WEA.

Rowland, M. Various selections. On *The Fairy Ring* [CD] ND-62801 or [CS] NC-62801 (1995). Universal City, CA: Enso, distr. by UNI Distribution Corp.

*Saint-Saen, C. "The Swan" from *Carnival of the Animals*. On *Classics for Children* [CD, CS] RCA 6718 2 RG. New York: RCA Victor distr. by BMG.

*Shostakovich. "Polka" [Recorded by the Royal Stockholm Orchestra]. On *The Golden Age—Ballet* [CD] CHAN9251/2 (1994). Tarrytown-On-Hudson, NY: Chandos, dist. Koch International, Port Washington, NY.

*"Sicilian Tarantella." On *Holiday Folk Dances* [CS] MAV; also on *World of Fun*, Vol. 6 [LP set]. Available: Wagon Wheel Records & Books, 17191 Corbini Lane #203, Huntington Beach, CA 92649 Tel 1-714-846-8169.

Sousa, J. P. "Semper Fidelis" and "The Stars and Stripes Forever" [Recorded by Boston Pops Orchestra/Arthur Fiedler]. On *This Is My Country* [CD] 09026-61545-2. New York, NY: RCA Victor, distr. by BMG.

"Spanish Circle Waltz." On *Joyful Folk Dances #6* [LP, CS]. Available: Folkraft Records and Tapes, P. O. Box 404, Florham Park, N.J. 07932 Tel 1-201-377-1885)

Strauss, J. Emperor Waltz, Roses from the South, and Voices of Spring. On *The Best of Strauss* [CD] TBO 406. Selcor Ltd.

Strauss, II, J., & Strauss, J. Seven of the most famous waltzes and polkas, including "Tritsch-Tratsch-Polka" [Recorded by Vienna Philharmonic Orch./Willi Boskovsky]. On *Pizzicato Polka* [CD] Decca Ovation 417 747-2DM (Recorded 1958-73). London: Decca Classics, dist. by UNI Distribution Corp., Universal City, CA.

Stravinsky, I. "The Rite of Spring" [Recorded by Paris Conservatoire]. On [CD] Decca Historic Series 440 064-2DM (1994). London: Decca Classics (distr. in US. by UNI Distribution Corp., Universal City, CA).

"Tarantella" [Recorded by various artists]. On [CD] Fiesta 1795. (Also on *A Tempo Di Ballo*, Fiesta FMC 2049; on *Music of the World*, Monitor MFS 71345; and on *Folk Dances of the World* [LP] Hoctor HLP 4003)

Tchaikovsky, P. I. "Waltz." On *Adventures in Music*, Grade 4, Vol 2 [LP]. Available: Folkraft Records and Tapes, P. O. Box 404, Florham Park, N.J. 07932 Tel 1-201-377-1885.

"When Johnny Comes Marching Home Again." On *Let's Square Dance #5* [CS or LP]. Available: Folkraft Records and Tapes, P. O. Box 404, Florham Park, N.J. 07932 Tel 1-201-377-1885)

Winston, G. Various solo piano selections. On *Forest* [CD] 01934-11157-2 or [CS] 01934-11157-4 (1994). Santa Cruz, CA: Dancing Cat Records.

*Available also on compact disk [CD] in Silver Burdett & Ginn's *The Music Connection*, 1995 series, Morristown, NJ, and from other leading music education resources.

Note: Recorded music may be found in local record stores or via mail-order services, such as Public Radio Music Source Tel 1-800-75-MUSIC or Tower Records Tel 1-800-ASK-TOWER. Physical education and dance supply companies and educational catalogue companies are also excellent sources.

EQUIPMENT SUPPLY CATALOGUES

Listed here are a few of the many companies (local, national and international) that carry movement education and educational games, gymnastics, and dance equipment and materials for young children. We encourage you to review this list and the physical education and dance supply companies in your locality; ask your school librarian or administration for additional resource catalogues on early childhood movement education.

Chimetime—Division of Sportime
Movement Products
One Sportime Way
Atlanta, GA 30340
1-800-477-5075 *or* 1-770-449-5700
Fax 1-800-845-1535 *or* 1-700-263-0897

Flaghouse
150 North MacQuesten Pkwy.
Mount Vernon, NY 10550
1-800-793-7900; outside USA: (914) 699-1900
Fax 1-800-793-7922 *or* (914) 699-2961

Porter Athletic Equipment
9555 Irving Park Rd.
Schiller Park, IL 60176
(708) 671-0110
(gymnastics apparatus)

Toledo Physical Education Supply
Box 5618
Toledo, OH 43613
(419) 476-6730 *or* 1-800-225-7749
Fax 1-419-476-1163

UCS
One Olympic Drive
Orangeburg, N.Y. 10962
1-914-365-2333 *or* 1-800-526-4856
Fax 1-914-365-2589
(gymnastics apparatus)

U.S. Games.
P. O. Box 117028
Carrollton, TX 75011-7028
1-800-327-0484
Fax 1-800-899-0149 *or* 1-214-243-0149

Wolverine Sports
745 Circle
Box 1941
Ann Arbor, MI 48106
(313) 761-5690

About the Authors

Bette J. Logsdon, PhD, has 37 years of physical education experience—5 years in public schools and 32 years at the university level, preparing teachers with special interest in elementary school physical education. She spent the last 15 years of her career at Bowling Green State University (Ohio). During this time, she taught regularly scheduled elementary physical education classes to learn more about children, test theories, and stay abreast of the challenges facing elementary school teachers. Bette lives in Toledo, Ohio.

Luann M. Alleman, MEd, has 25 years' teaching experience in public and private schools. She has worked with children, including physically challenged students, at the elementary and high school levels, and with college students in university teacher-preparation courses. She was the first intern consultant for physical education in the Toledo School System and provided in-service training for Toledo public school elementary physical education teachers. Retired after 17 years as department chair of elementary school physical education for the Toledo School System, Luann resides in Holland, Ohio.

Sue Ann Straits, PhD, has been a lecturer in the Department of Education at The Catholic University of America (Washington, D.C.) since 1993. Since beginning her career in physical education in 1972, she has gained extensive practical experience teaching physical education and dance in early childhood and elementary education settings both overseas and in the United States. She also has conducted workshops around the world on movement education. Sue Ann makes her home in Reston, Virginia.

David E. Belka, PhD, has taught physical education classes to elementary school students and pedagogy and elementary content courses at the college level. An expert in developing and teaching games, David is the author of *Teaching Children Games*, a practical guide that explains the why and how of teaching children to become skilled games players. For more than two decades, he has analyzed, critiqued, and reviewed elementary physical education texts. David lives in Oxford, Ohio, where he is a professor at Miami University.

Dawn Clark, EdD, is an associate professor and the coordinator of dance education at East Carolina University, where she teaches dance pedagogy. She taught physical education and dance at the elementary level for five years. In 1987 Dawn earned a certificate in Laban studies; this background has been especially helpful for the *Physical Education Unit Plans* books, whose units are organized around Laban's movement themes and movement framework. Dawn is a resident of Greenville, North Carolina.

Learning Experiences in Games, Gymnastics, and Dance

Adopted by school districts across the country, these highly acclaimed unit plans are tailored to meet the needs of elementary students at every level. Increase student learning and motivation—and decrease off-task behavior—with these time-saving plans!

1997 • Paper
184 pp
Item BLOGO781
ISBN 0-87322-781-6
$18.00
($26.95 Canadian)

1997 • Paper
Approx 184 pp
Item BLOGO782
ISBN 0-87322-782-4
$18.00
($26.95 Canadian)

1997 • Paper
Approx 184 pp
Item BLOGO783
ISBN 0-87322-783-2
$18.00
($26.95 Canadian)

1997 • Paper
Approx 184 pp
Item BLOGO784
ISBN 0-87322-784-0
$18.00
($26.95 Canadian)

Special package price!

1997 • All 4 *Physical Education Unit Plans* books
Item BLOGO697 • ISBN 0-88011-697-8
$59.00 ($88.50 Canadian)

Prices subject to change.

Human Kinetics
The Information Leader in Physical Activity
http://www.humankinetics.com/
2335

To request more information or to place your order,
U.S. customers call **TOLL-FREE 1-800-747-4457.**
Customers outside the U.S. use appropriate telephone
number/address shown in the front of this book.